IN QUEST OF A MEANINGFUL LIFE

Autobiography of a Civil Servant

IN QUEST OF A MEANINGFUL LIFE

Autobiography of a Civil Servant

PRASHANTA KUMAR MISHRA

Konark Publishers Pvt Ltd
New Delhi · Seattle

Konark Publishers Pvt. Ltd
206, First Floor,
Peacock Lane, Shahpur Jat,
New Delhi-110 049.
Phone: +91-11-41055065, 65254972
e-mail: india@konarkpublishers.com
Website: www.konarkpublishers.com

Konark Publishers International
8615, 13th Ave SW,
Seattle, WA 98106
Phone: (415) 409-9988
e-mail: us@konarkpublishers.com

Cataloging in Publication Data—DK
   Courtesy: D.K. Agencies (P) Ltd. <docinfo@dkagencies.com>

   Mishra, Prashanta Kumar, 1948- author.
      In quest of a meaningful life : autobiography of a civil servant /
      Prashanta Kumar Mishra.
      pages cm
      ISBN 9789322008857

         1. Mishra, Prashanta Kumar, 1948- 2. Civil service--India--Uttar Pradesh--Biography.   3. Uttar Pradesh (India)--Officials and employees--Biography. 4. India--Officials and employees--Biography. 5. Spiritual biography. 6. Meditation.   I. Title.

LCC HV28.M57A3 2017 | DDC 352.63092   23

Editor: Sivadas Sankar

Typeset by Saanvi Graphics, Noida
Printed and bound at Thomson Press (India) Ltd.

Contents

Foreword

I have known Shri Prashanta Kumar Mishra since 1979 when he was District Magistrate, Tehri Garhwal. He used to visit this holy place (Vasistha Guffa) from time to time every year. He is a simple, honest and spiritual person with no arrogance in his personality despite the fact that he had occupied many important posts including that of Chief Secretary, Uttar Pradesh and Member, UPSC. The book *In Quest of a Meaningful Life: Autobiography of a Civil Servant* written by him gives a fairly good account of his administrative and spiritual experiences. He has travelled to innumerable holy places of the country. He has trekked hundreds of kms in the Himalayas and never hesitated to stay in the Ashrams in the company of saintly persons and pilgrims. I am sure, his book will make a useful and interesting reading and will act as a guide to the younger generation and administrators.

I wish all the best to Shri Prashanta Kumar Mishra and am sure Shri Gurumaharaj Purushottamanand Ji will bless him in his spiritual mission and will continue to guide him in his journey on Mother Earth.

Swami Chaitanayanand
Sri Purushottamanand Trust
Vasistha Guffa Ashram
Gular Dogi, Tehri Garhwal,
Uttarakhand

A Few Words

For some time, I have been toying with the idea of writing a book on my administrative and spiritual experiences for the benefit of the younger generation and budding administrators. After demitting the Office of Member, Union Public Service Commission in August 2013, I got some respite to think creatively and started putting down my feelings and expressions in a more cogent way. For about a year, I strained my memory to jot down all the incidents and experiences that I had, right from my childhood till the present day. Then it took me more than one year to elaborate on these points which constituted the very basis of this book. Two volumes of my diary containing my spiritual experiences proved immensely useful while writing the book.

The book is primarily an autobiography covering within its ambit, my administrative and spiritual experiences. It goes back to my childhood days, the samskaras imparted by my parents, teachers and the elders of my village. It takes into account the role played by my village primary school, high school, college and university. My eldest brother, Shri Ramakant Mishra played a stellar role in grooming me for my future assignments and imparted the values and the discipline which helped me a lot to become a better human being. I have tried to give a fairly honest account of my experiences over these past long years. I have highlighted upon the cherished ideas and the principles of life without which man would be reduced to an animal. I have concluded the book with a spiritual optimism that we have the innate divinity and power to go beyond the frontiers of the Cosmic World.

While describing my experiences, it was never my intention to criticize any person or policy. The idea is to give a fair, just and honest account of various experiences so that the book can act as a guide for youngsters. I have tried my best to not hurt the feelings of any person, personality, region or sect. While I was extra vigilant and sensitive on this matter, if despite my efforts, somebody does feel hurt, then please excuse me and there lies the greatness of a person.

(ii)

It is the irony of life that I had my most intense spiritual development when I was the Commissioner (Sales Tax) in Uttar Pradesh. The period from 1991 to 2003 witnessed my spiritual development in the most meaningful way. Trekking for hundreds of kms in the Himalayas, meeting saintly persons and spending nights in the Ashrams, would not have been enjoyable but for the spiritual company of Shri N.C. Sharma, Shri C.S. Semwal and Shri Sarveswar Semwal. I can't forget the contribution of Shri N.C. Sharma and Shri C.S. Semwal in providing various photographs in this regard. I am extremely grateful to Shri Sarveswar Semwal who has enlightened me about the importance of Kedarkhand and more specifically about Panch Kedar. I cannot forget the role played by my wife Sarita and my daughter Pragya in giving suggestions from time to time to improve the structure, contents and the language of the book. In addition to her duty as a wife and a mother, Sarita never hesitated to accompany me to many places of spiritual importance, giving me company during the journeys. After dinner, both of us would sit together for hours to discuss the book, its contents and language. I have no hesitation in admitting that her

invaluable suggestions have helped me in improving the contents and language of the book.

The book titled *In Quest of a Meaningful Life: Autobiography of a Civil Servant* runs into 320 pages. The gigantic task of writing this book would not have been possible but for the painstaking efforts and cooperation rendered by Shri Bishnu Datt Joshi who has been associated with me right from my days in UPSC. He took dictations for hours each day and put neatly typed sheets before me on the following day! Shri Joshi's invaluable help allowed me to think in a more creative manner without being disturbed by any external factor. This helped my thought process to flow in an unbroken chain of expression. Without Mr Joshi's help, this book would not have seen the light of the day.

(iii)

I express my heartfelt gratitude to Shri Ganesh Shanker Tripathi whose loyalty and trustworthiness cannot be questioned. I am thankful to him for rendering necessary assistance in the publication of the book. I also thank Shri KPR Nair, Managing Director of Konark Publishers and the Board of Editors who have taken the pains to edit and publish the book in a beautiful manner.

This book is dedicated to my parents, eldest brother and bhabi, and Swami Chaitanyanand Ji of Vasistha Guffa who have influenced my persona to a great extent thereby shaping my administrative and spiritual life. I pay my obeisance at the lotus feet of Shri Gurumaharaj Purushottamanand Ji whose invisible spirit has always guided me on the right path. I cannot forget Acharya Shriram Sharma Ji, Swami Fakiranand Ji, Swami Premanand Ji, Swami Ram Ji, Swami Hansanand Ji, Swami Dineshanand Ji, Phalahari Baba and Nara Hari Baba who made a deep impact on my Spiritual Being. I am grateful to all those invisible Spiritual Masters and Teachers who often appeared in my dreams to guide me from time to time. I have written this book with all my sincerity depicting my quest for a meaningful life. Hope all of you will enjoy reading this book.

Prashanta Kumar Mishra

Chapter 1

······································· ❦

Introduction

Life is a continuous journey towards Godhood
and change is the essence of life.

*I*t was my good fortune to be born in 1948 in post-independent
India, in a village, Athmallik, in the erstwhile district of
Dhankanal in Odisha. When I scan over the entire period of my
life so far, I wonder what happened to our society during all these
years, both in the field of material and spiritual developments.
Significant developments have taken place during these decades
in many areas, in science, technology, economy, space exploration,
information technology and the industrial field. But the most
important development, with serious implications, has escaped the
attention of society as well as of the intelligentsia. In pursuit of
material development, we have lost sight of moral values that are the
bedrock of any civilized society. It is a pity that we are aware of our
value system and yet remain mute spectators to this development.
The world has suffered enough, not because of the actions of violent
people but because of the silence of good people. The all-pervading
corruption, prevalent in society today, at times makes me sick,
cynical and quite often furious with myself, with the intelligentsia,
society and the institutions that manage the affairs of the State. I
was determined to fight against this evil by forging a network of
committed individuals in different walks of life and if need be, to
charter the course alone against this monster.

Man is essentially spiritual by nature. There is an innate divinity in each one of us, but unfortunately, we have forgotten about it and divorced ourselves from our true nature. Spiritualism is the very essence of life and when it dies, we also perish along with it. In the words of Dr S Radhakrishnan, 'The world is suffering from scepticism in faith, anarchy in morals and unbelief in truth'. We do not know which way to follow and what to do in moments of crises.

Quite often I wonder, who am I, where have I come from and for what purpose? These questions have been occupying my mind quite often ever since I became an adult. I would like to mention an anecdote in this context that is amusing as well as philosophical. There was a gardener managing a mango grove. One day he found a man wandering in the place. He got suspicious and asked the intruder, 'Who are you, and where have you come from? What are you doing here?' The man replied with a smile, 'Well brother, for quite some time, I have been searching for answers to these same questions but have not yet found an answer'. This is life, simple yet mysterious.

I had an experience during my meditation in 1996 when I was suddenly transferred from the post of CEO, NOIDA to Lucknow as Secretary, Co-operation. I was staying in a room at the guesthouse at the fifth floor of the PICKUP building. As I was alone in the guesthouse on weekends and holidays, there was too much peace, which I found oppressive. So once I hit upon the idea of recalling my previous years while doing my meditation. After bath and breakfast, I would close my eyes and ruminate over the past experiences. I went back to my previous postings, the training in Mussoorie, preparation for IAS, university days, college and school days, even my childhood and sitting in my mother's lap. I tried to imagine and figure out my existence in my mother's womb. The moment I imagined my position in the womb, I experienced a jerk and a brilliant light startled me. I opened my eyes with awe and wonder. Tears were rolling down my cheeks and I found that three hours had already passed. I was absolutely calm. I analyzed this experience rationally; it may have

been a hallucination, it may have been a reflection of my obsession with spiritualism. Ultimately, I came to the conclusion that the light which I experienced was a life-giving force. Only when the embryo receives this force, does it grow to be a living one.

Life is a continuous journey towards Godhood and change is the essence of life. The un-manifested Brahman alone is Absolute and the moment it is manifested, it becomes relative. The static energy i.e. un-manifested Brahman when manifested into a dynamic energy, assumes various forms through the endless cosmic dance of life. Through evolution of millions of years, life has changed from a unicellular body to the complex human body. Yet the substantive living force behind all these forms remains the same. In this dance of life, every moment is precious, every day is laden with meaning and every happening has a divine design.

What is the purpose of life? Is it merely to eat, drink and be merry, or is it something more? To a sensuous person enjoying sensuous pleasures may be the real purpose of life. But he forgets this saying of Swami Muktanandaji:

I thought, I was enjoying my senses
Little realizing that the senses were enjoying me.
I thought, I was spending time nicely.
Little realizing that the time was spending me.

Sensual pleasure and material prosperity cannot be the purpose of life. Because of the exclusive emphasis on material prosperity, civilization after civilization has met its inevitable doom. India alone is an exception. It still stands in spite of centuries of slavery. A passion for material prosperity, love of luxury and wanton indulgence debase man. We are meant for much bigger things. As Tulsidas said, 'Manushya Yoni (human form) is a unique gift from God which is not available even to the gods'. This precious life must not be wasted. The lives of Adi Shankara, Swami Vivekananda and Ramanujam, all exemplify this. All of them died young but look at the lasting impact they left behind. The purpose of life is to understand life itself. When we understand this, we realize that our purpose is plain and simple i.e. to bring benefit to others. There is a pleasure in sharing and in giving to others. Look at the natural world, the sun, the wind and the water, etc., they all give away their benefits to all irrespective of consideration. We never thank God for all the benefits bestowed on us. We take all of these for granted. But the moment we understand and realize the real purpose of life, we would automatically bow our head in humility and gratitude.

Chapter 2

Childhood: Family and Surrounding

Compared to my childhood days, I often wonder
whether my children are the losers, being born and
brought up in big cities.

I was born in 1948 and the day happened to be the death anniversary
of my paternal grandfather. Therefore, my Bua (father's sister)
called me Sana Bapa (little father). As a child and later, I used to
dream a lot and there had been a profusion of snakes, oxen, carriage
of dead bodies, soldiers and Sanyasis in these dreams. I once saw in a
dream a cobra moving towards the temple without harming anyone
and in another an ox toiling in the field. In a dream, I had carried
bodies to the cremation ground in a tonga and I had fought many
a battle as a soldier and received injuries. Often, in these dreams
the serene and smiling face of a Sanyasi used to appear. I have often
wondered why such dreams keep recurring. I am not a psychologist
or an interpreter of dreams but it seems that the experiences and
samskaras of previous births might have been transmuted into my
being in a subtle form.

We have heard terms like transmigration of the soul, incarnation
and para-kayapravesh (entering into another's body). The soul – the
life-giving force, which resides in everyone is permanent, immutable
and indestructible. When I reflect on life, I find that the so-called
death is a mere hyphen between life and life. When we go on splitting
the so-called non-living particles, we arrive at sub-atomic particles

and, perhaps, the recently discovered God particle. When such particles are present everywhere, how can a thing perish? Endless destruction and creation take place even in the minutest particle of God's creation. The body consists of five elements; earth, water, fire, air and space. When the so-called death takes place, these elements merely disintegrate and re-integrate to facilitate the emergence of a different form of soul. Buddhism teaches that life and death are one and the same. In fact the entire 84,000 teachings of Buddhism are focused on the mystery of life and death. The mystic nature of life is truly incredible. 'Just as leaves fall from the tree in autumn and re-appear in spring as green shoots, the cycle of life and death and re-birth continues endlessly.'

I was born in a large middle class family. My mother recalls that when she was expecting me, a Sanyasi visited our house and stayed for a few days. When he noticed my mother was in the family way, he gave her a mantra for recitation, so that the baby would be very intelligent and spiritual. Sadhus and saintly persons were always welcome in our house and as a child I had observed many holy men visit our house to have their meals and take rest. Specifically I can recall the names of saints like Balia Dash, Dharam Dash, Daman Baba, Janaki Mata and Kainee Phullia Baba whose blessings have always been with our family. My parents never hesitated in serving these saintly persons with a smiling face and devotion. While my father was extremely religious, and spent a lot time doing puja, my mother, though religious, was practical in her approach to life. Though father was a first class Magistrate, he led a simple and austere life. When he retired at the age of 56, apart from the ancestral house and land he had inherited, he had just one table, four chairs and a cycle as his assets. He did not even have a transistor set. When during my university days, I got the national scholarship and bought a Philips transistor and presented it to my father, he was extremely happy. He retained the transistor till his death. He was a truly elevated soul.

My father, Kishore Chandra Mishra, was a devotee of Mother Kali and his entire life was devoted to the worship of the Goddess. As a child, I have seen him dancing during the Danda Yatra. I remember, he used to patronize Danda Nrutya by making it a duty to go to our village on the auspicious day of Meru to attend it. The word Danda Yatra takes me down memory lane of my childhood days when I used to perform the Danda Nrutya in my village. This is an important folk dance of Odisha and more so of the western part of the state.

We are a large family of five brothers and six sisters. My uncle has six sons and two daughters and my father's elder brother, three sons and three daughters. In my grandfather's time, all the brothers and their families stayed in the same house. With the enlargement of the family, in the same village in close proximity to each other, they resided in three houses but the management and the ownership of land was single. The joint family system has instilled in me values like love, affection, honesty, integrity and respect for elders, cooperation, discipline and emotional bonding. My eldest sister, Bulnani, used to look after all my comforts. In fact, she was the one who taught me manners, provided me emotional security and gave the love and affection of a mother. My eldest brother, Rama Kant Mishra, affectionately called 'Babula Dada', has been my mentor, philosopher, and guide.

Ours was a matriarchal joint family where my mother played a dynamic role in preserving, protecting and educating all the members. She was very intelligent, highly spiritual but practical and a strict disciplinarian. She was very straight, extremely honest and would call a spade a spade. But for my mother, father and eldest brother, I would not have been what I am today. Father's simplicity, spirituality and honesty and mother's discipline, straightforward and practical approach have all gone into making me what I am. My eldest brother's honesty, impartiality, and attention to minute details as an administrator, and above all his idealism, straightforwardness and selflessness have made a tremendous impact on me.

Most of my childhood days were spent in Athmallik, Bolangir, Sambalpur and Dhenkanal. Athmallik is a beautiful place surrounded by dense reserve forest on three sides and the great Mahanadi in the south. The Panchadhara range with its lustrous green forest and its streams murmuring down the hills had always been a source of joy. My formative years were thus spent in the lap of nature. Being close to nature brings joy, happiness and serenity in life. I have also seen extreme poverty in my village which has sensitized me to the plight of the poor. Village life taught me simplicity, compassion, fraternity, spirituality and thrift, and made me idealistic, sensitive to the cause of downtrodden and resilent enough to adjust to difficult situations in life. Alas! The innocence of village life has now been lost to the complexities of urban life which is mechanical, individualistic, selfish and devoid of socio-moral sensitivities.

I often wonder whether my children are losers for having been born and brought up in big cities. They may be intelligent, sharp and well informed but, as I observe, their development in life is lopsided, uni-dimensional and not holistic enough. My children seem deprived of the soothing influence of Mother Nature, the loving care of a joint family and the ground realities of life. I do not know who is the loser in this mad rush towards urbanization?

As a Director of the Government of India, I visited the United States of America in a delegation led by the Secretary, Social Justice and Empowerment, to study drug addiction problems among the youth there. We spent 14 days in different parts of the US and met the Director of National Institute of Health. When the US official asked our Secretary how long he had been living with his wife, the latter replied that they had been together for the last 32 years and would continue to do till the last breath. The US Director was taken aback and commented that in American society, they would have changed at least two or three wives in this period. Further, in his opinion, the real solution to drug addiction among the youth lay in having a strong, stable family life which provides sustenance and emotional bonding and security to the child. It is a pity that under the strain of economic development and materialistic pursuit, the joint family system has been disintegrating, being replaced by the nuclear family. Even at this stage, we can think of preserving a few important traits of the joint family system. If we make it a point to congregate at our ancestral place once a year to attend religious and family functions and to keep in contact with the members of the joint family through mobile, WhatsApp and email, then these efforts will definitely save the joint family system from breaking down. It may not retain the form in its entirety but definitely it can preserve its essence.

I spent the formative period of 17 years of my life in Athmallik. In retrospect, I felt I was fortunate to have such varied, rich experiences. I remember the pond near the house, where I used to take a dip every morning before going to school. I used to collect 10 to 15 lotus flowers from the pond and offer them to our family deity 'Rudra Bhawani'. This practice continued for years till I passed out of matriculation from Mahendra High School. I felt that this simple offering had a tremendous impact in the development of my spiritual feelings which have stood me in good stead through my life. Strange are the ways in which divine force operates.

Since my father held a transferable job, I also spent a few years in Bolangir, Sambalpur and Dhenkanal. Once when I was hardly four years old, on Ganesh Chaturthi my father took me to our worship room to initiate me into the learning of the alphabets. A new slate and pencil had been specifically bought for the purpose. While chanting slokas in praise of Vighnahraj and Goddess Saraswati, my father caught hold of my right hand with a pencil to write down the words 'Ridhi and Sidhi' (prosperity and wisdom). What a nice way of initiating a child to the world of letters, but alas, such a good practice of initiating learning has disappeared in the name of modernity.

I studied Shishu Shreni upto Class-II at the Sambalpur Police Line School. Like today's nursery and KG classes, even at that time, there was a system of Shishu Shreni where special attention was given to kids as they were attending school for the first time. I remember my first day in class. I was feeling out of place and started sobbing. The Head Master came and affectionately patted my head and handed over 3-4 biscuits. He consoled me and allowed me to sit for two weeks with my elder brother, Gama dada, who was studying in Class-II. After 14 days, I was transferred to my own class. This was a nice way of handling a child's psychology.

We stayed in our grand-mother's house and mother used to teach me every day. I vividly remember that I could not write the figure 7 in Oriya. I cried but my mother instead of rebuking me consoled and persuaded me to try again. After a few attempts, I succeeded and my joy knew no bounds. She made me understand that, in spite of failure, repeated attempts would definitely result in achieving the desired result. It is a great lesson in life.

My mother, Swaranlata Mishra, was very spiritual and used to take me to visit various temples in Sambalpur, particularly during Kartik Purnima. My father exposed us to the Ramayana and the Mahabharata by reciting to us slokas and telling stories from these epics at night. My father was not at all strict and showered his love and affection. Both parents were kind and broad-minded and allowed us to see one movie a month, particularly those with mythological and spiritual themes. I liked films like *Ram Vibaha*, *Rambaan Chodenge*, *Jai Hanuman*, *Veer Bhimsen* and other similar ones. I was so intoxicated with the likes of these that while still in Class-III, during summer vacation, I finished reading all the seven volumes of Ramayana written in Oriya. Watching Ram Leela and Krishna Leela during Dussehra and Holi festivals in the village gave me immense pleasure. I even participated in one of the Ram Leelas and played the role of the child Rama. Every morning and evening our house would reverberate with the chanting of Mantras and sounds of bells and the conch. The Car festival, the Ganesh and Saraswati Puja, Dussehra, Holi, Shivratri and Meru Yatra were all celebrated with much pomp and show. The religious and spiritual atmosphere that prevailed in my family and the village, determined my belief and trust in God and the cosmic force.

Athmallik was a typical agrarian society where people were simple and honest even though they were poor. The entire village was an extended family where everybody knew each other. We even shared the same room with the domestic help and farm labourers. The maid servant of our family, Pakni, was like a mother to us. She wielded the powers of the guardian to control us. Another help, Kanahia Kaka, lived with us from his childhood till his death. Even today, we maintain our relationship with his family.

When father retired in 1966, three of my brothers and I were still in college. The eldest brother, Ramakant Mishra, an IAS officer of the 1957 batch, and my bhabi Satyabhama Mishra, sacrificed their entire life to provide for our education and up-bringing. I regard them as my parents. They guided me from childhood days till I became an IAS officer in 1972.

Mother looked upon every guest as God (Athithi devo bhava). As a child, I had observed her inviting the first beggar who came for bhiksha every Sunday into the premises and treating him with food, clothes and money. No beggar, on any day, went back empty-handed. In fact, there was so much of competition among my brothers and sisters that each rushed to give the beggar something. My family did not even take any action when the poor from our village encroached upon the five acres of our land. In fact, father happily donated the entire land for building a school.

Chapter 3

······························ ✄

School days

I wonder whether modern-day teachers take such
care of their students like they did in our times. The profession
has been commercialized and the teacher-taught relationship
became the first casualty.

The description of my childhood days will be incomplete
unless I dwell upon my experience in the Town School and
Mahendra High School. When I was in lower primary school, the
school building was a kachha (thatched) one and we would sit on
the earthen floor. There was no desk, no bench and no modern
amenities. There was no fee either. Though by modern standards,
my school came nowhere as far as the infrastructure was concerned
but it produced IAS officers, engineers, doctors and professors. The
teachers were strict in enforcing discipline and imparting good
education. We were also encouraged to study nature by being
taken to the forest to observe birds and trees, to the riverside to
understand floods, etc. We were taught many lessons through
storytelling and drama. I received my first exposure to democracy
in this rural school. A boy would be nominated as monitor and his
responsibility was to conduct the mass prayer every day. Nobody
knew who would start the prayer on a particular day. Therefore,
everybody was well conversant with the prayer so they could avoid
facing an embarrassing situation in the assembly. Another boy

would act as health minister and his duty, after the prayer, was to see that the boys and girls had neatly combed hair and their nails were cut. These were lessons in preliminary hygiene. The students who failed this inspection would be reprimanded by the minister. Thereafter, a boy acting as information minister would request the students to update the gathering about the important happenings in the village like birth, death, marriage, disaster, celebrations of festivals, etc. There was a guest and culture minister whose duty was to ensure that every class had a pitcher of drinking water. There was an agriculture minister whose duty was to ensure that the plants in plots, allotted to small groups of students were watered and cared for.

Moral education was imparted to the children right from the beginning of the school days. Teachers were strict and dedicated. In the lower class, I studied the Ramayana, the Mahabharata, *Panchtantra*, *Katha Mala*, *Jatakagalpa*, *Birbal Kahani*, *Aesop's Fables* and *Childhood Days of the Great Personalities*. We also had exposure to the great teachings of Vedic India and the stories of great rishis. Apart from participating in festivals and yatras, we used to celebrate August 15, October 2, November 14 and January 26 with gusto. My eldest brother formed the 'Students Cultural Council' to motivate school children to participate in cultural and community activities. Through this we were exposed to social works like cleaning ponds, road repair, construction of small bridges and disaster management in case of fire. We had also participated in cremation of dead bodies and tree plantation in the premises of the school and play-grounds. A few saplings we planted have become gigantic trees providing shelter and food to hundreds of birds and shade to passersby. Whenever I visit my village, I make it a point to touch these trees. I have shown these trees to my children with pride.

During holidays we would go to the river banks or to the forest for picnic. Besides football, volleyball and cricket, there were a large number of other games we played during childhood, namely, Lunchur, Shikabhanga, Ghoghorani, Chor-Police, Gulichep - Guligala,

Bahuchur, Phuda, Seven desks, Gulidanda and marbles. Fishing was another pastime I enjoyed immensely. Since the village had an abundance of ponds and rivers, we became expert swimmers right from childhood. One day I went with my elder brothers to the pond for a bath. At that time, I was still learning swimming but slipped and sank to the deeper part of the pond. I did not know how to swim and just lay at the bottom for some time. Finding me missing, all my brothers started diving in search of me. Fortunately, I was rescued by an elder cousin. I could have died, but by the grace of God, my life was saved.

During the British days Athmallik was a small estate ruled by a king, Mahendra Singh Deo, and his son, Kishore Chandra Singh Deo, who later became the king. They were liberal, kind-hearted and used to take keen interest in the education of their subjects. Initially, there was a middle school in the village which, after Independence, became a High School and it was named Mahendra High School. I studied here from Class 4 until Class 11. Though it was a co-ed school I never talked to any girl. In fact, nobody would believe that I had not spoken to a girl till I joined the IAS! Though this trait has enabled me to focus more on studies, it has also adversely affected my sociability, particularly among ladies. This angularity got corrected after marriage when my wife, Sarita, made a conscious effort to make me more sociable.

There was much to learn from the teachers who were sincere and devoted to their duties and responsibilities. Particularly, Mrs Laxmi Rao, who was known as 'Mastarani Mama', had her residence right in front of our house and she used to keep an eye on my studies. She was a hard taskmaster but soft at heart. I used to study upto 01.00 or 02.00 am. At 11.00 pm, Mrs Rao would advise me to go to bed, cautioning me that unless I listened to her, I would fall ill. At midnight, again she would urge and tell me to go to bed immediately. At 01.00 am or 02.00 am, if she found me awake she would then just shout at me to go to bed! I wonder whether modern-day teachers would take such care of students. The teaching profession has been commercialized and the teacher-taught relationship has been the first victim.

My school was humming with activities even in those days. Apart from academics, there were PT classes, ACC and Scouts training, debating competitions every Saturday, and inter-house football, volleyball and kabaddi matches were held regularly. Ganesh and Sarswati pujas were celebrated with much enthusiasm followed by feasts at night. There were annual sports events to encourage the students to have a balanced attitude to life. They also participated in cultural activities and dramas. There was equal emphasis on study, discipline and extra-curricular activities.

I was not a good student till 3rd standard but suddenly I improved and got ranking in the Class 4 examination. In 5th class when I secured first position in the half-yearly examination, my confidence was restored and there was no looking back. Every year I came first in class by the grace of God and the blessings of my parents and teachers. I was very good not only in studies but collected various prizes in essay writing, debate competition and story writing, etc. I also became a champion in sports.

Generally the boys from a rural background, particularly those who have studied in their mother tongue, are not proficient in English. My English teacher made it a point to encourage good students and those who did well in English would find their name in the Bright Register and who were bad in English would figure in the Black Register. I tried my best and every time my name figured in the Bright Register!

According to a tradition in Odisha those who figured in the best ten in Matriculation Board Examination used to have their life history and photograph published in the paper. From 8th class onwards, I used to dream of seeing my photograph in the newspaper. I studied hard to achieve this objective, but alas, I could not make it as I committed a mistake costing me 10 marks in the Trignometry exam. I missed my spot in the paper. I was the first in my family to secure a first division in the matriculation examination but I cried bitterly. My uncle, father and elder brother consoled me by saying that it was a great achievement as I was the first in the family to secure a first division. The failure disheartened me but only momentarily. I was determined to secure a position in the University examinations. Failure teaches us a great lesson. Learning from the failure, we can make determined efforts to achieve our goal and therein lies the true spirit of a person.

Chapter 4

College days

The question is whether you would like to be a great philosopher like Bertrand Russell or a dignified clerk like me (IAS officer).

I was getting ready to enter into a more important phase of life i.e. college and university education. During those days, there was no mobile, no computer or smart phone. Even the telegraph system in the village post office operated on the Morse code. For everything, we had to depend on the post office. On the advice of my eldest brother, I applied for admission to pre-university science in Ravenshaw College. It was a reputed college and it is often said that anybody who is somebody in Odisha must be a Ravenshawian. My father, uncle and brothers had all been educated there. During my father's days, there was no proper road or transport facility to Cuttack. He had to undertake a boat ride from Athmallik to Cuttack through the turbulent Mahanadi. The boat journey used to take at least ten days one way. As a result, he used to come to the village only during summer vacation. This shows the high degree of commitment of our families towards education. The younger generation needs to understand the difficulties and struggles their parents underwent. Since they are in a much better position, they should make a conscious effort to go a step ahead of their parents so that the development of society continues.

While studying in Class-VIII, I remember, I went along with my eldest brother to see Pandit Jawaharlal Nehru, the Prime Minister who was to address the Indian Science Congress. While returning, my brother showed me the magnificent and imposing structure of the Ravenshaw College. From that day onwards, it was my dream to study there. That dream came true and I was admitted to the pre-University science class of Ravenshaw College in July, 1965. Coming from rural background, I was a bit nervous. So two days before my admission date, I visited the college to get myself acquainted with the place, roads and admission procedure, and ultimately was admitted into pre-university science with the Roll No. 1. I studied in Ravenshaw College for four years from pre-university science to graduation level in Political Science (Hon.). I was a good student and I took Physics, Chemistry, Math and Biology as my subjects in Pre-university Science. I love physics and mathematics even today. At that time, I had no idea about what I wanted to be in future. Occasionally I entertained the idea of wanting to be a lecturer, doctor, engineer or an administrator. But, slowly and gradually, under the influence and guidance of my eldest brother, I started nurturing the dream of being an IAS Officer.

I was staying in the West Hostel and, initially, there was a problem in adjustment. The spectrum of rural vs. urban life, family vs. hostel life, school vs. college life, Oriya vs. English, home food vs. hostel food, were quite unnerving and made me sad at times. I missed my childhood friends, the family atmosphere, particularly the spiritual atmosphere of my family and simple rural life. I remembered the advice my eldest brother gave me when I joined college. 'Prashanta, you will have many opportunities to aid the development of your career but at the same time, if you are not vigilant and cautious, you can slip into bad company,' he had said.

Ragging in college was unheard of at that time. There was an active students' union. Though an elected body, it never followed the path of confrontation. I liked the atmosphere prevalent during the college elections. Only during recess, the candidates came and addressed the students and would distribute the time table for the classes. One distinguishing feature about the election was that

every candidate had to address the students at a meeting, known as 'What I stand for'. It was like present-day television debates by candidates during elections.

I took my study seriously and did not participate in any games or sports activities. When the final examination of pre-university science approached, I was fully prepared. I did very well and hoped to secure a good position in the University. After the examination, the first half of my summer vacation was spent at my village. The second half was spent in Bolangir where my eldest brother was posted as District Magistrate and Collector. My brother used to take me along when he went on inspection tours. He used to explain to me the nuances of administration, field visits and camp life. The day was approaching for my results to be out. I was quite anxious. One early morning, I dreamt that after breakfast, I had gone to the market and a newspaper hawker was shouting 'PU result, PU result.' I purchased a paper and frantically searched for my name and position. I found that I secured the 11th position in the University. It was only a dream little realizing that it would be realized. The same morning, after breakfast, I went to the market and found a hawker actually shouting 'PU result, PU result'. I purchased a newspaper and was surprised to see my name exactly at the 11th position! Was it a strange coincidence or was it my sixth sense operating?

My uncle, Dr Ishwar Mishra, was the only doctor in our family. Therefore, there was a lot of pressure on me to get into a good medical college. I was not interested, as I did not like biology at all. In fact, while dissecting the frog during practicals my hands used to tremble. I was not made for such a discipline. The family's pressure was mounting, but my father and eldest brother advised me to opt for the course I liked best. I was interested to join Arts, as Humanities had always attracted me. Therefore, ignoring the pressure of my family I sought and got admission in Humanities in Ravenshaw College, in the first-year degree course.

I took Economics, Political Science and Mathematics as my subjects. Having come from the Oriya medium school, it was difficult for me to speak in English fluently. I found that groups of convent-educated girls and boys were confident and fluent in English. I was a bit nervous. To overcome my nervousness, I made it a point to participate in every English debate competition in the college and hostel. I did not get any prizes, but it bolstered my confidence. In pre-test examinations, I secured very high marks in English compared to the convent boys and girls. This further boosted my confidence. Since, I joined Humanities with the objective of ultimately appearing for the IAS examination, my eldest brother advised me to read one English paper, one magazine and the Careers Digest diligently.

I recall a discussion with my brother. He asked, 'Would you like to be a great philosopher like Bertrand Russell or a dignified clerk like me (IAS officer).' I was foxed and diplomatically answered that I wanted to be both. In fact, I liked to be an Administrator cum Philosopher. It reminds me of the quote of Plato 'that unless kings are philosophers and philosophers be kings, the city state will not be free from maladies'.

When I was in the first year, my elder brother Gama dada was in the same college in the final year Physics (Hon.). One day, we bunked class and went to see the movie *Guide* based on R.K. Narayan's novel. I did not realize then that watching a movie would help me later. In my IAS General Knowledge paper, there was a question in Part A that required the candidate to name the writers who had written the novels mentioned in Part A. Part B required the candidate to write the gist of any of the novels he had studied from the above list. I had never studied any of the novels mentioned in part A, but since *Guide* was one of the novels mentioned in Part A and I had seen the movie, I answered it on the basis of the movie. I realized that even an ordinary incident has a divine design behind it. In the final examination of First Year Degree Course held in March, 1967, I did well and secured 3rd position in the University. Though I got more marks in Economics

(70) than in Political Science (58) I liked the latter. So I took admission in BA Political Science (Hon.). Again, this decision proved a boon in disguise as I got very high percentage of marks (75%) in Political Science in IAS.

A few more incidents during the final year in college come to mind. Two sparrows had built their nest in the ventilator of my room. And they invariably made my room messy. At times, I got irritated and wanted to remove the nest, but the next moment, the plight of the poor birds would flash in my mind. This made me tolerate them. Another incident put me in an embarrassing situation; One day the postman came to the hostel to hand over a VPP parcel containing two HMT watches. I had never ordered any watch. When I told the postman, he said, 'It is in the name of P.K. Mishra, Ravenshaw College and so I am handing over the parcel to you.' At that time HMT watches were much in demand. Since I did not have money, I borrowed from my classmate and paid for the watches. I kept one and handed over the other to a friend. After a few days, the Head of the Department called me and told me that the watches were wrongly delivered to me as they were meant for his nephew, whose name was also P.K.Mishra. It was an embarrassing situation. I narrated the entire incident and said, 'Sir, I can return the watch with me but it will be embarrassing to ask my friend to return his.' Ultimately I returned my own watch to the Head of the Department which he gave to his nephew.

The Political Science Department of the College used to organize the annual function followed by an elaborate dinner. After one such function after dinner, Mr Acharya, my HOD, asked me to accompany some girls to their hostel since it was quite late into night. I wondered why I was chosen – maybe Mr Acharya had observed me to be a courteous student who would not indulge in any mischief. It was an embarrassing situation as I was shy and a poor conversationalist. Anyway, I accompanied the girls up to their hostel. We were silent almost all the way. To break the silence, I asked them whether they had studied the books by Finner, Laski and Barker, etc. The girls burst out laughing and said, 'Prashanta, you know only studies and nothing about how to converse with girls!'

Once I purchased a beautiful glass for drinking water. I went to the tap, filled it and was appreciating the glass and the reflection inside when I had a thought, 'The beauty of the glass is only temporary. It will vanish the moment it is dropped on the floor.' Exactly at that moment, the glass slipped out of my hand and broke. This was also a lesson i.e., as you think, so it shall be. Later, when I read the *Seven Spiritual Laws of Success* by Deepak Chopra, I came to know that Mother Nature was always eager to fulfil the wishes of her children. If it is a simple wish, it is fulfilled immediately, if it is complex, it may take few years or maybe a few births. This is called the principle of Effortless Ease. 'Nature's intelligence functions with effortless ease and abandons carefreeness.'

In my B.A. final year examination (Political Science, Hon.), I performed decently but not very well, as my performance in one of the papers was not that good. The result was out in June, 1969 and I got 66% in Political Science (Hon.) securing 5th position in the University. I was a bit sad as I could not secure a position in the first three. The difference was hardly 1 to 2 marks at each level. I consoled myself by philosophizing that one should accept gracefully whatever comes in life.

Chapter 5

University Days

Sycophancy was prevalent in my Department which
I did not like at all. Such a practice was against my nature,
ethos and upbringing.

After the results were declared, I wanted to study M.A. (Pol.
Science) in Delhi University, as I was confident of my admission
there on the basis of my high marks. To pursue higher education in a
city like Delhi, one needed solid financial backing. Ours was a large
family and my father had already retired years ago. The only earning
member of the family was my eldest brother. Therefore, financially
it was not possible for my family to send me to Delhi for higher
education. Perforce I had to be content to pursue my study in Uttkal
University at Bhubaneswar. I was a bit sad but then remembered
Harold Laski's remark that 'Education in modern times has become a
parental privilege.' I also remembered mother's statement that a large
family is a curse in India. Quite often, she used to say, 'O God, do not
make anybody poor as poverty destroys everything in life.'

I took admission in MA (Pol. Science) in August, 1969. The University
had a good campus with proper infrastructure and library facilities.
It was more in a rural setting. There was no trace of ragging, which
has become endemic in our educational institutions these days. There
was an introduction meeting followed by cultural activities and
dinner to introduce freshers to the seniors and the faculty. I wonder

when, how and why this pernicious practice of ragging has crept into our educational institutions.

I stayed in the hostel and except for the community life, the life there was not very enriching. Darbarigiri and chamchagiri (sycophancy) were widely prevalent in the Department and I did not like these. They not only destroy the self-respect of an individual, but also make him subservient and slavish in his approach to life. Destruction of self-respect means destruction of individuality which in turn leads to destruction of creative and independent thinking. This motivated me to appear for the IAS examination though I was merely a student trying to wriggle out of a suffocating atmosphere.

Chapter 6

Preparation for IAS

One may lose a few battles here and there but ultimately
one has to win the war of life. Nothing is impossible in life to
achieve.

While pursuing my MA degree in political science, I also studied
seriously for the IAS examination. It was burdensome and
taxing, but since the political science course was more or less the
same as that of the IAS syllabus, that helped me a lot. I started my
preparation in advance with proper planning and monitoring, under
the guidance of my eldest brother. I used to study for about 15
to 16 hours a day and kept a record of the hours through graphic
representation. This helped me to monitor my own consistency in
preparations. Base books in each subject, reference books of eminent
writers, reading English newspapers and magazines, using the
library facilities, collecting 10 years' question papers to find out the
trend, making copious notes, three revisions before appearing for the
examination, practising to write answers within the stipulated time
and, above all, my brother's guidance constituted the basis of my
preparation for IAS.

One of my father's friends who was a retired IAS officer and an
astrologer and palmist, came to my eldest brother's residence. At that
time, I happened to be in my brother's house at Bhubaneswar. When
my father's friend came to know about my preparation for IAS, he
caught hold of my hand and examined the palm. He predicted that I

would not get selected to IAS but I would become a great educationist. Though the prediction was quite shocking, I accepted the challenge and told him, 'Uncle, I will prove your prediction wrong!' By the grace of God and blessings of parents and teachers, I was selected in the IAS. I believe there is no substitute for hard work and we are the makers of our own destiny. Don't get perturbed by the adversities of life, accept the challenge, face it boldly and I am sure, you will come out successful. One may lose a few battles of life here and there but ultimately one has to win the war of life. Nothing is impossible in life. By sustained efforts, with determination and concentration, one can achieve one's goal. As Napoleon said 'Impossible is a word that is found only in a fool's dictionary.' Intense desire to achieve something is the key to life. The Upanishad says, 'You are what your deep, driving desire is. As your deep desire is, so is your will. As is your will, so is your deed. As is your deed, so is your destiny.'

I was so serious about the examination that I didn't realise that tension was gradually building up. I started to suffer from insomnia and often felt that somebody was hammering inside my head. Two days before the examination, I was so tense and tired that I could not even understand the sentences I had written in my notes. Immediately, I stopped reading and made a dash to the market. I saw a movie and came back in the evening to the hostel. Then I listened to some music from my transistor. I finally relaxed and managed to sleep through the night. The next day, my mind was fresh and everything became crystal clear. I did very well in the written examination. That day I learnt the lesson that mere study was not enough. Preparation for anything must be done with joy and relaxation. I always kept this in mind and even while discharging official duties on tour, I used to combine work with pleasure.

I was a serious student and particular about my study timings. One day when I got tired, I went for an evening walk then returned and showered. When I returned to my room, I found my eldest brother sitting on my chair. He looked at me and said, 'Prashanta, it is already past seven in the evening and you have not yet started your studies.' When I explained that I always started my studies by 6.30 in the evening but on that particular day because of the over-burdening of the mind, I just went for a walk, he replied, 'you must be consistent in your studies and time.' This only shows how serious and punctual my brother was in his approach to life and I imbibed this trait from him. Another time, my brother came to the library in search of me. I was in the library but had not entered my name in the register. When I came out of the library, he enquired as to why I had not entered my name in the register. When I said, 'Dada, it is a very small thing', he advised me that such small things matter a lot in life.

I had a friend, Sheikh Naimmudin, who was a good student of physics. Once when he came to my room, I persuaded him to appear for the Civil Services Examination. He expressed his inability as he was a science student and did not have the fees for the form. Fortunately, I had received my national scholarship and I offered him the amount. Very reluctantly, he filled up the form for the Civil Services Examination. I also shared my notes with him and when the result was out, he was selected to the Central Services (Income-tax). In another incident, while appearing in the Civil Services written examination, my scholastic lecturer made fun of one of our friends whose academic career was not so brilliant. The lecturer who was also appearing for the examination taunted that our friend would come first in the IAS. Lo and behold! When the result was out, the lecturer didn't even get a call for the interview but our friend secured the second position in the IAS examination. Strange are the ways of dispensation of justice by the cosmic spirit.

I did very well in the written examination and was sure to get a call for the interview and I got it. Before proceeding to Delhi for the interview, I went to my village to get the blessings of my parents. While bidding farewell, my mother gave me a piece of white cloth to keep in the pocket while appearing before the interview board. She said that this cloth was given to her by a saintly person and it would help me in the interview. Though I am not superstitious, I accepted it and assured her that her advice would be followed. I could have rejected it outright, but I did not because it was not a mere piece of a cloth but it represented the love, affection and the blessing of my mother. Apart from satisfying the wish of my mother, it gave me a psychological prop. When the IAS result came out, my name was in the list. Hard work, perseverance, blessings of parents, elders and teachers, faith in self and trust in God can create wonders.

Chapter 7

Life in The National Academy of Administration

My first journey to Gangotri and Gomukh probably laid a strong foundation for my further spiritual development.

*E*verybody in the family was happy but my mind was crowded with apprehensions. Not having been exposed to urban life, I was a bit nervous. Gama dada accompanied me from Bhubaneswar to Howrah, to see me off at the Railway Station for my journey to Dehradun and Mussoorie for my training. The bus journey from Dehradun to Mussoorie was quite enchanting. The zig-zag road, the coniferous forests of the Himalayan foothills and the sheer beauty of nature made the journey memorable. This was my first exposure to the Himalayas and I just fell in love with it.

On July 15, 1972 I formally became the member of the prestigious Indian Administrative Service. Life at the academy was peaceful and relaxed. The Foundational Course that lasted three months was attended by probationers of all the services i.e. IAS, IPS, IFS and Central Services. The idea was to forge a common brotherhood and camaraderie and *espirit de corps* among services which would stand them in good stead in future. Now I believe, this combined training programme of foundational course, for Central Services along with All India Services has been discontinued and each service has its own training programme. Surely, this modified system could not be in the larger interests of administration.

After this foundational course, which gave exposure to various aspects like law, culture, history, administration, management etc., the professional course began, exclusively for the IAS probationers. Followed by the professional course especially in the winter months, there was a Bharat Darshan and Army Attachment for the probationers. In my time, it was a truncated Bharat Darshan confined, to Punjab, Haryana and Rajasthan. Apart from the normal classes by the faculty, lectures were also given by important dignitaries. The whole atmosphere used to vibrate with intellectual activity. The other extra-curricular activities included football, volleyball, cricket, hockey, badminton, lawn tennis, etc. There was not a single day spent without a special event or activity being organized in the evening. I received mountaineering training at the Nehru Institute of Mountaineering, Uttarkashi. About 15 probationers were selected for this and life in the camp was quite adventurous, at times even harsh. We spent 15 days in the training camp learning the basics. Once during the training while climbing, I fell from a 20-ft. rock, fortunately, landing on a pile of sand. Everybody rushed towards me but nothing happened except a few minor scratches. After this training, we trekked to Gangotri and Gomukh, the origin of Mother Ganga. It was a difficult trek but we made it in record time. The distance from Gangotri to Gomukh is 20 km, but we completed it both ways in a single day. I was not very spiritual at that time nevertheless, I appreciated the stunning beauty of the Himalayas, it's snow-clad peaks, dense jungles, bhojpatra trees and the flowing river.

For the first time, I came across the bhojpatra jungle. Bhojpatra is the bark of the tree and it is so thin that one can write on this bark. When we reached Gomukh, I was wonderstruck to see the glacier and Shivlinga peak. Though I wanted to take a dip, I dared not as the water was too cold. Maybe my spiritual yearning was not strong enough at that time to give me the necessary courage to have a dip. Many years later, the desire was very strong and I fulfilled it. This first journey to Gangotri and Gomukh, probably, laid the foundation for my future spiritual development.

Another milestone that helped me to look at life in a holistic manner was the journey with a group of probationers to Kedarnath and Badrinath. At that time, the road to these places was very narrow and gate systems were prevalent, to facilitate and regulate the flow of traffic. From Phata, we trekked to Kedarnath. The trekking was no doubt arduous, but I enjoyed it. The beauty, grandeur and the imposing structure of the Himalayas, its snowy peaks teaching us to remain white and as pure as possible, and the roar of the river Mandakani, the merging of the forest streams into the great river, like individual souls merging into the great cosmic spirit, all enthralled me. I could observe even old persons trekking towards Kedarnath by sheer will power. The presence of the forest chattis made our journey comfortable with their 'hot cup of tea'. The never-ending stream of pilgrims only showed their tremendous faith in God. My friend Subodh Nath Jha and I literally ran up the winding and difficult path to Kedarnath and were the first to reach it. I was tired but the panoramic view, the pristine glory of the Mandakani and the very sight of Kedarnath temple, transported and elevated us to an entirely different plane. We spent the night in a dharamsala. It was very cold at night with snow all around. Early next morning, we managed to get a good darshan of Kedarnath. At that time, the area was not as congested as now. The beauty of nature was intact but greed, unplanned, unscientific development and the encroachments have not only spoilt the area but created tremendous environmental problems. The most tragic incident of June, 2013 might be likened to a mini Pralaya designed by the divine to teach mankind a lesson.

From there we went to Badrinath by road. There was no difficulty at all as the bus could reach Badrinath without any trek along the journey. The roar of the Alaknanda and the magnificent view of the peak – Neelkanth created awe and reverence. The darshan of Badrinath i.e.

Lord Vishnu, was elevating and created a deep impact. This journey to Kedarnath and Badrinath nurtured the seeds of spiritualism which developed into a beautiful tree later.

Life at the academy was enjoyable with each day humming with intellectual and cultural activities. It was not uncommon for many probationers to drink during parties at the campus. I was a teetotaller. At one of the parties, four of my friends literally dragged me to the bar coercing me to drink. Despite the pressure, I refused and told my friends that since I had no objection to their drinking, why were they concerned about my non-drinking. I also told them that unless they refrained from forcing me, I would report it to the authorities. My friends desisted from coercing me, but they were disappointed that their efforts to convert me failed miserably. This incident taught me a lesson; It is easy to say 'yes' to everything but one must have the courage to say 'no' when the situation demands. The present plight of the bureaucracy is because it has not cultivated the courage to say 'no' to the wishes and directions of the boss when the situation demands.

Present-day administrators and highly placed persons hesitate to perform physical labour as if it is below their dignity. During the training in Mussoorie, we were practically taught the value and importance of Shramdan (contribution of labour). Every day, we used to contribute physical labour while singing the song 'chal dana-dan faware'. We even prepared the horse riding track through shramdan under the guidance of our Director.

While at the academy I suddenly got a jolt in October, 1972 when I received a telegram about the passing away of my father. In fact, just the other day, we had a football match with the college students. I was also a member of the team but we were beaten, 3-1 by the youngsters. While returning to the academy after the match, I was sharing my thoughts with my friend that since my father was getting old, I must be mentally prepared for the worst. The next day, while getting ready for the morning classes, a bizarre thought entered my mind, as to what would happen to our family if father expired. When I was coming out of the dining hall, I was handed over a telegram. Little realizing what it contained, I opened it casually and got the shock of my life when I read that my lovable father was no more. How can I explain my premonition about the death? Human beings as imperfect as we are, we do not understand the invisible forces that operate in the cosmic world.

I proceeded immediately to my village by train. It took me more than 48 hours to reach home. By then the body was already cremated. All my brothers, sisters and relatives had gathered in the house to participate in various rituals on the 4th, 10th and 13th days etc. When I was in the village, I was informed by the Academy that I was allotted to the UP cadre. The comment of my brother, an IAS officer of the 1957 batch, is worth mentioning here. He said, 'I am happy that you are going back to your ancestral State. UP is one of the best administered states in the country.' I often wondered what had happened to my UP during all these years. A State which is politically very sensitive and powerful, a State which has produced so many Prime Ministers and which is rich in culture, has come to such a stage that people often poke fun by calling the state 'Ulta Pradesh' (Upside down State). Such uncharitable comments pain me. What are the reasons for such a slide? Maybe it is the population explosion or lack of infrastructure or lack of proper education and health coverage. Maybe our political representatives, bureaucrats and intelligentsia have all collectively failed to provide a role model for the development of UP. The state is the melting pot of civilizations and cultures and it has a large heart. I joined the UP Cadre as an outsider from Odisha but the people at large were so hospitable, so courteous and so large-hearted that I got myself assimilated into it through a process of imperceptible assimilation. I came, I saw but I was conquered by the love and affection showered by the general public in a profound manner. As an outsider, I never felt like a stranger in UP. There is practically no feeling of regionalism in the state but unfortunately caste plays an important role. What a contradiction! Probably, we have forgotten the maxim that a large heart and a small mind cannot go together. The experience at the academy will be incomplete without the mention of Harish Canteen, Library Point, Whispering Windows, Kulri, Camel Backroad and Landore. Harish was a legendary figure, praised by every civil servant who had received training in the Academy. His canteen was a place of recreation and relaxation where hot pakora (croquettes) and tea/coffee were served. Harish catered to all our diverse needs. Quite often, probationers also visited Whispering Windows which served food and wine. The name seems to be apt as after a few drinks, the probationers could only whisper. I remember a conversation with one of my friends belonging to the Bihar cadre. This friend hailed from a respectable family and probably had never seen poverty in life. Once he saw me sending a money order to my parents and wondered how it was possible for me to send money home, when every time he demanded money from his parents. Even though my salary was hardly Rs 500, I still managed to send Rs 100 to my parents every month. I joked 'You are a drinker and a chain-smoker. Very often, you eat out and many times, you entertain women probationers in hotels. I never do any of these things and hence all this money is saved.'

It is often said, 'What is in a name?' But my experience shows otherwise. There were two P.K. Mishras in the Academy; one was Prashanta Kumar Mishra, that is myself and the other was Pramod Kumar Mishra. Both of us were from the 1972 batch, both from Odisha and good friends. But he was from Gujarat Cadre and I was from UP Cadre. Having the same name created enough confusions in the academy and then later also. I used to take extra lunch items like dosa, vada and eggs but Pramod generally did not. At the end of the month, on receiving our mess bills, he would look at me. With his usual innocent smile, he would ask, 'Prashanta Babu, I have not taken these items, but they are reflected in my mess bill.' With a mischievious smile, I would reply, 'Pramod, I have taken these items, but fortunately they are not in my bill.' When he left the Academy, he took some advance which was reflected in my account. It took me quite sometime to get it corrected. When Pramod became the Additional Principal Secretary to the Prime Minister in 2014, I received congratulations from many persons. In fact, one of the leading newspapers wrote about Pramod but published my photograph. This was quite embarrassing and I brought it to his notice and he, in his own way, laughed it away. I still like and respect him as he remains the same Pramod of the Academy days with the same disarming smile.

Horse riding was compulsory during our time. One had to pass the riding test also. Mr Naval Singh was a legendary instructor who had taught horse riding to thousands of probationers. Many of them were afraid of riding as a few accidents had also taken place during these classes. Once I fell off the horse during cantering and was unconscious for a few minutes. One of my friends lost four of his front teeth during horse riding. I remember a hilarious incident. When a probationer could not control his horse, Mr Naval Singh charged towards him and shouted, 'Mister if you cannot control a horse, how can you control a district?' What is the rational behind this horse riding? It is a British legacy and was useful during that period when there was not much of infrastructure facility. Many feel that this training has lost its *raison d'etre* in the modern context of availability of transport facilities. The other view is that it is still relevant as mounted police is often used in maintaining law and order and for crowd control. Moreover, even today, there are inaccessible areas which can be accessed only through the horse or mule. It also gives a sense of adventure and boost to the officer's confidence level.

The Prime Minister, Mrs Indira Gandhi, visited the National Academy at Mussoorie and addressed us. When the session was opened for questions, I asked her, 'Madam Prime Minister, we belong to the All India Services but why is it that we are allotted a particular State and confined to it? Why can't we serve in any part of the country?' She smiled and in a pleasant voice replied, 'What you have suggested is quite ideal but considering the linguistic diversities, the re-organisation of States on a linguistic basis, and the complexity of District and State Administration, it is better to have a State cadre in the interests of efficiency, public dealings and public relations.'

Apart from the school and university days, it is the training period which I often remember. It is one of the best periods in the life of a civil servant. I enjoyed my life and at the same time learnt a good deal in terms of manners, courtesy, knowledge, and confidence. I never neglected study of the training materials and did fairly well in the examination improving my position to a considerable extent. Now we were getting ready for the district training in our allotted State.

My ancestral house in Athmallik, Odisha

My parents Kishore Chandra Mishra and Swarnalata Mishra

My eldest brother Rama Kant Mishra, mentor, friend, philosopher and guide

Five brothers

Receiving certificate of mountaineering training from
Mrs Sathe, wife of the Director, Academy

At Kedarnath temple as a probationer

With II.G. Dabral, Vice-Principal, OTS, Nainital

With George Bush (Senior), the then Vice President of USA

At the Mazar of Sufi Saint Salim Chisti with family, Fatehpur Sikri

At Kainchi temple (near Nainital) with my wife

After a refreshing bath in the river Saraswati near Kalimath

At Badrinath temple with C.S. Semwal

At Alka Glacier (Vasudhara) with the Semwal brothers

With N.C. Sharma at Surya Sila, Yamunotri

Panoramic view of the river Ganga from Vasistha Ashram

Swami Chaitanayananda ji worshiping Lord Shiva

With Swami Ramji at his Rishikesh Ashram

C.B. Sathpathy, IPS (Retd.), a great devotee of Sirdi Sai Baba releasing
my book '*Ek Drishtikon*' in 1996

My family with R.K. Trivedi, the then Governor of Gujarat

Taking charge as Chief Secretary, UP

With Dr A.P.J. Abdul Kalam, former President of India

Taking oath as Member, UPSC

With Vice-President, Hamid Ansari

Meditating at the bank of the
river Ganga near Vasistha Guffa

Chapter 8

....❦

District Training

(April 1973 – March 1974)

The DM is the key person in the district even today and if he takes interest, everything falls in line.

*N*ormally probationers are allotted small and medium type districts for grassroots training. Originally, I was allotted District Bahraich for such training, but it was subsequently changed to Gorakhpur and I was not informed about it. Before reporting for the training, I went to Odisha and after spending a few days with my family, headed for Bahraich. It was a tedious journey. First, I boarded a train from Bhubaneswar to Howrah and then to Lucknow and from there to Gonda. At midnight, I reached Gonda by AT Mail and in the morning boarded a passenger train and reached Bahraich by 9.30 am. Since I did not know anybody, I went straight to DM's residence by rickshaw. Mr S.N. Shukla, the DM of Bahraich, received me warmly at his residence and then informed me that I had to proceed to Gorakhpur as my district had been changed. I had my breakfast and lunch with him and his family and at night left for Gorakhpur. It was highly courteous on Mr Shukla's part to see me off at the railway station.

I reached Gorakhpur in the morning and went straight to the DM's residence. He allotted me accommodation in the Officers' Hostel which was close to the Collectorate. Life there during training was difficult since I was a bachelor and there was not much of lodging facility available for a probationer. I had my breakfast, lunch and dinner at a dhaba. With a meager salary, I could not afford the luxury of a hotel. During my stay here, my stomach was constantly upset because of the oily and spicy dhaba (roadside restaurant) food. The stomach ailment I contracted there persists even now. The training module consisted of judicial, revenue, criminal, civil, tehsil, block and treasury training and attachment to various officers like ADM (E) and ADM (P) and SDM. Occasionally, the DM took me along when he went on tour. As a probationer we had to prepare assignments on law and order, socio-economic survey of a village, report on the development project and a report on the block, tehsil or a district. I believe that even today, these kind of assignments are given to the newcomers though decades have elapsed. If it is so, then there is need to have a fresh look at the training module and assignments to probationers, keeping in view the present dynamics of district administration. The training for me was quite fascinating. My knowledge of Hindi, learnt at the Academy, improved considerably. I recall an incident; the DM told me to accompany him during his 'daura' (tour), but I could not understand the word and asked him to explain what it meant. He was annoyed and remarked, 'You are a Mishra and you don't know Hindi. It is a shame.' Immediately, I understood that the DM had confused me with a person coming from the Hindi belt. I clarified, 'Sir, I hail from a non-Hindi speaking State i.e. Odisha and I first learnt the Hindi alphabets at the Academy.' Once, I received an application where the DM had written, 'Forun isko bhej deejiye.' (send it immediately). I could not understand the word 'forun' (immediately) and mistook for a foreign country. So, I went personally to ask him which foreign land this application was to be sent. He had a hearty laugh and explained that it was an Urdu word meaning 'immediately'. I used to observe the DM's dealing with the public. I noticed that whenever somebody came, he would say 'tasreef rakhiye'. Once somebody came to meet me, I also said 'tasveer rakhiye'. He laughed and gently corrected me, 'Sir, it is not "tasveer", it is "tasreef". "Tasveer" means picture

and "tasreef" means to be seated'. It was hilarious to learn Hindi in the course of my training. I picked it up quickly as there were many common words in Hindi and Oriya. Later I went on and even wrote a spiritual book in Hindi, *Ek Drishtikon.*

I did not sleep well for about one year while preparing for the IAS examination and as a result developed insomnia and migraines. The migraine was so severe that I would at times end up crying. There was no cure for this in allopathy. When I came to Gorakhpur for my training, my uncle Dr I.C. Mishra, a World War II veteran, advised me to visit Dr Mukherjee, his friend, living in Gorakhpur at that time. Dr Mukherjee was an allopath, but also famous as a homoeopathic doctor. One evening I called on him, and ended up having dinner with him. While bidding farewell, he enquired whether I had any problems in Gorakhpur. I replied 'Uncle, I have no problems except for a terrible migraine every now and then'. He told me that there was no cure for it in allopathy. The various pills would bring temporary relief but not a permanent one. He advised me, 'Take 1 litre of water with 100 grams of mishri (crystallized sugar lump) dissolved in it. Leave it uncovered under the open sky. Next morning before sunrise, drink it without brushing your teeth. Do this for 3 months and observe the result.' I did this and surprisingly the migraine vanished, and it never recurred again. India is replete with such traditional wisdom which, if researched and recorded, would go a long way in providing relief to the millions. During my stay here, I came to know of the Gita Press which was doing yeoman service in the field of spiritualism. I visited the Press and was impressed by the work they were engaged in. A lot of good spiritual books were presented to me. I went through these books which helped me immensely. The training pattern in UP was a sandwiched one; it involved district training, institutional training at OTS, Nainital, agricultural training at Pant Nagar Agriculture University, driving and weapons training at Sitapur PAC and secretariat training at Lucknow. The first part of training at Gorakhpur lasted till August, 1973. Then I proceeded to OTS, Nainital for institutional training. All the IAS probationers of the UP cadre and the PCS probationers of UP received their training here. Thus, it provided a good meeting ground between IAS officers and PCS officers. We were exposed to various laws of UP, schemes of development and the problems that the State faces. Though Rampal Bhardwaj, IAS, was the principal of OTS Nainital, I would specifically mention Mr Hargovind Dabral, Vice-principal and a senior PCS officer, later promoted to IAS as the sole spirit of the training school. He was a dedicated and a thoroughly intelligent person. Apart from various laws and development papers, we had one paper on personal conduct and behaviour. I secured the highest marks in this paper i.e. 95%. I was not satisfied with it and rushed to Mr Dabral's room and asked, 'Sir, why have you deducted 5 marks? What are the deficiencies in me?' Mr Dabral smiled and patted my back and replied, 'I have given you the highest but I like your spirit.' He explained that the whole life was a process of continuous learning and every moment, every day, presents a situation where the individual has to learn something or the other.

Life in OTS, Nainital was peaceful. The beauty of the Himalayas, the greenery, the ice-cold breeze, the winding roads and the lakes and the serene, beautiful faces of the Kumaonis make the atmosphere more enchanting. I enjoyed every bit of my stay there. Walking along the winding roads of Nainital in the evening, enjoying a boat ride in the lake, walking in the congested market places, observing the never-ending stream of tourists from different parts of the country and relishing the hot tea and bhutta etc., these memories are still fresh in the mind. When I get tired and sad, I ruminate over my good old days as a probationer in Nainital to refresh and energize myself. I remember one trekking trip to Nainadevi peak. Since I was young, I was walking fast. Mr Dabral advised me to take small steps and at a slow pace to conserve energy for the final ascent. He said, 'Mishra, you must always remember that in hilly regions, you should walk slowly, steadily and surely, otherwise you will be tired and exhausted soon.' This advice still rings in my ears. It helped me a lot later in life when I was posted as DM of Pauri Garhwal and Tehri Garhwal and had to trek a lot in the districts. The picturesque landscape of Nainital is always there in my mind. But when I visited Nainital later, in June, 2013, I was aghast to see the congestion, degradation and pollution of the city. No doubt, tremendous development has taken place but concrete jungles have emerged. One notices a lot of vehicles and people but the pristine glory of the Himalayas, the beauty of the lakes and the environmental cleanliness of the area have all been compromised.

Our stay at OTS Nainital got over in November, 1973. In December, all of us proceeded to Pant Nagar Agricultural University for our next training. It was a reputed university and had a good faculty. We were taught not only various branches of agriculture, its practices and nuances but at the same time we were trained in tractor driving and ploughing. The training here was highly useful. A few days before our departure from Pant Nagar, one of the Professors invited all the probationers for dinner at his residence but he didn't invite me. I was surprised and pondered over the reason. But the next day, I was invited alone for dinner. I could smell something fishy and I was right. The Professor put forth before me the marriage proposal for his niece which I politely refused.

From Pant Nagar, we left for Sitapur. We stayed at the Sitapur PAC Guesthouse which had good accommodation and facilities. We learnt jeep driving and weapons training (pistol) during our 10 days' training there. When after the training, a test in firing was conducted one of my friends was a total wash-out. But when after the test, a firing competition was held, miraculously most of his bullets hit the target and he stood first. We were all surprised, but life is like that.

After Sitapur, I came back to Gorakhpur in January, 1974 to complete the unfinished part of the district training. I stayed at the Officers' Hostel. During this period, I finalized all my four assignments which were appreciated by the Academy. I was fortunate to have an exposure to the Assembly Election in UP. In Gorakhpur district I was attached to ADM (Plg.) for election duty. I was surprised at the way the elections were conducted with thorough preparation and in a just and fair manner. The Indian electorate may be illiterate but are intelligent enough to exhibit a keen sense of understanding of the problems and the importance of the elections. Advanced European countries had taken hundreds of years to come to the stage of universal franchise but we had done it in one go.

In mid-March, 1974, I left for Lucknow for secretariat training. The whole batch of the UP Cadre 1972 was there for the training. It was a pleasure to meet all friends after a lapse of many months. I was attached to the Secretary (Education) for my secretariat training for one week. It was good of the Secretary to have taken keen interest in my training. He explained to me about the budget preparation, plan and non-plan outlays, continuing schemes, new schemes, revenue budget, capital budget and budget monitoring.

The one-week stay in Lucknow was quite enjoyable. This was my first visit to the city and I was impressed by the magnificence and grandeur of the Lucknow Secretariat building. Every evening, we used to go to Hazratganj market for 'gunjing' (strolling) and feast on delicious kabab and kulfi with faluda, for which Lucknow is quite famous. Unfortunately, we could not meet the Chief Secretary and the other Secretaries of the important Departments as they were too busy with their day-to-day administration.

The district training had come to an end. During this period, I came to the conclusion that unless the DM showed interest in the training of the probationer, nothing would move in the right direction. In fact, the DM is the key person in the district even today and if he takes interest, things will fall in line. We used to send a monthly report to the Academy giving a vivid description of our training programme

and impressions. We did not know what happened to these reports. Hopefully, the Academy in the present time must be calling for such reports and after careful analysis, give necessary directions to the DMs under whose guidance the probationers receive training. I also observed that particularly in UP, the district training pattern was so devised that it was hopelessly fragmented and sandwiched with little time for actual training. No independent charge of any Tehsil or Block was given during the training. But I feel such training, by giving independent charge, would certainly enhance the confidence of the probationer. In big important districts, the DM and ADM are so busy in maintenance of law and order, VIP duties and meetings that they have no time to give serious attention to the training of the probationer. In my opinion, probationers should be posted in small and medium districts where they can learn the ABC of administration under the guidance of the DM. We were told that in old days, the DM used to look after the comfort of the probationer as a member of his family. But alas! That is rare now.

After the secretariat training in Lucknow, we proceeded to the National Academy of Administration, Mussoorie for our sandwiched pattern training. Here there was no examination. There were only sharing of the district experience of each probationer and presentation of group papers. It was quite relaxing as there was no examination and no evaluation. An interesting feature of my stay during this period was that my elder brother Gama dada who was selected for Central Services, joined me as an IRTS probationer in the Academy for his training. During this period, both of us trekked to Nag Tiba which was quite an adventurous one. We also participated in the marathon race organized by the Academy. The presence of my elder brother made my stay in the Academy even more pleasant.

The sandwiched pattern training continued for three months, from April to June, 1974. During this period, Mr Vishwen, the Appointment Secretary of UP, came to the Academy and met all probationers of the UP cadre. He asked each one of us about our preference for the district to be posted. I replied, 'Sir, you post me anywhere in UP.' He was surprised and impressed. In fact ignoring the preferences of other probationers, he posted me in Agra, a key district of the state. When I was leaving the Academy to join my posting in Agra, our Director called me and briefed me about UP. He further advised me to be careful about a few officers posted in Agra. This advice, which I bore in my mind, came in handy throughout my stay in Agra.

Chapter 9

···

Sub-Divisional Magistrate, Baha and Agra

(July 1974 – July 1975)

Crises will come and go in a person's life. Strange situations will arise but it is you and you alone who have to face up to the challenge with all your might, discipline and samskaras to weather it out.

The two years' training period was over and it was time to work independently as SDM in a Sub-division. I didn't know to what extent the training had equipped me to handle the functions of the sub-division, but I was confident that with sincerity, integrity and willingness to learn at every stage, I would definitely be able to discharge my responsibility with efficiency. After the training, I first went to Delhi to spend few days with my eldest brother and bhabi. Thereafter, I arrived at Agra Cantt. by the Taj Express. Since I was a complete stranger, and there was nobody to receive me at the railway station, I had to take a rikshaw and go straight to the DM's residence. Mr J.N. Pradhan was the DM. I waited for some time to meet him. When I met him, to my utter surprise, I found that he was under the impression that I had come to the district for training. When he came to know that I had already completed my district training and this was a regular posting, he directed the ADM (E) to put up a proposal for my posting as SDM in some sub-division. I had lunch with the DM at his residence and I was allotted a one-room suite in the Officers' Hostel which was 6 km from the Collectorate but near the Taj Mahal.

I was posted as SDM, Baha — a ravine and dacoit-infested sub-division. At that time, all SDMs used to stay in district headquarters and once a week, go to the sub-divisional headquarters to hold court and meet the public. Such a practice was, perhaps, a legacy of the British Raj and continued for a long period after Independence. This was contrary to all canons of district administration. I never followed the practice of visiting the Sub-divisional headquarters weekly and would spend half my time in the sub-divisional headquarters and half in the district headquarters. It had greatly facilitated my interaction with the local public and the officials and helped me understand their problems much better.

There is a good practice in the district administration to call on the DM, SSP and the District Judge by the newly appointed officer. I called on the DM and SSP and when I went to the Judges' compound to call on the District Judge, he was not at home. While returning from there, I saw the name-plate of an IAS officer who was senior to me. I thought it proper to call on him and he was happy to receive me. It was evening already and he took me to Sadar Tehsil building to review the progress of compulsory levy of wheat. He rebuked the Tehsildar left and right with slang unmatched in any vocabulary. That was his style of getting things done. He forgot the elementary principles of public administration to motivate and encourage officials. I always believe in Maslow's theory of motivation and hierarchical needs of the personnel. You can drag the horse to the water but cannot force it to drink. During my 42 years in administration, I had little occasion to use the stick. There is no point in harassing or humiliating subordinate officials. Most bureaucrats even today believe in the danda (stick) forgetting that the problems and nuances of modern-day administration are too complex to be handled by this policy. A demoralized organization cannot ensure good results.

After the review, the senior officer took me in his jeep to the Collector's Compound where all Magistrates were staying. On the way, he advised me that there was no need to work hard to get a good posting and promotion. To quote his words, 'Just hook yourself well with the politicians and everything will be all right.' What an advice to a new entrant! At that time, I did not realize that such advice would be taken seriously by most bureaucrats. The senior officer took me to one of the houses in the DM's compound to give me a treat along with some other officers. From here my ordeal began. There were two or three officers who came to the residence. Drinks were served along with snacks. I was a bit nervous but politely declined the drink. The officers made fun of me and commented, 'Don't behave like an Oriya. You have not learnt anything in the Academy.' Very politely I retorted, 'I am an Oriya and I have to behave like an Oriya!' I tolerated the situation so long as they did not compel me to drink. I was content with snacks but after some time to my great horror, I found that a blue film was being screened. My samskaras (inherent values), discipline and the values imparted to me from childhood, revolted and I stormed out of the place, walking the 6 km to the Officers' Hostel. Crises will come in a person's life. Strange situations will occur in life but it is you and you alone who have to face the challenge with all your might, values, discipline and samskaras to weather it out.

The institution of SDM/SDO is an important one in revenue administration and it is the real prop of the District Administration. The SDM has multifarious roles to perform in his Tehsil. The primary functions are (a) maintenance of law and order, (b) collection of land revenue and other dues, (c) court work involving revenue cases and preventive cases under Cr.PC and cases under the Special Act, (d) conducting identification parade and taking the dying declaration, (e), public distribution system (f) VIP duties (g) distribution of Gaon Sabha and ceiling surplus land to the weaker sections and to ensure their possession, (h) keeping an eye on supply of fertilizer, agricultural inputs, power and irrigation facilities, (i) removal of public grievances (j) disaster management like flood, drought etc. (k) tour and inspection. During our time, the SDM's role in the development of the blocks within his jurisdiction was minimal. In fact, the institution of SDM was more or less excluded from the process of development. Probably the same trend continues even now. This is not desirable. The SDM's position in his sub-division should be like that of a District Magistrate, coordinating and guiding all the activities from law and order to development. If it is done, it will definitely streamline the development administration in the blocks.

My narration will not be complete without an account of some interesting episodes on when I worked in Baha and Agra Tehsils. I was a newcomer to administration, still learning Hindi and my DM allotted almost all the sections of the Collectorate to me. I was over-loaded with official work and would wind up office at 9 to 9.30 pm almost every night and then walk to the Officers' Hostel, a distance of 6 km. At that time using the official jeep for commuting from residence to office was considered as private use and I strictly adhered to this principle. As a result, I had to walk 12 km every day.

One can appreciate my ordeal. One evening when I was leaving the office at 9 pm, an experienced old Deputy SP of Intelligence who was on the verge of retirement, came to me and said, 'Mishra Sahib, why are you working so hard? Nobody is going to recognize your hard work. My sincere advice to you is, "Pose busy and take it easy"'. I took it in a lighter vein, and thought that Mr Negi was joking. But after putting in many years of service, I felt that Mr Negi's comment was not far from truth. In fact, in the services hardly 15% of the personnel work creatively, with sincerity and dedication without making a noise. The rest try to pose busy achieving very little, yet feathering their own nest.

I was so over-burdened with work that one day I went to the Commissioner to complain about it. With a paternal smile he patted me and said, 'Mishra, you are a young IAS officer and will be DM soon. Unless you know the functioning of every branch of the Collectorate, you will not be a successful DM. By over-loading you with work of all sections, your DM has correctly exposed you to experiences of different sections of the Collectorate. It only shows his confidence in your ability to cope with the problems.'

I was also trained by my DM in delivering public speeches. He took me along to a public function on Independence Day where he had to deliver a speech. To my surprise, he asked me to deliver the speech before hundreds of people. I was nervous as I had never faced such a crowd in my life but reluctantly I went to the dais and addressed them mostly in Hindi with a little bit of English. When I finished the speech, I received a thunderous applause and the DM congratulated me on such a good speech. After this, the fear of the crowd vanished.

I recall an interesting case of a famous doctor who was a friend of the DM. While constructing his residence he had encroached upon some Gaon Sabha land. He probably assumed that since he was a friend of the DM, no action would be taken. But when it was brought to my notice, action for eviction was started. The doctor approached the DM who, in turn, advised me to regularize the encroachment by taking an equivalent amount of land from the doctor's private holding. I was aghast at this interference by the DM in the revenue proceeding which was a judicial one. I did not yield to his pressure and decided in favour of the Gaon Sabha. First it was an encroachment, secondly the doctor remained silent for a considerable point of time and thirdly when it was detected by the revenue administration, he wanted to wriggle out by offering an equivalent land in exchange. This incident enhanced my reputation as a fearless and fair-minded officer.

The DM used to take monthly staff meeting to review the work and performance of the officers. I was meticulous but nevertheless on a few occasions, had failed to provide some information. The SDM of Firozabad used to provide all the information that was sought.

Whenever a question was put to him seeking some information, he would open a diary and give precise and definite figures. At one meeting while reviewing the work of Firozabad, the DM sought some information. When the SDM, opened the diary and uttered the figures, the DM snatched the diary and, to his utter surprise, found that the page was blank. Thus, the SDM was exposed. Don't bluff. Always side by the truth.

Tour and overnight stay have become uncommon now in the District Administration. In UP, there was a mandatory provision for making a monsoon tour, in August and a tour during winter. The officer had to stay in the village either in a tent or in a school or Panchayat Bhawan at night. Though some officers did not follow this practice, I followed it both in letter and spirit. Since I was a new entrant, I used to read the revenue manual for guidance. At one such inspection when I asked the Tehsildar to parade all the 4th class employees before me, he tried to evade the situation. After lunch, when I again asked him to do so, he reluctantly revealed that a few of the Tehsil staff were deployed at the DM's/ADM's and other officers' residences. This is a normal practice in UP which continues even today. It may be necessary to provide comfort to the officer but it is not desirable in this form. This is not only illegal but also makes one feel guilty. I believe a few States (in the South) probably have made provisions for keeping domestic servants by providing certain allowances to the officer concerned. I think this is a better way of handling the situation.

While going through the revenue manual relating to inspection of the record room, I came across an interesting point. It required the officer to enquire about a cat and its health. I could not understand the sense of such a provision. When I posed the question to my Tehsildar, an old, mature and honest person, he laughed and said, 'Sir, the practice of keeping a healthy cat in the record room was started back in the British days. This was to prevent rats from damaging the records.'

Agra provided a solid training ground in administration, exposing me to its different facets. I not only learnt judicial and revenue work but also came to know about the sufferings of the poor, their problems, the interference in administration, the corruption, handling of communal riots, disaster management and myriad problems confronting the public at large. Agra attracts a lot of international tourists and important dignitaries. I had a good experience in handling VIP duties and responsibility. In a nutshell, my tenure there provided me with ample opportunities to get a bird's eye view of district administration and its problems.

Agra was a turning point in my life. As a University student, when I visited Agra in 1971, I was greatly impressed by the beauty of the Taj and wondered how fortunate were the people there to witness the beauty of the Taj every day, little realizing that one day I would be posted there and later get married in Agra.

Love knows no bounds and Cupid strikes everybody at some time. During my stay in Agra, I came across a beautiful girl, the daughter of the Senior Superintendent of Police, named Sarita with whom I fell in love. The courtship lasted about two years. This was a period of romance and excitement, leaving an indelible imprint in my mind. I first saw her at the SSP's residence reciting the Ramayana at her family function. I was impressed with her simplicity, elegance and beauty. The moment was auspicious as the Ramayana was being recited and was an opportune moment to take a vital decision in life. It was all divine design, otherwise a boy from Athmallik, Odisha could not have come all the way to Agra, UP to marry a girl outside his region. I used to walk to the Collectorate and Sarita used to cycle down to St. John's College for her classes. We used to criss-cross each other and exchange glances. Mr J.N. Awasthi was the SSP of Agra and he was extremely fond of me. I also liked the family immensely. They were all cultured and affectionate people. As the days rolled on, my visits to the SSP's residence increased and I would also go to see movies and attend parties and picnics with the family. At that time, there was no mobile, no facebook, no WhatsApp and no technological advancement. The only interactions happened either during a party or while watching a movie or at social functions. Once we all visited the Bateswar Mela. Bateswar is known for its large number of Shiva temples situated on the banks of the Yamuna. It gave me a good opportunity to interact with Sarita. With the passage of time, the attraction got intensified. Sarita was a good student, a good shooter and a painter. One day, at the Kailash Mela near Sikandara, in order to impress her, I took a mis-adventurous trip on a horse to Sikandara, a distance of 15 km from the city. The ride was painful and I suffered bruises near the ankles and thighs. So much so that I had to return by jeep and get treated at the Police Lines Hospital. After that, my horse-riding became the joke in the Awasthi family.

Agra is known for its extreme climate. In June, under the scorching sun, as the SDM I had to mobilize my Tehsil and field staff to collect compulsory levy of wheat from the farmers. It was a good experience and one had to be on tenterhooks to sort out the problems connected with levy procurement. By mid-June, I had almost achieved 95% of the target and I was sure to achieve more than cent per cent. During this time, Mr J.N. Awasthi and his family along with some friends decided to take a trip by road to Kashmir. I was invited too, by Mr Awasthi himself, but I declined since I was busy with levy procurement. The same evening I got the first telephone call from Sarita who jokingly taunted me, 'Only levy is coming in your dreams and nothing else.' The next morning I went to her father and expressed my desire to join the trip to Kashmir. He readily agreed and finally after getting the necessary leave sanctioned by the DM, I became a part of the entourage. It was an extremely fruitful and enjoyable trip. We visited Jullundar, Bhakra Nangal Dam, Jwala Devi, Kud, Srinagar, Gulmarg, Khilan Marg and Pahalgaon. Kashmir with all its natural beauty, streams, lakes and beautiful faces truly represents heaven on earth. At that time, it was not turbulent and we moved freely. We also trekked from Katra to Vaishno Devi during the trip. I was greatly enthralled by the chanting of 'Jai Mata Di' by the pilgrims. At that time, the surroundings were undeveloped and unhygienic. There was a lot of congestion and since there was only one opening to the cave, there was always the danger of suffocation. Somehow, we managed to get Darshan and I prayed before the Mother to bless me with Sarita. Later, Sarita told me that she too made the same prayer. Two souls were coming together and a strong bond never to be broken was established. I found a good family in UP and an excellent life-partner.

While on this trip the National Emergency was imposed and we had to rush back to Agra. The trip to Kashmir brought us very close. When Mr Awasthi sent the marriage proposal of his daughter to our family, a few members of my family vehemently opposed it, as it was outside the region. My eldest brother who was posted as Director in the Ministry of Agriculture at the Centre, enquired from Mr R.K. Trivedi, Secretary in the DoPT, about Mr Awasthi's family. Mr Trivedi was Vice-Principal of Metcalfe House when my brother was receiving his IAS training in 1957. He knew my brother very well and advised him to go ahead with the proposal as the Awasthi family enjoyed a high reputation in UP. Still the language barrier came in the way. I did not want to displease my mother and the elders. I wanted their support and so, I had to wait for two years before I convinced all of them. My mother, who had studied up to 7th standard only, had a broad mind and a large heart. It was her words that her son's happiness was her happiness that actually clinched the issue in my favour.

Chapter 10

....❧

Joint Magistrate, Mahoba

(August 1975 – July 1976)

> Politeness and courtesy beget politeness and courtesy
> from the other side. It is always better to be polite even
> when being firm.

*I*n August, 1975, I was transferred from Agra to Mahoba, District Hamirpur as Joint Magistrate. Mahoba is a beautiful place with small hillocks, lakes and reservoirs in abundance. It looks even more enchanting during the rainy season.

The position of Joint Magistrate is a unique one to UP. Few sub-divisions like Mohoba, Karvi, Kashia, Ranikhet etc.; are earmarked for initial posting for young IAS officers as Joint Magistrate. In Mahoba, this institution is called as 'Jointee' in popular parlance. The Joint Magistrate is different from an SDM in the sense that the former is a young IAS officer looking after more than one important Tehsil. For instance, in my case, there are four Tehsils in District Hamirpur and as Joint Magistrate I was looking after two important Tehsils, Mohoba and Charkhari, more or less independently.

The residence of the Joint Magistrate was a huge bungalow with a sprawling lawn and trees round the premises. Bundelkhand area being a hilly terrain, there were a lot of snakes including black cobras, scorpions and insects in the residential campus. While coming back from office which was just across my residence, I used to notice black cobras and other reptiles in the compound. The peons guarding the bungalow were equipped with not only lathis but also guns. I was told that the peons had already shot two or three black cobras. When I heard this, I scolded them and directed them not to harm or kill such creatures, particularly nagas when they were not causing us any harm. One evening after returning from office with a heavy head, I was relaxing on the cot with a peon pressing my head. Suddenly, my peon screamed that a Kala Nag was entering the bed room from the side of the bath room. I saw the serpent cross through the bath room door. Both of us ran out of the room screaming. Probably, the snake got frightened by the noise and turned back. Another time, I saw a huge 12-feet snake move very fast towards the dilapidated wall of the compound. The chowkidar of the bungalow pierced the snake with his spear but the snake had so much strength that it still moved towards the pile of bricks despite being pierced into two halves. That was a ghastly scene. I noticed a bunch of spikes arranged in a circular fashion just above the tail of the snake. I was told by the locals that such snakes caused irreparable damage by ejecting these spikes into human beings. The portion of the body which receives these spikes begins to rot and the victim eventually dies.

I had heard of scorpions and their poisonous bites. I personally experienced it when I was posted in Mahoba. Soon after marriage, my wife had gone to Kanpur to her parents' place, and was returning that particular day by bus. It was summer and I was resting in the verandah on a cot, when I noticed a bus coming from Kanpur side, stop near the gate. I rushed to wear my slippers, without even inspecting them slipped my foot into the slipper and got a shock. A small grey scorpion lying on the slipper stung my right foot. My wife didn't come that day but I got the scorpion sting. It was a painful experience and the pain moved upwards gradually. To avoid any complication, I tried to contact the Dy.CMO on telephone but could not and hence went to the hospital nearby. The Dy.CMO came and in his nervousness, without even testing the reaction of the injection administered it. It was half over when my head starting reeling and my tongue started to choke my throat inside. I was unable to speak and with a gesture of my hand, I indicated my discomfiture. The doctor realised that my body was reacting to the injection and immediately administered another injection to nullify the reaction. I was put in emergency for 24 hours with a lot of ice on the right leg to numb the pain. During this time, I observed that the pain of the scorpion's bite slowly moved upward for 12 hours and in the next 12 hours, it came down slowly and by the end of the 24 hours the pain was over. It was a 24-hour ordeal.

The work of the Joint Magistrate was challenging but interesting as well. At that time, on the recommendation of the Patil Committee, great emphasis was laid on distribution of Gaon Sabha and surplus ceiling land to the weaker sections. I used to hold Gaon Sabha meetings even at night in the villages to ensure proper allotment and distribution of patta. Despite my sincerity, I had to face scathing unjustified criticism from an important politician at a public meeting which was attended by the Cabinet Minister in charge of the 20-points Programme. A raid had been conducted under my instruction against the politician to unearth his nefarious activities of smuggling out wheat and cement to a neighbouring state. His trucks were seized and an FIR was lodged against him. I could understand the bitter feelings the politician had towards me but he took advantage of the Minister's presence to malign me in the eyes of the public. I requested the Minister to give me a minute to say something. With his permission when I exposed the politician and his misdeeds before the public, a chorus of shouts rose that their Joint Magistrate was honest, and worked round the clock, but the politician was a crooked fellow. The Minister could sense the gravity of the situation and abruptly ended the meeting. He took me along to the inspection bungalow nearby and requested me to have dinner with him. I refused saying that we were advised in the Academy not to mingle freely with politicians and to keep them at arm's length. The Minister, without taking any offence, smiled and asked me to have tea with him. I refused that too as I did not drink tea. The Minister then requested me to have at least lemonade which I readily agreed to. He sent away all his hangers-on from the room and had his dinner in the room while I sipped my lemonade. In a fatherly tone he said, 'Son, you are an IAS Officer and member of a prestigious service. You will one day be a DM, Secretary, Chief Secretary and occupy important posts. If you are so sensitive and blunt, it will be difficult to work within the system. I am not asking you to do anything illegal, but I must advise you to be a little discreet and to express your views in a manner that will not humiliate others.' I pondered over this advice for a second and thought that the Minister was correct. I told him, 'Sir, I have noted it for the future and I am sorry.' Bluntness does not pay in the long run. Politeness and courtesy begets politeness and courtesy from the other side. It is always better to be polite but at the same time be firm. Had I told these things to a present Minister or a politician, probably I would have been reprimanded, but the old politician did not take amiss at my utterances and like an elder, he counseled me correctly. This is the difference between the behaviour of the present day politicians and those of the old generations.

During my tenure, I evolved a novel way of handing possession of land to the allottees. I used to receive a lot of complaints from the weaker sections about the dispossession of the allotted land by powerful and influential sections of the villages. I observed that the report called for from the police or tehsil never saw the light of day or was so delayed that the real purpose of allotment was defeated. I hit upon an idea and in all cases of the complaints of the allottees who belonged to weaker sections, I straightaway issued show cause notices to the influential parties under Section 107 of Cr.PC for likely commission of breach of peace. I took the advantage of the words 'receiving information and likely to commit' to issue such notices under Cr.PC to bind them down to maintain peace. By following this novel method of handing over possession to allottees of the weaker sections, I succeeded to a great extent, despite the sluggishness of the police and tehsil.

It was the days of the Emergency and the staff was punctual in attending office. There were instructions from the Government to collect market intelligence about prices of essential commodities from mandis and the weekly market. I would visit the mandis and weekly markets and when even I would enquire about the rise in price of any particular commodity, immediately the sellers would reduce the price to the level of the previous week. Potato prices were rising in my sub-division and I took a review meeting of the cold storage owners to find out how many tons of potatoes were stored in such storage and not released to the market. After the review, I ordered them to release a certain percentage of stored potatoes in the market. Since this instruction was applied uniformly to all storages, the potatoes of my DM which were stored in one of the cold storages of Mahoba, was also released for public consumption. The DM rang me up and with a laugh told me, 'You are really working in the public interest and you have also released my potatoes to the public!'

During this period, I received a written instruction from my District Magistrate to send a report about two mischievous advocates so that appropriate action under MISA could be taken against them. I told the DM that there was no need to take any action. Since they were practising in my Court, my counseling would be good enough to check them. As a result, no action was taken. Thus, I averted the possible misuse of MISA in my sub-division.

I was very particular about redressal of public grievances. Every day I would listen to the grievances, even on Sundays and holidays. On one such occasion, a 75-year-old woman came to my residence weeping. She complained to me that her son who was working in Tehsil was not giving her enough food and was threatening to throw her out. The complaint was purely a personal one and I could have outright rejected it. Being illiterate, she could not understand whether the Joint Magistrate was legally competent to issue any instruction to his son to look after her properly. She had merely looked up to the Joint Magistrate as a dispenser of justice. I could have avoided it just by referring it to the Tehsildar. Instead, I immediately called the Tehsildar and the son. I rebuked the son and went to the extent of threatening him that he would not receive his pay unless he looked after his mother properly. He promised me to keep her with him and to look after her properly. After a few months, the woman came to my office and showered her blessings on me. In my administrative career, I found that a little bit of effort on the part of the officer to go the extra mile in public interest would provide great relief to the poor and the marginalized sections.

One evening while relaxing in my lawn, I received a telephone call informing me that a passenger bus from Charkhari to Mahoba was being looted. I immediately got into my jeep along with four of my peons armed with guns and drove straight to the alleged spot of crime. We did not find anything there; it was obviously a fake call. When I narrated this to my father-in-law, he cautioned me, 'Prashanta, it was foolish on your part to proceed on an anonymous call without verifying it or without proper planning. Had there been dacoits on the spot, what could you have done with your four peons?' I always bore in mind this sane advice. Whenever any crisis or emergency took place, I always made it a point to proceed to the scene after proper consultation and planning. To rush to the spot without proper planning is not an act of valour, but one of foolishness.

Quite often it happens in a civil servant's life that he is unnecessarily troubled by recommendations and pressures from relatives. When I was Joint Magistrate, Mahoba, a relative of my 'would-be father-in-law' approached him to put in a word to me about the ceiling case pending in my court. My father-in-law knew what sort of Administrator I was. Hence, he declined and advised the relative not to approach him. Later, the same relative approached one of my father-in-law's cousins who, in turn, requested me to look into the matter. I scrutinized the case and declared the entire land (about 30 acres) as surplus under the Ceiling Act and vested it in the State. Many such occasions will come in the life of a civil servant but his real test lies in dispensing justice according to the law and merits without any fear or favour.

As a Magistrate, I had observed that the Tehsildar and his staff were often over-burdened with making VIPs' arrangements. Their visits as well as tours and inspection of the senior officers entailed a lot of expenditures which were impossible for the Tehsildar and his staff to bear from their pocket. This resulted in corrupt practices and demeaning of VIPs and senior officers in the eye of subordinates. During my entire career, I was particular to pay the expenses I had incurred. As Joint Magistrate and later as DM, I used to carry a kitchen box with necessary provisions and my wife used to cook for me while on tour.

While I was holding Court one day, a, relative from my in-law's family came to the Court Room and addressed me as Mishraji and requested for consideration for some recommendations. It was an embarrassing situation and, in order to uphold the court's dignity and the prestige of the Magistracy, I rebuked him and ordered him out of the Court premises. He was offended but this was absolutely essential to preserve the dignity of the institution.

Mahoba, no doubt, was a beautiful place but there was not much of a social life here. While in Mahoba, I got married to Sarita in January, 1976. When I came back to resume my charge after a month's vacation, to my surprise, I found my residence decorated with lights of different colours. When I enquired, my steno said the decoration was made to receive the Sahib and Memsahib. I did not appreciate it and directed him to remove all the decorations. When Sarita came to Mahoba, my life became comfortable as I used to get good food and company. I learnt to drive the scooter from her and we used to go to Vijaya Nagar Reservoir for swimming and fishing. We also visited Belatal and Lahachura dam and other scenic places. Life was continuing in a peaceful manner except for the summer which in Bundelkhand can be quite unbearable. There was erratic power supply and no provision for cooler. We had to manage with hand fans. In the evening, we used to sleep under the open sky on our premises and it was quite enjoyable.

At that age, my lifestyle was not very spiritual although, the seed of spiritualism had already been sown and was gradually taking shape. We would visit Chandrikadevi, the presiding deity of Allaha Uddal every week. It was an imposing deity in a cave. Near Chandrikadevi, there is also a place where there is a beautiful statue of Lord Mahavir. It is a testimony to the fact that probably at some point 'Jainism' prevailed in this area. We also visisted Chitrakoot in Banda District. I was overwhelmed when I visualized the vanavas of Rama, spending his days in Chitrakoot. There are many places and temples in Chitrakoot which devotees used to flock. We visited only a few and could not go to Hamuna Dhara and Gupt Godavari. However, I enjoyed the serene hilly atmosphere in that area.

Chapter 11

···
✄

Deputy Secretary (Co-operation)

(July 1976 – August 1978)

Observe the principle of intellectual honesty and
objectivity while submitting notes to higher authorities and
never buckle under any pressure.

In July, 1976, I was promoted to senior scale of IAS and posted as
Deputy Secretary (Cooperation) in the Agricultural Production
Commissioner (APC) Branch of the Secretariat. The APC is a senior
post of the rank of Additional Chief Secretary with jurisdiction over
a number of Departments like Agriculture, Horticulture, Animal
Husbandry, Fishery, Minor Irrigation, Rural Engineering Services,
Rural Development etc., for efficient coordination and functioning
of the agriculture, and related sectors. During my two-year tenure as
Deputy Secretary/Joint Secretary, I came across three APCs and three
Chief Secretaries.

Life for young officers posted for the first time in the Secretariat
at Lucknow was tough as there were not enough infrastructural
facilities available. It was difficult to get residential accommodation
in Lucknow, and there was no transport facility either. We had to
make all arrangements for ourselves. With great difficulty, I got a
single room accommodation in Gautampalli Guesthouse near the
Secretariat. At that time, my father-in-law was also transferred from
Agra to Lucknow and he, along with his family, stayed with us in the

same room for a year. There were eight persons living in that room and there was only one bathroom and a make-shift kitchen behind the almirah. We all used to sleep on the floor. I wondered how we spent one year in such a small space. Even though it was inconvenient, yet we enjoyed our stay together, playing cards, going to parties, picnics and movies.

It was a memorable experience for me and my wife to attend the 'IAS Week' for the first time in my career. A unique feature of UP, the IAS Association every year organizes a week called the 'IAS Week'. During this period, the Chief Minister addresses the IAS Officers, exhorting them to work sincerely for the development of the State. The law and order situation and the progress of development schemes are analyzed in-depth and suggestions invited for improvement. The Chief Minister also invites the officers and spouses to a luncheon at his residence. This provides an opportunity for the officers to interact with each other and with Ministers and political representatives. An evening tea party is organized in the Botanical Garden, with music by the Police and Army bands. The Governor, the Chief Minister, his Cabinet Ministers and political representatives and officers participate in this function. It is a colourful evening with high-tea and everybody enjoys this. The IAS Association also holds its Annual General Meeting during this period and elects its office-bearers. The Members of the Association organize a colourful cultural evening at the Raj Bhawan, followed by a sumptuous dinner hosted by the Governor. During this period the IAS Association also organizes its 'Service Dinner' at Mohd. Bagh Club. The distinctive feature of this function is that after the dinner, the junior-most member of the service has to address the gathering and at the end the senior-most officer also addresses the gathering sharing his own experience and wisdom gained during his long service career. On the last day, a friendly cricket match between the IAS Eleven and IPS Eleven is also held amid fanfare. It is hilarious to listen to the commentary of the cricket match. I don't think any State observes such a 'Service Week'.

While working in the Secretariat, I came across an interesting character who was the Deputy Secretary in APC Branch. As a senior officer from the Co-operative Service I presumed he would be knowledgeable about cooperative matters. Whenever I went to him for advice, I found his table absolutely clean without a single file. I wondered how he could manage his work so efficiently, whereas in my case, I was forever drowning in heaps of files. One day, I asked him about the secret of his efficiency. He smiled and answered, 'Mishra Sahib, you are a young IAS Officer and do not know the functioning of the Secretariat. In the Department, there are Section Officers and Under Secretaries under me and there are also higher officers, like Special Secretary, Secretary and APC. Since all are Government servants, they are responsible for their acts of omission and commission. Therefore, when a note from the Section Officer and Under Secretary comes to me, I merely write 'Aadesharth' (for order) and send it to the Special Secretary. When the file comes back with order and observations of the higher officers, I simply write 'anupalanarth' (for compliance) and send it downwards. With these two magical words, I have succeeded in clearing the files in minutes.' While dwelling upon the question of responsibility, he commented, 'The fundamental principle of Government administration is "More work, more responsibility, more chance of committing mistakes and more punishment; Less work, less responsibility, less mistakes and less punishment. No work, no responsibility, no mistake and no punishment." It is for you to choose.' I laughed and thought what an advice this veteran was rendering to a young officer. The tragedy of the system is that it tolerates such deadwood that actually needs to be weeded out.

A few encounters during this period come to mind. I was attending a capsule course on agriculture and irrigation. The then APC was the key-note speaker that day and he was advocating more exploitation of groundwater through tube-wells. During question hour, I asked him, 'Sir, with increasing use of groundwater, there is a possibility that it will be depleted considerably. So there is need for coming out with a legislation to regulate its use and installation of tube wells.'

The APC was annoyed and told me harshly, 'You, young officer, do not know anything about agriculture or irrigation.' I kept silent but developments in subsequent years clearly vindicated my stand. I sincerely believe that every individual is a creative being and officers, however young, must be encouraged to come out with creative suggestions and out-of-box thinking.

Once, I submitted a detailed note, after careful analysis, on some disciplinary proceedings to my Special Secretary. He did not like the note. He called me to his chamber and advised me to change it in a particular fashion. Very politely I refused and told him that it would be intellectually dishonest on my part to change the note. I requested him to make his own observation and decision as he deemed proper. I had come across many such situations, but I always observed the principle of intellectual honesty and objectivity while submitting my notes and never buckled under pressure.

The Emergency was lifted in 1977 and General Elections were held soon after and the Janata Government came with a massive majority at the Centre and most States. I was transferred as DM, Rai Bareilly and a few of my seniors advised me to take charge immediately, otherwise there would be political manipulation. I never believed in these manipulations (bureaucratic or political) just to get a good posting. I handed over my charge in the Secretariat and decided to take over my new assignment after availing of the joining time. Just one day before taking charge, I was telephonically informed by the Appointment Secretary not to proceed to Rai Bareilly but to wait till further orders. It was followed by a written communication. So I was compulsorily wait-listed for a month and thereafter the Government, in its wisdom, posted me as a Joint Secretary in the Department of Food at the Secretariat. I had hardly worked for 15 days as Joint Secretary, Food, when I again received a transfer order as DM, Pauri Garhwal. These developments in the corridors of power gave me a bitter taste of administration which was subject to so many pressures and manipulations.

Meanwhile, a baby girl was born in our family bringing us immense joy and happiness. After the necessary rituals, we named her Pragya, with the nickname Chavi. The arrival of the baby changed the entire spectrum of our happiness and our attitude towards life. It is a unique experience to become a father and experience immense love and affection for the new-born. Only when one attains parenthood, does one understand the parents' concerns for the child's safety, happiness and health.

Chapter 12

....

District Magistrate, Pauri Garhwal

(September 1978 – May 1979)

It is man alone who is responsible for the destruction of
forests in the name of Development. We have forgotten that we
cannot sustain ourselves for long if we divorce ourselves
from nature.

When Chavi was hardly four months old I was transferred to Pauri
Garhwal as D.M. I did not take my family to the District. Known
as British Garhwal, it is a beautiful district in the Himalayan region.
With its ever-green coniferous trees, snow-clad peaks, rich flora and
fauna and beautiful tourist spots Garhwal has always remained an
attraction for tourists. The Ganga flowing down with pristine beauty
has always added a special charm for the pilgrims to important places
like Swargasram, Geeta Bhavan, Parmarthniketan, Laxman Jhoola,
Neel Kanth, Dev Prayag etc. I liked my posting here.

There was no direct connectivity to Pauri and I had to travel by train
from Lucknow to Nazibabad to Kotdwar, an important town in the
Bhabar area. After landing in Kotdwar, I experienced the difficulties
the hilly people face in their daily life. It was raining heavily and
there were landslides at many places blocking the road. I had to walk
20 km to reach Pauri to take charge. It was a difficult trek but quite
enjoyable. The Himalayas have a special charm for me and whenever
I come to this region, I feel myself transported to a different plane

altogether. The purity and the holiness of the region and the presence of the Ganga in her pristine glory have always sent waves of invisible vibrations.

Pauri is situated at a height of 7000 feet and the winter here is biting. After 3 pm, the icy cold breeze begins to blow and sends shivers down the spine. There were fire places in the residence of the DM where we used to sit in a semi-circle to get the warmth. For the first time, I observed that the pine cones were used in place of wood. It was a nice experience to draw warmth of the fireside having hot pakora and roasted groundnut over a cup of hot tea.

In the bureaucratic world it is often said that the first charge of the DM is like the first love which can never be forgotten. I still remember the days I spent in Pauri. The institution of DM is an important one as it represents the eyes, ears and brain of the Government at the district level. He is considered the maa-baap of the people and the protector of the down-trodden and marginalized sections. The district was generally peaceful from the point of view of law and order. I never faced any problem here. More attention was given to development works, public relations and removal of public grievances. In the district, people loved those officers who toured the interior and when necessary covered many places by trekking. I toured a lot and inspected almost all tehsils and sub-tehsils and most blocks. Pauri is ideally suited for development of horticulture and potatoes. During my tenure here, I emphasized on the plantation of walnut and apple in this region. With the help of the Local Area Development Fund, I took the initiative to introduce mushroom cultivation. One retired brigadier and another young educated person, who was a progressive farmer, were selected and financed by the District Administration for this purpose. I believe, this initiative had resulted in spreading mushroom cultivation in Pauri. Lots of emphasis was also given to minor irrigation, gravity irrigation and the hydram system of irrigation. Apart from massive construction of roads by the Border Roads Organisation I took interest in spreading the network of small roads and bridle paths to connect the interior of the district. Afforestation was a major thrust area here and the local people, through the Panchayat Forest, played a significant role in promoting and extending the forest coverage. I noticed that wherever the Forest Panchayat was active, they did a commendable job. There were different kinds of forests in the district namely, Reserve Forest under the Forest Department, Civil Swayam Forest under the DM, Panchayat Forest and private forest. At that time I did not find any coordinating agency among these institutions except the DM. The villagers had certain rights in the forest and they used to apply for cutting trees for construction of houses etc. There was a healthy practice in the district that whenever permission was given to fell a tree, the beneficiary was directed to plant at least 10 trees in its place but this practice remained more or less on paper only. There has been no effective monitoring and implementation of this vital aspect. I recall an interesting meeting taken by our Commissioner to review the programme of afforestation. When he invited suggestions from the public, the Sarpanch, Shri Negi, who was a dedicated worker, suggested; 'If all of us vacate Pauri for about 10 years leaving the area to itself one will find a dense forest in this area.' Everybody started laughing but I found the statement quite interesting. It is man and man alone who is responsible for the destruction of the forest in the name of development. We have forgotten that we are all products of nature and cannot sustain ourselves in the long run if we divorce ourselves from the proximity to nature. We can now see the visible impact of climate change in different parts of the world. It is high time that the eco-friendly aspect of development be given top priority to ensure sustainable development. Nature has everything for us to fulfil our needs but not our greed. Need and not greed should constitute the very basis of the development strategy. Conservation, promotion and protection of medicinal plants and herbs present an area where a lot of work has to be done.

Tourism is another area which has great potential. Apart from pilgrimage tourism, trekking, adventure tourism, eco-tourism, home stay and river rafting can constitute the core of development in this area. The British administration must be given due credit for having established a chain of forest Inspection Bungalows in every nook and corner of the district. The most interesting feature of each such bungalow is that it has a library with books on the flora and fauna of that area.

I was fond of touring and trekking. During my tour the first half of the inspection was devoted to office work and the second half to field work. I remember when I was inspecting an interior block I expressed my desire to visit the demonstration plot of soyabean. After lunch when I was about to set out on my journey, the BDO tried to dissuade me on the ground that I had to walk about 5 km. I told him that he need not bother and I would be able to cover the distance with ease. We walked and walked and it was evening yet there was no sight of the demonstration plot. When he eventually took us to a plot, I found that there was no trace of any soyabean there. I returned, suspended the BDO and started disciplinary proceedings against him.

While reviewing the development programme of the district, I found that the performance of a particular BDO was nil. I asked him, 'What are the the reasons for it?' He confidently answered, 'Sir I don't like to do hanky-panky in development works. I am an honest fellow. Whatever I do, it will be in a straight manner.' I was impressed by his statement. After a month when I again reviewed the progress I observed that the pace of development works in that block was proceeding at snail's pace. When I enquired about it, he replied in the same vein. I felt that the BDO was just bluffing and a shirker. I tried to get the feedback about him from different sources and it came to my knowledge that he was not a good worker and whiled away his time drinking. With great difficulty, I transferred him to another district – Tehri Garhwal, little realizing that I would be posted there after a year. I realized then that transfer was not the solution and a bad worker needs to be punished and a good one rewarded.

The women folk in the hill district were hard working and honest. Many families faced the ordeal of drunken menfolk. During my tenure in Pauri I encouraged the women to get together and start campaigns against the evils of drinking and to destroy the illegal bhattis of kachha sharaab (furnaces of country liquor). It was to their credit that they participated enthusiastically in such campaigns. I salute them because they do the household work, fetch water from the streams, bring fodder, collect firewood apart from working in the field. The success of any programme depends on the true involvement of the women folk. Without their participation the hill development would come to a standstill. I also noticed that the able bodied men mostly joined the defence forces or migrated to the plains in search of jobs. The hill economy is often termed as 'money order economy' as there is less development in the area. The Government of India at that time introduced the concept of 'Hill Area Development Agency' (HADA) to give a push to the development programme in the district. During these years, much development has taken place as a result. Since the Himalayan region is a fragile one, being the youngest mountain region in the world, it is susceptible to disasters like landslides, flash floods and earthquakes. Therefore, while pursuing the development agenda, components of sustainable development to mitigate the bad effects of global warming and environmental degradation must also be kept in mind. Otherwise if the Himalayan range gets disturbed and its perennial sources of water dry up, this will wipe out the entire civilization of the country.

I had read Jim Corbett's *Man Eaters of Kumaon* and also read in the newspapers about the man-eater of Duggada. At that time Mr George Joseph, a dynamic officer of the UP Cadre, was posted as DM, Pauri. He was my predecessor. When the tiger menace increased, Mr Joseph made a vow that he would not shave till the tiger was killed. Great efforts were made and ultimately, thanks to the efforts of the Forest Department and the District Administration, the tiger was caught. When I met Mr Joseph while taking over the charge as DM, I found him with a thick beard. I enquired about it and he laughed and said,

'Since the tiger was not killed but caught and caged, as per my vow, I have not shaved.'

I came across tigers many times during my stay in Pauri Garhwal. While travelling to Kotdwar, with my wife and child one evening we got out to ease ourselves when we heard a roar. Terrified, we rushed to the car and when we drove just after few yards ahead, a tiger leaped in front of the car. We were thankful to God that we were inside the car.

After attending a meeting at Dehradun, I was returning to Pauri by the Dev Prayag road one evening when I spotted a tiger relaxing on a cement bench. I got frightened as I was in an open jeep and instructed the driver to drive very slowly without disturbing the animal. The tiger suddenly got up and majestically walked ahead of the jeep for quite some time. It was not bothered by the presence of the vehicle, and after a while just disappeared into the jungle. This also teaches us that the animals generally do not attack unless provoked. I was henceforth advised by the local staff to not alight from the vehicle especially in the evenings in a jungle area. It is always prudent to get down where there is human habitation or a small market. I scrupulously followed this principle whenever I travelled in the hilly region.

Two incidents come to mind, during my tenure in Pauri. One was about the Australian Prime Minister's visit to Dikalla Jim Corbett Park and the second relates to a strange case of a long-standing dispute between two villages over forest rights and the drinking water sources. First, let's talk about the Australian Prime Minister's visit. Every tourist thinks that the Jim Corbett Park is exclusively in the district of Nainital. In fact, the most important tourist infrastructures, buildings, rest houses, restaurants etc. are located in Dhikala under the jurisdiction of Pauri District. I received a wireless message from the state Government about the Australian Prime Minister's visit. The entire entourage had to be accommodated in Dhikala. At first, I was under the impression that Jim Corbett Park was under the

Administration of DM, Nainital District and therefore he would make the arrangements. I was surprised to discover that the most important place in Jim Corbett Park i.e. Dhikala, was under the jurisdiction of the Pauri DM. So I had to supervise all the arrangements. Five days before the visit, I was on the way to Dhikala to see the arrangements. A police Sub-Inspector stopped my car and without saying anything, sat by my side, even though I was travelling by an official car. He asked, 'Where are you going'. 'Dhikala' I replied. Then he asked, 'What are you doing'? I replied, 'I am in Government service'. Then he asked, 'What is your post?' When I replied that I was the DM of Pauri Garhwal, he was startled! He asked the driver to stop, got down, saluted me and started apologising profusely. I did not mind it and took the Sub-Inspector along to Dhikala. Quite often, when a person has power, it goes to his head and he loses his balance of mind.

When I reached Dhikala, I found the whole place teeming with tourists. The place needed to be sanitized from security point of view. I requested the Forest Department to cancel permits immediately and hand over the campus. When I realised that the Forest Department was not doing anything in this respect, I, as DM, issued notice of vacation to all the tourists lodged there and directed the police to ensure that the place gets vacated since there were hardly three days left. I am sure, this decision of mine must have caused inconvenience to the tourists but it had to be done to ensure the safety of our important guest.

The second incident relates to a long-standing dispute between two villages about their rights over forest and drinking water sources. This had been pending in the DM's Court even before Independence. When I came to know of it, I was determined to sort it out. It was at the argument stage and the British Officer who had conducted the spot survey, had gone back to his country after Independence. The survey report he submitted was not exhibited. This caused a bit of a problem, nevertheless, with the consent of both parties, I proceeded with the hearings. I heard the arguments continuously for three weeks without a break and took down copious notes extending to at least 50 pages. I took another one month to go through the files and evidences to make up my mind. At that point, my steno told me, 'Sir, many DMs have come and gone. Nobody has touched this file. Whosoever has tried to sort out the matter has been transferred.' I just laughed it away and told my steno to come to the campus the next day fully prepared to take dictation for a long time. The next morning, when I sat down to dictate, I was informed about my transfer as DM, Tehri Garhwal. Was the file jinxed? I do not know what happened to it; it is still a mystery.

Life in Pauri was peaceful with no tension but it was highly restricted as social life revolved around a few officers only. The DM's residence had a billiards table and most evenings were spent playing billiards. There are many scenic places like Pauri, Kotdwar, Srinagar, Rudra Paryag, Lansdowne, Khirsoo and Mundaneswar. I had visited Lansdowne many times as the Garhwal Rifles Headquaters is located there. It is a beautiful place for long walks. I also visited Kimkaleswar, Kamleswar Mahadev of Srinagar and Jwalpa Devi, Kanyo Ashram and, above all, the famous Neelkanth Mahadev as well as all the ashrams like Swargashram, Gita Bhawan and Parmarth Niketan situated by the banks of the Ganga. Such visits to holy places made me calm, serene and happy.

In Pauri, for the first time, I learnt about the tradition of writing Charge Note by the out-going DM for the benefit of the successor. It was a general practice during the British regime for the out-going DM to write a detailed charge note giving a clear picture about its topography, population, political and social leaders, fairs, important personalities, development potential and various problems of the district. This was a very good practice which continued for some time but, I believe, has been given a quiet burial.

Chapter 13

District Magistrate, Tehri Garhwal

(June 1979 – June 1980)

Impressed by the natural surroundings and the pristine glory of the Himalayas little did I realize then that this visit would result in a long association with Vasistha Ashram.

After serving in Pauri Garhwal for nine months, I was transferred to Tehri Garhwal in the last week of May, 1979. I did not know the reason for this, maybe it was to accommodate a married couple belonging to my service. I served as DM in both Garhwals but the difference between the two was quite substantial. Pauri Garhwal was under the direct administration of British Raj, whereas Tehri Garhwal was under the King of Tehri. Probably that explained the difference in attitude and state of development between the two. Pauri was more progressive and developed and the people exhibited a more positive attitude towards administration and development process. In Tehri one could find more of politics, agitations and arguments. But essentially the problems of both districts are the same i.e. backwardness, lack of infrastructure and connectivity, drinking water shortage, degradation of forests, lack of health and educational facilities and frequent land-slides during the monsoon season. As DM of both Garhwals, I had a good exposure to the problems of the hilly regions and got an excellent opportunity to contribute towards development of both.

The headquarter, Narendra Nagar, was a small and beautiful town with the advantage of both the hill station and the plains because of its close proximity to Muni-ki-Reti and Rishikesh. The DM of Tehri used to visit Tehri town once a week to hold court and interact with the people. The peculiarity of the hill district administration is that this region has developed a well established practice of revenue police administration which, I believe, is still in existence. During my time, the whole district had a skeleton force of regular police which had jurisdiction only alongside the main roads. Predominantly, most areas were under revenue police. It had Patwari Chowkies which acted as police stations. The Patwari, Supervisor-Kanungo, Naib Tehsildar, Tehsildar had all the police powers to handle the law and order situation and investigate crime. Considering the simplicity of the people and less crime in these areas, the revenue police system has withstood the pressure and requirements of time. But with increasing development activities and more inflow of tourists and people from other parts coming to hill areas, this has negatively impacted the otherwise peaceful conditions here. These necessitate a fresh look at the policing system. The revenue police system lacks infrastructure, training, investigation capabilities and the necessary equipments and weapons. From time to time, efforts have been made to strengthen the revenue police system but these have not been sufficient to cope with the complexities of modern life. A package to strengthen, re-orient and modernize the revenue police coupled with a programme to increase the coverage of the regular police to infuse professionalism and efficiency is the need of the hour.

Official life in Tehri was peaceful and there was no law and order problem whatsoever except for the occasional disturbance by Tehri Dam agitators. It provided me opportunities to pursue the development programmes with single-minded devotion. Quite often, I observed that there were disputes among villagers on the source of water. When such occasions arose, either it was to be resolved through negotiations among villagers or through adjudication. The acquisition of land for Tehri Dam and the rehabilitation of those displaced posed a serious challenge. Together with Mr George Joseph, Tehri dam administrator, we both worked togther to ease the situation to a great extent. There was not much social life here either except the occasional gathering in officers' club, sports competitions once a while and a bit of badminton in the evenings. To add a little flavour to the social life, all of us colleagues took active interest in making the winter festival (cultural) a grand success. We also took the initiative to introduce football league matches in Narendra Nagar which were quite a hit.

The Himalayas are the abode of Gods and Uttarakhand is the Dev Bhoomi. The entire Himalayan area is surcharged with spiritual energy and the vibrations are palpable. The spiritual life is virtually elevating. The Ganga demarcates the boundary line between the Pauri and Tehri Garhwals. Muni-ki-Reti which is close to Rishikesh is in Tehri Garhwal and lies on the Yatra route. It abounds in famous Ashramas like the Shivananda Ashram, Omkarananda Ashram, Vithal Ashram etc. During my tenure here, I came in close contact with the Shivananda Ashram (Divine Life Society) and particularly with Swami Premanandaji who was the embodiment of simplicity and serenity. He introduced me to the books by Swami Shivananda. My association with this ashram not only gave me an opportunity to read a lot of his spiritual works but also increased my yearning for spiritual development.

At Patti, Gulardogi, there is a famous cave, Vasistha Guffa. It is believed that Vasistha Maharshi, the guru of Ramchandraji, had meditated here with his wife Arundhati for many years. It is also believed that Vasistha brought Ram and Laxman to this region to meditate and do penance to ward off the evils of brahamhatya as they had killed Ravana, his sons and relatives. Vasistha earmarked the area of Laxmanjhula as a meditation site for Laxman and the Dev Prayag (confluence of Alaknanda and Bhagirathi to form the Ganga) for Ram and guided them from this place. At Dev Prayag, there is a beautiful statue of Ram as Raghunathji. This seems to be a folk tale but nevertheless highlights the importance of Vasistha Guffa, situated between Laxmanjhula and Dev Prayag. This cave was later discovered by Swami Purushotamanandaji in 1923 and he used it as his tapasthali (place of meditation). It is a beautiful place with lustrous forests and the Ganga flowing down swiftly with a musical note. The place is vibrant with spiritual energy, infused with natural beauty and the pristine glory of the Ganga. Swami Purushotamanandaji was the disciple of Swami Brahamanandaji who, in turn, was a Gurubhai of Swami Vivekananda and disciple of Ramakrishna Paramahamsa. After Swami Purushotamanandaji attained samadhi, his disciple Swami Chaitanyanandaji is now the current head of Vasistha Ashram. Swami Chaitanyanandaji is 86 years old and is the embodiment of simplicity and compassion. As a child, he had been associated with Swami Purushotamanandaji and renounced the world quite early in life. He came to Vasistha Guffa as a young Sanyasi and learnt yoga and spiritual knowledge under his spiritual guidance. He has trekked all over the Himalayan areas, Tibet, Uttarakhand and other parts of the country.

My association with Vasistha Ashram dates back to 1979 when I was District Magistrate in Tehri Garhwal. One evening while camping at the Swiss Cottage of Maharaja Tehri on the banks of the Ganga, one of my officers told me that there was a famous cave, known as Vasistha Guffa nearby and advised me to visit the place. At that time, I was not very spiritually inclined but a tremendous desire arose in me to visit the cave as it would be an adventurous trip. I readily agreed and visited the cave in the evening. The evening had cast its shadow and the Ganga was flowing with a beautiful musical note. I instantly liked the simple cave and the natural environment. The place was indeed peaceful and serene. Impressed by the surroundings and the pristine glory of the Himalayas little did I realize that this visit would result in a long association with Vasistha Ashram, bringing immense spiritual growth within me.

Since 1991, I used to take 10 days' leave in May and June to trek in the Himalayas and to meet holy persons during the journey. Since then I have been regularly visiting the Vasistha Ashram to seek the blessings and the holy presence of Swami Chaitanyanandaji. Whenever I visit this place, I am transported to an entirely different world. Generally, when I am here, I attend the morning and evening Aarti in the cave as well as in the Guru Maharaj temple. The evening Aarti, with the sounds of conch and bells is quite thrilling. The food served here is simple but the affection with which it is served makes it delicious and enjoyable. Swamiji enquires about the health, comfort and difficulties of everybody who happens to be there. The Monday puja of the Shiva Linga of the cave as well as the temple is quite elaborate and touches the spiritual core of the devotee. After the Aarti, we used to take the blessing of Swamiji. Usually, I spend the evening sitting in meditation on a big rock facing the Ganga. It is so exciting, relaxing and spiritually enhancing that I forget about the material world and the trials and tribulations of life. I watch the swift flow of the Ganga and often feel I am also floating down the stream. This experience can only be felt and not described in words.

Many miracles about Vasistha Guffa have been mentioned. I have seen a photograph of the cave emitting a stream of light and merging with another point and covering triangularly the Shiva image. A few personal experiences while staying in the Ashram come to mind. Once after coming back from my spiritual journey in the Himalayas, I briefly halted at Vasistha Ashram. I went to the cave to meditate before the Shiva Linga. Generally while in meditation, I never ask for anything from the Lord but that day suddenly a thought came to my mind about my daughter Chavi who had appeared for the examination a second time for admission to the Tata Institute of Social Science, Mumbai for MA (Social Work). She had attempted earlier but at the final round could not succeed. Therefore, I was a bit anxious this time. When my anxiety about Chavi's admission surfaced during meditation, I immediately dispelled it by concentrating on Lord

Shiva. In the evening, I left for Delhi and reached by 10.00 pm. I was tired and after dinner, went to bed immediately. At midnight, I was woken up by a huge shout from the adjacent room. Chavi was calling out in excitement, 'Papa I have made it, I have made it.' I got up and enquired what had happened. With a hug, she told me that she was selected for admission to the Tata Institute. I profusely thanked God for fulfilling my wish.

In 2004, my nephew (sister's son) was diagnosed with intestinal cancer which had slightly damaged the liver also. My brother-in-law, a doctor practising in Odisha, came to my residence in Delhi and broke down. I advised him to proceed with the treatment and at the same time pay a visit Vasistha Guffa and pray before the deity. My brother-in-law and sister went to the cave and met the Swamiji who assured them that he would pray for his well-being and by the grace of Guru Maharajji, he would be all right. The boy recovered and soon there was no trace of cancer. My sister and brother-in-law revisited the Ashram to express their heart-felt gratitude and pray to Lord Shiva. The boy is absolutely fine now.

When I resigned as State Chief Secretary for my principles, I immediately rushed to Vasistha Guffa to seek solace for my restless and tormented soul. I told Swamiji that I had quit and was a completely retired person. I expressed my desire to devote myself to spiritualism full-time. The Swamiji shook his head and said, 'You will serve another five years at the Centre.' I was surprised at this because I had already taken voluntary retirement. But lo and behold, the Swamiji's prediction came true. I was appointed by the Centre as Member of the Union Public Service Commission (UPSC), a constitutional post.

On another occasion, on a visit to Vasistha Guffa and after lunch, I was relaxing on a chair facing the Ganga when I suddenly heard the beautiful sound of a flute. It was so enchanting and so melodious that I forgot my bodily presence. After a minute or so, it stopped and I thought, probably, some cowherd was playing his flute. In my heart of hearts I hoped it was divine music. So I thought within, 'Oh Krishna, if you are playing the flute, please do it again for me.' Again, I heard the same melodious flute note. After a few seconds it stopped. Again I requested just to test whether it was a fluke and again I heard the same melodious note. I was ecstatic and tears rolled down my cheeks. At night, I narrated the incident to Swamiji asking whether it was music from the cowherd's flute or something else. He smiled and said, 'Many such things happen in this place!'

With the passage of time my association with Swamiji and the Guffa began to grow. I consider myself fortunate to have been associated with this holy place and a great yogi like Swami Chaitanyanandji who has guided me since 1979. I bow down to his lotus feet and offer my obeisance with all humility.

Apart from Vasistha Guffa, the other important spiritual and tourist places in Tehri Garhwal are Kunjapuri, Surkunda, Chandrabadani (all Shaktipeeth), Dhanaulti, Bhilangna valley and Chamba. I believe, after the submergence of old Tehri town, the new township has become a tourist spot because of the vast expanse of the dam reservoir.

As mentioned earlier, there was not much law and order problem in Tehri but occasionally it was disturbed by agitation against the dam. One night, I received a call from my SDM at Tehri that an image of Lord Ganesha had been installed at night on the road leading to the dam site. As a result, the dumpers and vehicles going towards the site had been stopped by the people. The SDM wanted my guidance on what should be done, because this might develop into a religious conflagration. I immediately told him to remove the idol from the site. The SDM told me, apologizing, that he was a devotee of Lord Ganesha and he might not be able to remove the idol. I told him curtly that since Lord Ganesha appeared from nowhere at night, similarly, Lord Ganesha should disappear before morning. I directed him to carry out the order. It was done and the problem, probably created by mischievous elements, fizzled out.

Once there was an agitation by workers of the Tehri project demanding better working facilities. The dam management did not listen to their grievances and went on a witch-hunting spree. Day-by-day the problem was getting murkier. I intervened and sorted it out by persuading the management to accept the workers' genuine grievances. My experience as DM of four of these districts has taught me that strong-arm methods to suppress labour agitations were not an effective way of tackling them. It is always better to negotiate and bring both parties across the table. Repeated persuasions and discussions definitely ease the situation. At the same time, the intelligence system should be strong enough to give correct feedback and information so that effective strategies can be worked out. At times, it is better to go for preventive arrests so as to send the signal that though the Administration is ready for negotiations this should not be taken as a sign of weakness. It is also necessary to ward off possible sabotage and violence. The higher authorities and the Government must be appraised of the situation from time to time. But ultimately it is the responsibility of the DM and SP to tackle any problem regarding law and order.

During my tenure in Tehri Garhwal, I had the opportunity to interact with Mr Sunderlal Bahuguna, the protagonist of the Chipko movement. He complained about the unnecessary auction of the forest trees, which included felling of a lot of young trees over vast areas. I intervened immediately and directed the DFO to sort out the matter urgently. The DFO in turn, wanted me to take stringent action, including the arrest of the leaders, so that the agitation by the local people would fizzle out. I sensed that the DFO was not looking at the problem in a broader prospective and had become parochial in his approach. I suggested that he should find out whether young trees on a massive scale were being auctioned. If it was so, then he should exclude all these trees and must provide a plan of massive plantation of the area from where the old trees were to be auctioned. I flatly rejected his suggestions to arrest the leaders and directed him to remove the genuine grievances of the people. The matter was sorted out in a few days. After that Mr Bahuguna and Mr Chandi Prasad Bhatt became my well-wishers. After many years, when I met them at a seminar in Nainital, Mr Bahuguna addressed me as DM of the Chipko Movement. I have a firm belief that when an officer is dedicated and sincere and keeps public interest uppermost in mind, then he will eventually succeed in his efforts because not only does he get public cooperation but divine blessings will also always be with him.

The Himalayas being the youngest mountains of the world are prone to landslides. During the rainy season, it is a common feature in this part of the State. One evening while I was working in the Collectorate I got the information that due to excessive rain, there was a huge landslide in a village killing 15 people. The village was approachable only from the side of Dehradun. I asked the Deputy S.P. Incharge to accompany me to the site so that necessary relief could be rendered to the bereaved families. The Deputy S.P. In-charge said, 'Sir, I am an old person and may not be able to trek many kms in the hilly terrain to reach the village.' This did not stop me and the next morning along with my driver and PA, equipped with the relief fund, we proceeded towards the place. At that time, I did not realise that I had to trek about 15 km to 20 km on a treacherous path crossing rivulets. We left the vehicle and started towards our destination on foot. On the way, we were lashed by rain. But our drenched clothes soon dried on the way when the sun came out. I had carried just four parathas and some fried potatoes. My driver and PA did not bring any food. Despite their refusal, I shared my parathas with them. After the light lunch, we resumed our journey until we came across a huge boulder by the side of a small rivulet. The current was strong and fast and we could not muster the courage to cross it. The boulder was slippery and we were hesitating to climb to the other side, as one mis-step could have hurtled us into the fast running current. I was helpless and frustrated. Just at that moment, like a Godsent messenger, I observed a local person climbing over the rock and coming to our side. When I enquired about the reported deaths in the village, he said he was coming from that village to meet the DM. When I revealed my identity, he was extremely happy and literally carried me on his shoulders across the rock. He was so overwhelmed with our response that he insisted on carrying me on his back all the way to the destination. I refused and asked him to guide us to the village safely. I visited the landslide site, talked to the bereaved families and handed over the cash amount on the spot. On enquiring about the visit of any revenue official to the village, to my utter surprise, I found that not even the Patwari had come there. I suspended the Patwari and took action against the Supervisor Kanungo. At night, we stayed on in the room of a dilapidated school building. It was extremely cold and the Pradhan (village head) was kind enough to provide me with a quilt. At night, I had thick rotis, salt, onions, green chillis and burnt potatoes for dinner. I was so hungry that the dinner tasted like amrit (nectar). In the morning I had a hot cup of tea and when I left the place, the entire village came to see me off. In fact, many of them walked with me covering the 15 km till I reached my vehicle. When I bid farewell, I could see the tears in the eyes of many people. That was an unforgettable experience.

In June, 1979, in the first week itself I was struck by personal tragedy like a bolt from the blue. At that time, I had only one daughter, Chavi who was one year old. On June 7, we went to Muni-ki-Reti and Rishikesh along with our daughter. It was a warm and humid day. We had our lunch at Chotiwaala Hotel and returned to the rest house. In the evening, much to our dismay, Chavi started vomiting and became seriously ill. We rushed to Narendra Nagar and called the CMO to examine her. He arrived with team and gave her an injection to stop the vomiting. The vomiting stopped but the next morning, we found her stomach distended like a balloon. Since there was not much medical facility available in Narendra Nagar, we immediately rushed her to Doon Hospital, Dehradun and got her admitted in the emergency. Even after five days, the doctors there failed to diagnose the cause of distention. The baby was not responding to treatment and her condition was getting worse. Finally, on the fifth day, the MS told me hesitatingly that the child's pulse was getting weaker and it would be better to take the baby immediately to AIIMS in Delhi.

We rushed to Delhi by road with a doctor accompanying us. Even in the car, the child was on an intravenous drip. After a six-hour drive we reached AIIMS. Thanks to the help of Mr J.N. Chaturvedi, the then Police Commissioner of Delhi, a friend of my father-in-law, the baby was immediately admitted in the emergency. Since I was totally new to Delhi and had no relations or acquaintances here, we were forced to spend the night in a room of the nearby Police Station, kindly offered to us by the SHO. The baby was in a very critical condition and even the doctors at AIIMS could not diagnose the cause. The case was discussed by a team of doctors who took the decision to operate. The operation lasted for five hours and our mental state during those five hours cannot be described. There was nobody with us to provide us solace and psychological strength. Both of us were shedding tears and prayed to God to save our child. I was having an internal dialogue with God. 'Oh God, I have scrupulously maintained an honest, sincere and dedicated life with tremendous faith in you but what are you doing to my innocent child? If she dies, I will lose complete faith in you and turn into an atheist.' At that very moment, the head of the Paediatric Surgery came out and informed us that the operation was successful but the condition of the baby was still critical and anything could happen to her. He said that her large intestine had been perforated at the sigmoid joint and since the child continued with normal life unaware about the damage caused for five days, the fecund materials kept getting deposited on vital parts of the body and she developed acute septicaemia. Though the operation was successful but according to the Head of the Department, the chances of survival were just 10%. The baby was kept in an oxygen chamber in the ICU and we were not allowed to see her. Information about her condition was given daily by the ICU doctor.

Every day, we would visit AIIMS and enquire about her condition. On the second day after the operation, the head of the Department informed me that the antibiotics available in the hospital were not effective and advised me to get some medicines from London. I told him, 'I cannot go to London nor do I have any friend there to send this medicine. You treat my child with whatever medicine is available.' The next day, when we reached AIIMS, the Head of the Department informed us that the medicine had arrived from London! I was wonderstruck! Was it a mere coincidence? Or was there something more? God had listened to our prayer. The medicine arrived from London and in the duration of two months, my daughter recovered completely. In the words of the Head of Department, it was nothing less than a miracle because they had already lost all hope. But she survived miraculously though the survival chances in such cases were hardly 10%.

This incident has tremendously increased my faith in God. I firmly believe that a sincere prayer cannot go unanswered. He always stands by the side of his devotee and adversities in life are like purgatorial suffering which test the faith of the individual and cleanse him further to make him a better human being. Life will always move in direction for the best. On the way, you may find some rough roads, but they will lead you to a better life. There is always something divine about a crisis in life. But at that moment we are so consumed with fighting it out that in the melee we miss the divine aspect. At the same time, we were blessed with a second daughter bringing us immense happiness. We named her Runu.

Chapter 14

District Magistrate, Mirzapur

(June 1980 – June 1983)

The posting to Mirzapur was a turning point in my life. It not only established me as an able and honest administrator but it also provided me with a great opportunity to move forward on the path of spiritualism.

I was transferred as DM Mirzapur in June, 1980 and worked there till June, 1983, for three long years. This was perhaps one of the best periods of my service life as it provided me enough opportunities to prove my worth as an administrator. Mirzapur is a drought and flood-prone district which demands much planning, team work, determination and sincerity to tackle these problems efficiently. The District Magistrate is still the kingpin of the administration and everyone looks to him for leadership and guidance. In Mirzapur, my efforts to tackle drought, flood and to implement the government's development schemes in an efficient manner, earned appreciation from all quarters. It was a turning point in my life in the sense that it not only established me as an able and honest administrator but also provided a great opportunity for me to move forward on the spiritual path.

The DM's bungalow here is quite impressive and beautiful. It is an old bungalow of the British Raj situated near the bank of the Ganges with sprawling premises of about a few acres of land dotted with fruit and timber trees. The erstwhile Mirzapur was a huge district, more or less the size of the state of Haryana. A new district called Sonbhadra has now been carved out of the old district. Being a drought-prone area, it has serious drinking water problems. It is a backward district in terms of economic and human development index. It abounds in forests, hills and hillocks, rivers, reservoirs and waterfalls. The irony is that though the inhabitants of erstwhile Mirzapur are predominantly of the Scheduled Tribe they are categorized as Scheduled Castes. During my tenure here, I tried my best to bring them under the category of Scheduled Tribes but could not succeed. Perhaps they still continue as Scheduled Castes. The tribals of Mirzapur used to lead a miserable life as they had no right over the forest land on which they lived. I observed that successive forest settlement works to demarcate the boundary line between the forest and the tribal possessed land had been so faulty that it had been scrapped many times. Influential persons in connivance with the revenue officials had usurped these tribal lands. I shall narrate a case which will highlight this modus operandi. In one revenue case, I observed that all entries in the revenue register were recorded in the name of one particular influential person. His advocate argued that the recorded entries were in favour of his client and that his client was in possession of the land and cultivating it. I listened to the argument and mentally decided to take a surprise inspection. When I went to the spot, I found a tribal person cultivating the land with his small hut also on the same premises. My enquiries from the tribal and the local people, revealed that the same tribal had been cultivating this land for many years. The influential person, in connivance with the revenue staff, had succeeded in recording his name in the Record of Rights. Obviously, when I came back from the inspection, I ordered entry of the tribal's name in the Record of Right. Had I not done the inspection, I would have never been able to unearth the nefarious design of the influential person and my revenue staff. I had the satisfaction of ensuring justice to the tribal people.

Mirzapur is a beautiful district and it looks even more beautiful in the rainy season with its lustrous forests and the roaring of its rivers and waterfalls. I travelled extensively in the district touring 15 days a month. Mirzapur is dotted with many beautiful spots which can attract tourists. To mention a few, they are Vindhyachal, Ashtabhuja, and Kalikho temples constituting a triangle, and Geruatallav, Motiatallav, the Hanuman temple near Motiatallav, the Virbhadra temple in Virohi village, the Vindham and Sirsi falls in Mirzapur, the Mukha falls, the Eco Valley and the fort in Robertsgang, the Dongi falls, Arohora reservoir, Ashoka's rock edicts near Arohora on a hill top, the Chunar fort, Bhartihari's Samadhi in Chunar fort, the Rihand dam, Pant Sagar, Bina coal mines, Shakti Nagar and Obra Power Complexes, fossilized rocks of Markundi hills and Shivdwara of Robertsgang. Mirzapur has a rich cultural heritage full of temples. It has a tremendous potential for tourist attraction and I sincerely hope that the integrated projects covering all the important places of old Mirzapur, are formulated to give a push to tourism development.

I went to Lucknow Secretariat to meet a friend Mr Pandey who was from the judiciary. He was an honest and fearless judge who became famous for his judgement of the opening of the lock of the Ramlala temple in Ayodhya. Being a very spiritual person, he said when I met him, 'Prashantaji, you are fortunate to be posted as DM, Mirzapur which is the seat of Maa Vindhyawasani. You will do a great service to the people if you take steps to improve the management of the temple and develop the area of Trikon. Lakhs of people from UP, Bihar, MP and Delhi visit Vindhyachal during Sharad and Chaitra Navratra Melas, so you should concentrate on the management of the Mela and provide the necessary infrastructure facilities for the yatri's comfort. If you do it, you will earn a good name for yourself, and also get the blessings of Maa Vindhyawasani.' I kept his advice in mind during my entire tenure in Mirzapur.

I was fortunate to have Mr Uma Shanker Vajpayee as my S.P. and Mr Jain as District Judge, Mirzapur. They were competent, and upright people who had earlier worked with my father-in-law. They were like family friends and we discussed all problems to evolve a strategy for Vindhyachal. Mr Vajpayee did a magnificent job in controlling the crime situation in Vindhyachal and bringing the Pandas around for discussions to improve the situation. The District Administration floated the idea of the Vindhya Vikas Parishad to look after the management of the Vindhyawasani temple with active cooperation from Pariwal and Pandas. The Vindhya Vikas Parishad was headed by the DM. Initially, there was opposition from the Pandas but ultimately they too supported this idea. A few influential Pandas even went to Allahabad High Court to get a stay order but at the first hearing itself, it was rejected outright, as the steps taken by the District Administration were intended to provide relief to the lakhs of pilgrims expected to visit without harming the legitimate interests of the Panda community. We concentrated on controlling the crime situation, preventing harassment of pilgrims during the Mela period, introducing scientific management of queues and crowd control, ensuring cleanliness around the temple premises, and providing necessary relief to pilgrims. In the first year itself there was visible improvement in the management of the Mela and the District Administration earned the appreciation and confidence of the public.

During my tenure, the Prime Minister, Mrs Indira Gandhi, visited the District three or four times. Her first visit was absolutely a private one which was communicated to me only in the morning and she was to land in the evening. The time was short but nonetheless, we succeeded in providing her presentable accommodation at the Asthabhuja Inspection Bungalow. My wife took pains to do the decor of the room where the Prime Minister was to stay. Mrs Gandhi performed a long puja at night at the Asthabhuja temple, then returned to the bungalow.

The next morning, she expressed a desire to have hot jalebee, mathri with pickle, for breakfast. I was surprised, as I was not prepared for such a demand. The ITDC had been given the responsibility of catering for the Prime Minister's visit and I felt helpless. I called my Tehsildar (Sadar) and expressed the Prime Minister's desire and he said promptly, 'Sir, don't worry about such a small thing. Immediately I will go to the Vindhyachal area nearby and get all these items.' He rushed and procured hot jalebee prepared in desi ghee, mathri and pickle. I heaved a sigh of relief. I was told later that the Prime Minister was happy with this desi (local) breakfast. For the first time, I realized that the Tehsildar was a multi-tasker who could rescue a superior officer by such prompt action.

After the Prime Minister left, the Commissioner told me, 'Prashanta, the Prime Minister's visit has just got over. Many other important dignitaries also visit this place during the Mela but the condition of the road is very bad and the area needs a fresh look.' I took his words seriously and in the second and third year concentrated on the area's development. One day, along with my driver and peon I went to the Asthabhuja Inspection Bungalow at the hill top and spent the entire day roaming around the area. I walked most of the area of Trikon and the hills, conjuring up a vision of development of the area at the hill top as well as the base. I thought of undertaking a massive plantation programme in the denuded forest, a good network of pitch roads connecting the Trikon and nearby areas, provision of drinking water, repair of temples and construction of a helipad etc. To make doubly sure, I once invited all District-level officers along with their families for a lunch at Asthabhuja and to discuss the possible framework of the area's development. After lunch, I took them around and explained my vision for the area's development. They all laughed at my idea and said, 'Sir, it will remain only an utopian document and we have serious doubt about it's success.' I was not disheartened. With the help of my officers, I prepared a detailed plan, with resources from NREP, Municipalities, Zilla Parishad and District Plan. The resources were pooled together and the project was launched without any fanfare. Slowly, but steadily, the project took shape. I would visit the site even at night. I used to tell the contractor, 'Maa Vindhyawasani is a powerful deity and you are doing a very important work

(Punyakam) for the deity. If you indulge in corruption, I am sure Maa Vindhyawasani will not spare you or your family.' This had a magical effect on the contractor who assured me that he would ensure the quality of the work as per specifications. While reviewing the project, ADM said, 'Sir, it will be difficult to go for the pitch road at the top of the hill under NREP scheme as the scheme provides for 75% labour component and 25% material component. But to provide a pitch road, we need more material component, may be to the extent of 75% or more.' After listening to the problem, I got an idea and I suggested, 'The area where the road is being constructed is a hillside with rocks and stones over a vast expanse. Why don't you engage labour to break the stone into chips and that way you will convert the material component into a labour component.'

This out-of-box suggestion really enabled the project to be completed without compromising the labour-material percentage. When the Chief Secretary, along with a Member of the Planning Commission, visited Asthabhuja temple during the Mela, they were astonished to find such a good network of roads at the top of the hill. The CS asked me, 'Prashanta, how did you do it?' I replied, 'Sir, it was done under the NREP.' The Planning Commission member replied immediately that construction of pitch road is not possible under NREP as it would have been difficult to adhere to the prescribed labour-material percentage of components. I then explained my idea of converting the material component into labour component by engaging labour to break the rocks to get the material component. Both were happy and remarked, 'Well done, it is a brilliant idea.' Quite often, we bureaucrats are accustomed to stereotype thinking and refuse to see beyond our nose. As a result, the creative faculty of the officer gets stifled. Since there is no encouragement to think and act out-of-the-box, many of us follow the traditional wisdom of sticking to precedents and rules which might have been outdated in the present context.

South Mirzapur, now known as District Sonebhadra, has become the hub of power generation. The presence of coal mines and the projects of power plants have uprooted the tribal people of this area more than once in their life time. When I was DM there, thousands of hectares of Gaon Sabha land and those of private individuals had to be acquired for NTPC's Shakti Nagar Mega power project. With their bitter experience of land acquisition proceedings, the tribals who faced being uprooted began agitating against the project. With my experience in rehabilitation of the Tehri Dam Project, I insisted that NTPC first provide a rehabilitation package to the affected people. They must re-settle these people in a planned manner, providing all facilities like roads, housing, school, hospital, police chowki, post-office, drinking water and marketing. Since the project cost thousands of crores, it would not be difficult for the NTPC to earmark a few hundred crores for rehabilitation. Further, I observed that the contractors engaged had brought labour from outside and were reluctant to employ the local people. This was causing much bad blood. I advised the NTPC management to engage the local people as un-skilled labour. With training, the same people could become semi-skilled and skilled workers and could be a part of the project. The NTPC co-operated with the District Administration and we were able to settle the matter amicably. The project work went on with speed and was nearing completion. The NTPC was passing through a critical period of its project as a single day's delay in the commissioning would cost hundreds of crores of rupees but the labour leaders would not understand the implication of the timely completion of the project. They started agitations on some pretext or the other and the working atmosphere was getting vitiated. Considering the criticality of the project schedule and the law and order situation, the District Administration externed such trouble-makers. These leaders complained to the Chief Minister against the District Administration. And when the Chief Minister talked to me on the telephone, I explained about the situation and the criticality of the project's commissioning. I requested him to let the matter to be handled by the District Administration and not to get unnecessarily worried. There was no interference whatsoever from Lucknow and the agitation fizzled out.

I visited Mirzapur, Sonebhadra and Myorepur in March, 2016, after 33 years. No doubt, more power plants have come up in Sonebhadra and infrastructural facilities, particularly roads, have improved vastly but I was sad to see the thin forest cover, air pollution due to continuous mining and the poverty of the local people. I visited the Banwasi Seva Ashram and was informed that the air pollution as well as contaminated water have adversely affected the yield as well as quality of crops, particularly pulses, and the health and fertility of the people here. I was also told that in a few villages, babies were born with deformity. Development is welcome but not at the cost of environment and health. Mother Nature has everything to fulfil our needs and if we ignore nature and the environment, it will only spell disaster for the species. Eco-friendly development is the need of the hour.

I used to visit Vindhyachal temple quite often as I derived much solace from this. Inside the temple, the walls were covered with silver sheets and I observed that there were patches where the sheets were missing. I got suspicious about these patches and hit upon the idea that if the silver could be converted into a throne (Singhasan) for the deity, this would not only solve the problem of possible theft but at the same time, it would be a befitting tribute to Maa Vindhyawasani. Along with the SP, I discussed the matter with the Panda representatives who were opposed to it. They said that any change in this respect could be be carried out only with the consent of the royal family of Vijayanagaram or their representative as silver was donated by the family on this condition. One evening, Bajpayeeji and I went to Varanasi to meet the royal family and requested the queen to give her consent for making a throne for the deity with the silver her family had donated. She was very happy with this proposal. She not only gave her consent for such a cause but at the same time promised more silver required for making the throne. Armed with her consent, we went to the temple to bring all the silver for the making of a throne. The Pandas resisted initially but after seeing the consent letter, did not oppose. In the presence of the public witnesses, the silver sheets were removed from the wall, weighed and deposited in the treasury of Mirzapur under a doube lock and with signatures from the witnesses. The next day under police escort, the whole silver was transported to the residence of the queen who took pains to get made a beautiful throne for the deity. The solid throne was installed, after required preparation, on an auspicious day in the temple. The public was happy and so were the Pandas, as it enhanced the beauty of the sanctum sanctorium.

The Vindhyachal area, girdled by the Ganga and Vindhya Hills has been a great centre of the tantric cult. During Navratra Melas, one could observe the presence of many sadhus and sanyasis here. It was my good fortune to come across and interact with many saintly persons. One evening when I was walking towards Asthabhuja temple on the hill top, I came across a sadhu who said to me, 'Son, the arrangements made here are excellent. There are good roads, power connection as well as drinking water facilities for pilgrims. You are doing good work and I am sure one day you will be the chief of the Uttar Pradesh Administration.' I did not take his words seriously and in the din and bustle of administrative life, I entirely forgot about it. When in July, 2007, I became the UP Chief Secretary, I suddenly remembered the remarks of the sadhu which took 24 years to materialize. The blessings of parents, elders, teachers and saintly persons never go in vain. Their blessings are added to your invisible credit bank. We mortals cannot understand the way such invisible forces work. The day we become pure and selfless, we can feel the operation of these invisible forces.

I recall another interesting encounter with a saint, Narhari Baba, who was a wandering monk, and used to come to Ashtabhuja during Navratra Mela. One night, he was explaining to me about the nature of the Government at different stages of society. According to him, in Satyuga, all human beings were like Devas (gods). They were governed by the principles of Devamat. In course of time, the population increased and a little bit of degeneration started. During this period, the rishis and the sages came out with the Vedas which became the fundamental basis of governance. The governance was done on Vedamat. With the further increase in population, more deterioration took place and at this stage, the people were governed by Lokmat i.e. direct democracy. With still further deterioration in the value system and standards, Bahumat i.e. majority became the rule to govern. There was further deterioration resulting in Alpamat i.e. coalition government. Then the saint said, 'God forbid, I hope there should not be any 'Nomat' Government (Government without any consent). If such a Government comes, then it will be disastrous for the entire nation.'

During my tenure in Mirzapur the Divisional Commissioner was not happy with me for reasons known only to him. He constantly sought explanations from me. Once he visited my district to verify the actual possession of land by the allottees. On verification, 99% of land allotted was found to be in possession of the allottees. But the Commissioner was not satisfied and called for my explanation on this point that the land reform here had not been seriously taken up. I had unearthed bogus and fake transactions of ceiling and Gaon Sabha lands to the tune of hundreds of acres which were restored to the State Government. The Revenue Secretary was so happy with my performance that he sent me an appreciation letter for effectively implementing the land reform in Mirzapur. Therefore, I sent the explanation to the Divisional Commissioner along with the appreciation letter. It was quite a rebuff to the explanation the Commissioner had sought. Similarly, during a strike by the workers of Power Sector in UP, along with the SP, I camped at Obra Thermal Power Complex to ensure continuous supply of power to the state. During the strike period in fact the power generation went up and I received a congratulatory message and appreciation from the Chief Secretary, but unfortunately one sub-station in Mirzapur City went out of order during this period. It was suspected to be due to sabotage. The Commissioner immediately jumped on me and called for an explanation. I simply sent the congratulatory message and appreciation letter of the Chief Secretary to the Commissioner as my explanation. In administration, on many occasions, one comes across such bosses who unnecessarily try to harass sincere officers for no rhyme or reason. But one should not be unnecessarily worried or perturbed, as I am sure, his good deeds, his reputation, his clean image and above all God's protective hands will definitely come to his rescue.

Having been brought up in a liberal atmosphere, I did not have an idea of caste being so important in UP. I got a taste of it when I was posted in Mirzapur. One of the Cabinet Ministers who hailed from Mirzapur was very powerful. When I first met him during his visit to my district, I was aghast at his utterances. He addressed me as Panditji. At first I did not understand who he was addressing but the MPs, MLAs and the political representatives told me, 'Sir, the Minister is calling you.' I said, 'The Minister is calling some Panditji and not me.' They had a hearty laugh and said it was the practice in these parts to address like this. This was an eye-opener for me and for the first time, I realized how deeply the caste system had penetrated our system. It is a pity that once a cradle of civilization, UP is now riddled with petty politics and caste considerations. What is more important is not the caste a person is born into but the quality of head and heart he possess. A good person is good and a bad person is bad irrespective of caste, creed or religion. The sooner the caste system is given a decent burial, the better it will be for the country.

I was born in a Brahmin family and I had no control over it. Because of this caste tag, many times I faced embarrassing situations. At Mirzapur I was surprised to receive a letter from my Divisional Commissioner calling for an explanation with regard to a complaint alleging that I was pursuing a policy of Brahamanvad in the district. I was shocked and hurt. Within few days, the state Chief Minister visited my district. After lunch, he was having discussions with the local Minister and officers, when he asked me if I was facing any problems. I politely asked him, 'Sir, is it a crime to be born in a Brahmin family?' He was startled and asked, 'Why are you saying so?' I then told him about the complaint I got and he assured me that nothing would happen. The Chief Minister returned to Lucknow and within a few days, the Commissioner was transferred.

Another experience comes to mind. I was Commissioner (Sales Tax) in UP in 1991 and the same kind of allegation was leveled against me in a complaint which was then forwarded to me for comments by my Principal Secretary (Institutional Finance). When I talked to him, he informed me that it was the Appointment Department which had asked for the comments. I reflected over the complaints and sent an apt reply. In the comments, I pointed out that in India everybody was born into some caste or the other. I was born in a Brahmin family and I had no control over it. I further observed that to me a Brahmin means a person who was a seeker after the ultimate truth i.e. Brahman. If Brahminism is taken in this sense, definitely I was pursuing a policy of Brahmanvad. If it was merely a caste tag, then the complaint was fit to be thrown into the dustbin. When Mr Rizvi, my Principal Secretary, got this reply, he telephoned and congratulated me and said, 'You have thrown a bombshell.'

Politics is not my cup of tea and I have always remained straight and frank while dealing with politicians and Ministers. Mr Pandey, a local politician considered himself a big shot as he was a bit close to the Cabinet Minister (Cooperation). He applied for allotment of a co-operative fair price shop which he could not get as per the rules. That particular shop was allotted to someone else. When the Minister visited my district, Mr Pandey met him and got an order from the Minister that this particular shop might be allotted to him. Armed with the Minister's order, Mr Pandey came to my office and in a belligerent mood asked me to allot the shop as per the order. I explained my inability on the ground that the Minister's order was not proper as it was not authenticated by the Secretary. It was not a Government Order at all. Moreover, it violated the government's guidelines for such allotment. Mr Pandey was quite agitated and asked me to write this on his application. I took the paper and wrote the reasons for rejecting his request in the application itself. Mr Pandey went straight to the Minister again to complain against me, but this time he did not listen to him.

The Cabinet Minister in-charge of the district came to Mirzapur for a review meeting. While reviewing the public distribution system with officers and the public, an important politician of the district and a freedom-fighter complained that a lot of black-marketing was taking place in the public distribution system. When the Minister looked at me, I said, 'Sir, it is a fact. Black-marketing does take place in the public distribution system. When we get such information, stern action is taken against the offenders.' In the presence of the Minister and the peoples' representatives, I immediately telephoned all the SDMs to conduct raids the same day. As ill luck would have it, the younger brother of the politician who made the complaint, was also booked along with others for irregularity in the distribution of rations. The politician came rushing to my residence and requested me to not take action against his younger brother. I showed my helplessness as it was done on his complaint and under my direction in the presence of the Minister. He then rushed to the Minister and made the same request. The Minister laughed and advised the politician to proceed as per the law.

A Lok Sabha by-election was to be held in Mirzapur and three days before the scheduled date, I went to inspect the election arrangements. I went home for lunch when I received a call from the Additional District Magistrate that 2000-3000 BJP supporters had gathered at the Collectorate, led by important leaders. They alleged that ballot papers were being forged. Such an inference was made on the basis of an allegedly forged paper recovered. This news had been published in the morning's paper following which I had already requested for a detailed report. Leaving my lunch, I rushed to the Collectorate, but before meeting the delegation, I had received all the information about the so-called forged ballot papers. A delegation of six or seven leaders led by Mr Atal Bihari Vajpayee, met me in my office. I listened to them patiently then explained the whole situation to them. I pointed out that the so-called forged ballot paper was indeed a defective one; the number on the counterfoil did not match with that on the main ballot. I explained the entire procedure. When the district election office received the ballot papers from the security printing press at Allahabad, they were all counted, defective ballots were removed and a list of these papers was prepared. Further, when the ballot papers were deposited in the double lock of the treasury of the District, they were again counted and the defective papers, if found, were further listed. I showed the delegation the list of defective ballot papers in which the so-called forged ballot paper was also mentioned. So it was a case of defective ballot paper and not a case of a forged one. Mr Vajpayee was convinced, being a stalwart and a statesman. He immediately grasped the situation and never exploited it for electoral gain and the crowd dispersed quietly. A country with such a leader and statesman at the helm of affairs cannot falter on its march towards development.

During my tenure here the Opposition had called for a Bharat Bandh and the state government gave directions to make arrangements to meet the situation, including arrest of the political leaders. The Divisional Commissioner, an ex-army officer, monitored the situation closely. When he enquired about the number of arrests made, I replied, 'Sir, there is no need to arrest any political leaders. Leave it to me to handle the situation'. He was not satisfied with the reply and warned 'If any untoward incidence happens, you will be held responsible'. I accepted the challenge and on the eve of the bandh I called leaders of political parties and, during discussions, told them, 'In a democracy you have a right to agitate and ventilate your grievances in a peaceful manner, but not with violence.' I informed them about the instruction of the Government and said, 'If all of you behave in a peaceful and responsible manner on bandh day there is no need to make any preventive arrest. You can shout anti-Government and anti-DM's slogans but please do not incite the crowd to indulge in violence. If you give me an assurance to this effect, I am not going to make any preventive arrests.' The leaders assured me the agitation would be absolutely peaceful. There were slogans against the Government and District Administration but, as promised by the opposition leaders, there was no violence.

Right from day one, I was determined to provide a clean and honest administration and it was also my strategy to create an element of fear in the minds of anti-social elements. Even though the instruction of the Government was to listen to the grievances of the public on a particular day of the week, I used to listen to their grievances every day from 10.00 am to 2.00 pm. At that time there were no computers or other technological devices, but I used to maintain a register and note details about grievance redressals. The complainant was given the next date of visit to enquire about the status of his application. If the complaint was not sorted by then, the reasons were explained and another date given for final disposal of the complaint. This system of introducing a master calendar of public grievances streamlined the procedures.

I used to tour a lot in this sprawling district and gave pointed attention to the PDS system and development works. I didn't hesitate to use the DM's power to detain anti-social elements under the Prevention of Blackmarketing Act. Likewise, I used the NSA against the bad elements who created terror and in this context I would like to narrate the episode of Lal Sahib. This Sahib was a terror in Mirzapur. He was in the police but was dismissed from service and a number of cases of murder and dacoity were lodged against him. On the basis of the report, he was detained under NSA for one year which had a salutary effect. When he was released, he wanted to see me. Being a dreaded criminal, my security staff wanted to deploy a large contingent of policemen in the premises before the meeting. I told them categorically, 'He has come here to meet me and I will meet him. Call him.' He entered my office and said, 'Sir, are you not afraid of me? The S.P. had deployed a lot of force when I went to meet him today but you have not done anything like that.' I looked into his eyes and said, 'You are a criminal and you should be afraid of me. Why should I be afraid of you? I know you have floated the rumor that the District Magistrate tours a lot and he can be easily blown off by a bomb. But my life is not in your hands but in the hands of God. If I am not destined to die, I will not die even if you hurl hundreds of bombs. If I am destined to die, I can die in a fraction of a second even while walking on the street. So my life is not in your hands.' These words had a magical effect on Lal Sahib and he flatly prostrated before me and started sobbing. He expressed his desire to lead a normal life. I advised him, 'Lal Sahib, society at this juncture will not accept you as you are a criminal. You lie low for a few years and try to help people at the time of their need. Slowly and gradually, you will be accepted into mainstream society through your good deeds and behaviour.' To my surprise, he accepted my advice and tried to change himself.

Tehsil Sadar and Chunar are prone to floods. During the rainy season, particularly August and the first week of September, the Ganga assumes the shape of an ocean with giant waves lashing at the banks. During my tenure the flood was threatening the lives of hundreds in the villages of both tehsils. There was already a drill in District Administration to review the preparedness for disaster management. The District Administration was working round the clock to meet the challenges but it was of such a serious magnitude that even after deploying a few hundred boats in the affected areas, we fell short by about one hundred boats. There was no alternative but to procure boats from Varanasi and Allahabad Districts. When the tenders were opened, the lowest price offered was still much more than the rate approved by the State Government. The ADM (Finance and Revenue) put up a note to recommend rejection of the offers. I called him and said, 'My dear sir, it is an emergency situation. Legally you are correct, but can you assure me, there will not be any loss of life if your advice is accepted.' He showed helplessness in the face of the approved rate. I took the file and approved the lowest tendered rate, even if it was more than the Government rate. I gave a detailed written justification on the file for this decision. Under such emergency situations, I had no other alternative but to approve the lowest rate. At the same time, I also informed the Government about the decision to ensure transparency.

Often, I wonder if laws are made for human beings or the other way. Greek philosopher Cicero said, 'A person who is not governed by laws, rules and regulation is either a beast or a god.' Since we are neither, we are supposed to be governed by rules and regulations. There is another school of thought that stipulates that laws are made for human beings and human beings are not made for laws. In administration, we come across many situations where an outdated law will stand as an obstruction in the implementation of a decision which is in the public interest. In such a case, what is to be done? Apparently, there seems to be a conflict between the two views. Extreme rigidity or extreme flexibility is not in the interest of good governance. A balance has to be struck and the Aristotelian policy of the golden mean seems to be the best option. Often outdated laws act as obstacles to the realization of public good. Such antiquated laws must be identified and repealed as soon as possible.

While undertaking flood relief work in Chunar, I came across a local leader who used to criticize the Government actions. Naturally he was a bitter critic of the relief work in Chunar Tehsil. I tried to convince him that the administration was working round the clock even at the risk of the lives of the officials to provide relief. I asked him to accompany me on one such mission and he readily agreed. We took a big boat loaded with relief materials at about 9.00 am. After visiting many villages, we were returning to Chunar in the evening. While in mid-stream of the Ganga, it started pouring and due to strong winds and big waves the boat began rocking. I remained calm and prayed but the politician was gripped with fear and started to tremble and cry. He moved closer to me and in a choking voice begged, 'Sir, please save my life.' I told him, 'Our lives are in the hands of God, remain calm and pray to God and I am sure since we are on a noble mission, nothing will happen to us.' Somehow we manoeuvred the boat towards the bank and got down safely. The politician was in tears and said, 'Sir, we politicians only know how to criticise the administration. Now, I realize how the Government officials are discharging their duties even at risk to their lives.' After that incident, he started behaving more responsibly.

I enjoyed good relations with the press all through my career. As indicated, Mirzapur is a drought-prone district and every year drought affects it. In 1981, there was a serious drought. A massive employment generation programme was launched under NREP and I personally monitored the situation at the ground level. From May to June, virtually there was no work for the administration except to ensure the proper implementation of drought relief work. A list was prepared showing various projects undertaken under NREP in different villages and it was displayed at the Collectorate, Tehsil and the Block levels. The local press was critical about the relief work and so they met me in a group to complain about it. I figured the best way to dispel their doubts was to take them around to the interiors of the district. Every day, I used to inspect the relief works undertaken, right from the morning till midnight without lunch or dinner. Journalists in two jeeps accompanied me to the various sites. We started at 8 am and proceed to the interior parts. The roads were bumpy and at many places we had to find our way to the site. I did not take any lunch deliberately during these visits. Since I did not have lunch, the journalists also did not have it. After travelling for 16 hours on bumpy forest roads, finally we reached back at Dalla Cement Guesthouse at midnight. The dinner was cold and the journalists were so tired and exhausted that they could not enjoy it. Two of them even fell sick. The next morning, they were supposed to accompany me but excused themselves saying, 'Sir, we are satisfied with the relief work being executed even in the interior parts and you have taken stern actions wherever irregularities have been detected.' They requested me to drop them at Mirzapur city and I readily agreed.

In the first week of April, anticipating drought and acute drinking water shortage I requested the State Government to send a few rigs for drilling borewells. I followed it up with reminders but the machines were nowhere in sight. I hit upon an idea and took the journalists so that they could see for themselves the plight of the villagers. I did not say anything and when they returned from the trip, they reported the ground realities. The next morning, I got a telephone call from the Chief Secretary enquiring about the drought situation. I explained in detail and told him that whatever had been reported in the newspapers was the ground reality. I added that despite my best efforts and repeated reminders, the rigs had not arrived at Mirzapur. The Chief Secretary assured me that these machines would be made available within 48 hours. The Chief Engineer of the Jal Nigam/Jal Sansthan was in panic and contacted me. As promised by the Chief Secretary, the rig machines were provided in 48 hours and it came as a great relief to us. I used to encourage the media to report about the bungling and shortcomings in implementation of development schemes. Such an approach helped in two ways; it gave me a feedback about the status and implementation of the schemes and, secondly, it enabled me to call for explanations and take action against defaulting officers.

There used to be a lot of complaints about IRDP schemes from almost every block. Of the 20 blocks of Mirzapur, on the basis of complaints received, I identified three blocks for hundred per cent verification and engaged my entire team of young Magistrates, probationers and district-level officers for the purpose. To my horror, I found that 65% of the beneficiaries under IRDP schemes were either fake or did not receive any benefit. In fact, in many instances, the same items were shown repeatedly under different names. Such a mal-practice was known in the popular language as Khunta Badla. I thought mere suspension or departmental proceedings would not be sufficient to deter such corruption. I directed the enquiry officers to lodge FIRs against officers/officials numbering about 30 and to get them arrested. FIRs were filed and the accused were put behind bars. As anticipated, this had a salutary effect on the rest of the 17 BDOs who took back their files of subsidy for further verification. I also took serious action against my ADM (Projects) who was directly responsible for the implementation of such schemes. I recommended a vigilance enquiry against him. After many years, I came to know that this officer not only got his promotion but also got posted as DM. I was surprised and wondered how such corrupt officers manipulated the system to escape the consequences. Considerable delays in completion of the enquiry/investigation and in giving sanction for prosecution, go in favour of the accused. It will be in the interest of the administration that such delays must be curtailed at every stage and the manipulation plugged. Instead of following the complicated, procedure of departmental proceedings and investigations, we may introduce a summary approach to the proceedings of the case so as to ensure justice expeditiously.

I believe the institution of DM is not merely for maintenance of law and order or revenue collection or implementation of developmental schemes, it is in fact the DM who is the head of the district administration and the common people look to him for justice and removal of their grievances. I used to hold court at Robertsganj Tehsil once a week and would observe that whenever I was there I always heard someone abusing the Executive Officer, Municipality, SDM and Tehsildar outside the premises. When this happened for the third time, I enquired about who was hurling those abuses. I instructed the ADM, Roberstganj to produce him. A boy was produced and I asked him the reason for using such language. He said, 'Sir, I am a graduate and unemployed. I have parents and sisters to look after and despite repeated requests, these officers have not given me a job even on daily wages but they are appointing their own kith and kin.'

I noticed the boy was not in a proper state of mind. It was none of my business to ensure a job to the boy, even on compassionate grounds, but I instructed the executive officer and the SDM to employ him on a casual basis on municipal road construction. Since he was a graduate, he could be given some supervisory work. This was done and after a week, I found the boy was in a better mental state and no more filthy language was heard outside the office premises. When I got transferred to Agra in 1983, the boy was removed from this casual employment. One morning I found the boy at my residence. He had come all the way from Mirzapur to narrate his problems and I observed that he was in the same earlier mental state. I telephoned an industrialist I knew to request him to engage the boy as a factory worker. He readily obliged and the problem was sorted out. This was not my job but since the boy had come with expectations, I had the greatest satisfaction that I saved the family.

Once an old man came to my house in the morning and complained that his only son had gone on a hunger strike as he could not meet Mrs Indira Gandhi. The man was worried as his son had not taken food for two days. He came all the way from his village so that the DM could solve his problem. From the way the old man narrated I could guess that the boy was mentally disturbed. I told him, 'Please tell your son that you have met the DM who has promised that at the first opportunity, he will arrange a meeting with Mrs Gandhi whenever she visits Mirzapur next.' The old man went back and the next day met me again and said, 'Sir, the boy has ended the fast.' I was thrilled.

While meeting the public in the Collectorate once, a person entered my room and started hurling choicest abuses against the CMO. I asked him to sit down calmly. He said, 'Sir, I am suffering from acidity and gastric problems and have met the CMO many times but he gives me a few tablets and some liquid. These are quite ineffective. They are all useless fellows.' I advised him, 'Go for a morning walk, do not take tea, coffee or spicy and oily food, take food on time, take cold milk intermittently and do a bit of Yoga.' After patiently listening to me, he again started abusing the CMO and said, 'Sir, he never gave such a piece of advice'. He left quite satisfied.

One evening a person wanted to meet me alone. He started in a low voice, 'Sir, I have some doubt about the loyalty of my wife.' I was furious but still heard him out. I asked him, 'Do you have only doubt or you have some evidence?' He said, 'I do not have any evidence but she is not taking care of me. She is neglecting me.' I asked if he had ever given any gift of a sari to his wife and he said, 'No'. I again asked if he had ever taken her to a movie or for a walk. He again shook his head. I told him that the relationship was a two-way street based on trust and loyalty. 'You please look after her the way I have suggested and come back after 15 days.' After a fortnight the man came and reported that everything was all right and there was peace at home now.

Another time a woman came to the Collectorate carrying her child and, in a choked voice, complained that her husband was a drunkard and he was selling his land to buy liqour. The husband had come to the Collectorate with an advocate to sell the family's last piece of land of about two acres. She pleaded that if this piece of land was sold, she would not have anything to fall back upon. I was in a dilemma as it was purely a legal matter. I pondered over the matter and called ADM (Finance & Revenue) and instructed him not to register the sale deed. In the meanwhile, I called the advocate and his client to my office where the public was also present. The advocate was agitated and complained against the ADM (F&R) for not registering the deed. I explained the whole situation and its future implications to the advocate and the public and asked them whether it would be proper to destroy the life of the mother and child. They all agreed not to register the same and the family was saved from impending disaster.

One morning, an old person came to see me at home and said, 'Sir, I was your Naib Tehsildar and retired 20 years ago. I am more than 80 years old but I have not enjoyed my pension so far. It seems I will die without getting the benefits.' I was taken aback and requested him to wait for 3 days so that I could find a solution. He said, 'Sir, I have patiently waited for long 20 years and so can wait for another 3 days also.' I went to the Collectorate and handed over his application to the ADM (Executive) to treat it as urgent. After some time, the ADM, accompanied by OC (Combined Office) and the Office Superintendent, returned and said that the file was not traceable. I directed the ADM to suspend all the activities of Magistrates and officials and to join in the search of the file. After a few hours, the file was found lying in the dustbin in a corner of the record room. It was reported the file lacked some information sought by the AG. When I told them that pension cases were now being handled by the local Head of the Department, and not the AG they could process the file. The information on the file was sufficient to take a decision. I sanctioned 90% of the sum as provisional pension along with arrears. The next day when I handed over the order to the Naib Tehsildar I could see tears in his eyes. He blessed me profusely. I had the greatest satisfaction that God chose me as His medium to dispense justice to the old retired Naib Tehsildar. I was grateful to God.

Another incident that shook me was the death of one of my Magistrates' wife. It was summer and I was supervising relief work in the interior part of Robertsganj. At about 2 pm or so, I got a wireless message that the wife of the Magistrate had died of burns in the kitchen. I rushed back to Mirzapur and by the time I reached there, the body was already on the funeral pyre. At the burning ghat, the father of the girl came to me and said, 'Sir, I suspect some foul play. In fact, I am convinced that they have killed my daughter.' I advised him to lodge an FIR at the police station. At night, I received a call from the girl's father that the police station was refusing to register the FIR as it involved a Magistrate. I talked to the Police official and directed him to register the FIR. At midnight, I was woken up again by the security who informed that the SP had come to discuss something urgent. I was surprised by the SP's visit at such an odd hour. The SP said, 'Sir, an FIR has been lodged against the magistrate and you don't worry about it.' I was surprised and told him that I was not worried at all. 'You proceed with the investigations and decide on the merit of the case.' The SP replied, 'Sir, it is a case involving a Magistrate and, as you know, the relationship between the police and Magistrate is a delicate one and if the District Police handles the investigation, it may sour our relationship.' I then suggested to refer the matter to the CID. The next day, all the Magistrates of the District met me and expressed their dissatisfaction at the reference of the case to the CID. I explained the reasons and persuaded them not to do anything that would distort the image of the magistracy. After many years, I came to know that the Magistrate was convicted and was in jail. I do not know what happened ultimately. We must understand that nobody is above law.

The Mirzapur DM's bungalow is a magnificent structure right on the banks of the Ganga. But unfortunately, due to soil erosion, the river had come dangerously close to the residence. My fear was that in a few years, the building would collapse. I called the PWD Engineers and instructed them to make a project to strengthen the river bank so that the bungalow could be saved. After a fortnight, the Executive Engineer came with a proposal of Rs 1 crore for the purpose. It was well nigh impossible to get this amount sanctioned just to strengthen the river bank. I rejected the proposal and instructed the Executive Officer, Nagar Palika and OC, Nagar Palika to dump truckloads of garbage at the crevices and gullis (lanes) along the banks. My idea was to fill up the weak portion of the bank with the garbage so that it could settle down after a few showers. Thereafter, some pitching of stones and massive plantation work including elephant grass would be undertaken to further strengthen the bank. The project did not cost much and was completed in time. A simple innovative approach saved a lot of Government money.

One evening I was surprised to be invited by my Commissioner for a special drink party he was hosting. I told him, 'Sir, you know I am a teetotaler, and so what is the point in my joining this party.'

He laughed and said, 'The public and I know that you do not touch liquor but someone had complained that you are fond of drinking and always remained drunk.' In a lighter vein, he continued, 'If nothing else, a few elements will definitely complain against you. It is better that you come here and enjoy the drinks.' I had a hearty laugh and politely declined. The matter ended on a jovial note.

It is not only politicians who can make life difficult for an honest officer, sometimes even relatives can create problems. One of my relatives was interested in a mining lease in the district and met me in this respect. I dissuaded him as I was the DM of Mirzapur and did not want to leave any scope for anybody to point a finger at me. He understood the situation and did not insist and I have no regret for taking this stand of mine. The basic principle of ethics is that a person should be honest in every action. Reputation is not built in a day. It takes years and years to build up one's reputation. It is the cornerstone of the strength of a person.

When I became Chief Secretary, UP in 2007, my daughter Pragya came to Lucknow to appear for an interview for the selection of National Co-ordinator for an important international NGO. She had done her Master's degree in Social Work at TISS, Mumbai and was working with the Indian Red Cross Society. Out of 200 candidates, eight were short-listed and Pragya was one of them. During breakfast, my wife asked me whether it will be proper to put in a word for Pragya. Before, I could say, Pragya jumped up and said, 'No Papa, never. You have not done it in your lifetime, now why should you do it for me.' I appreciated her attitude and did not speak to anybody. My daughter was not selected. I told her, 'Whatever has happened would be in your interests. Take it that way.' After this, she was selected for an assignment in Nepal by an International Civil Society Organization and she has now landed up in the UNDP. This is the grace of God.

Mirzapur also proved another turning point in my life. The invigorating atmosphere of Vindhyachal transported me to a higher plane. I visited almost all the temples and important places of Mirzapur and had the good fortune of interacting with saints like Narhari Baba, Adagadanandaji, Devraha Baba, Yog Expert Raj Bali Mishraji, Ram Kinkar, Maa Anandmayee and a host of others. During Holi, a group of small boys came from Mathura to perform the Krishna Leela at the SP's residence. Many officers and their wives were also invited on this occasion. After the performance, as per tradition, Krishna and Radha were to be worshipped with an Aarti. After the Aarti, I touched their feet and felt that I was holding the feet of my Lord. I was in a state of ecstasy with tears rolling down my cheeks. I was in a different world and did not want to let go the feet of the Lord. The spell must have lasted for a minute. But for the first time, I realized that there are different planes of existence and one could travel to such a higher plane with devotion and surrender. I used to visit Vindhyachal once a week and whenever I was at Vindhyachal, Kalikho and Ashtabhuja, I always felt elevated to a higher plane. The experience at Mirzapur laid the foundation for my onward spiritual journey.

Chapter 15

District Magistrate, Agra

(July 1983 – July 1985)

If we work for a noble cause, 'the all-pervading Divine Force'
is always there to help you.

My three years in Mirzapur were one of the best periods in my
life. After three years I was expecting a transfer any time and in
July, 1983, I was informed by the then Appointment Secretary, that
I was transferred to Agra as DM. He directed me to take over charge
of Agra immediately. Soon after I received a Government order and
without waiting for a substitute, I handed over charge to the senior-
most ADM and proceeded to Agra the next day. A lot of public and
officials came to the Railway Station to see me off. I was touched. I felt
the pang of separation and tears came to my eyes. I reached Agra the
next day and took over. A new life, new friends, new people and new
challenges awaited me here.

Agra has always been an important district from the point of view
of law and order, VIP visits and influx of foreign tourists. Of course,
Agra is the city of the Taj. I had to look after law and order, VIP
visits, development works, meeting the public, judicial functions and
collection of taxes etc. Agra was sensitive from the point of view of
law and order as it had a large population of Muslims as well as those
belonging to the weaker sections. During my initial period here, I
found that most Magistrates and the Police officers used to spend

their evenings in the chain of hotels for which Agra is quite famous. From the point of view of a quick response to law and order situation, this was not a good sign. In consultation with the SSP, I set up joint groups of Magistrates and COs (Police) who were directed to maintain constant vigil on the city's law and order problem by intense night patrolling. Initially, they resisted this but with strictness from both the side of SP and DM, they fell in line. This had a positive impact on the law and order situation in the city.

For effective maintenance of law and order it is essential that the DM and SP work in tandem, trusting and respecting each other and ego must not come into play. If trust is not there, if cordiality is missing and if ego comes to the forefront, then God alone can save the district. Throughout my tenure as DM in four different districts spanning seven years, I succeeded in forging a good personal rapport with my police counterparts. Whenever I had found laxity on the part of the police, I never hesitated to pull them up. A few days after my taking over, the SSP transferred a few SOs without consulting me and I came to know of it from newspapers. Immediately I sent a letter to the SSP that it would have been better if he had consulted me at least on telephone. The SSP immediately assured me on telephone that henceforth he would definitely consult me while transferring SOs. In the next chain of transfers, he consulted me but when I saw the list, it was a longer one. I again brought it to the SSP's notice and giving details, informed the Secretary (Home) and DG (Police). I did not know then that my letter would create such a problem for the SSP. After two years, when I was posted as Director (Youth) in the Government of India, the SSP came to my office at Shastri Bhavan and narrated his predicament. He said my letter had created a problem regarding his promotion and he wanted me to talk to the Home Secretary and DG (Police). Since the SSP had changed his attitude after this letter, I spoke to the Home Secretary and the DG (Police) saying that I had no grudge against him and, in fact, we functioned as a close knit team during a critical period. I believe this cleared his path to promotion and he later thanked me for that.

The greatest challenge we faced was after the assassination of Mrs Indira Gandhi. On that fateful day, my Commissioner was chairing a meeting of the agricultural development in Agra Division with officers and Central Government representatives. At about 10 am, I received a call from my confidential office informing me that Mrs Gandhi was shot at and seriously injured with little chance of survival. I put down the telephone, came to the Commissioner and requested him to spare me from attending the meeting as there might be a law and order problem in the District. I dashed straight to my confidential office. Here the staff informed me about the tragic incident and told me it was true. I was sure in my mind that this would have serious repercussions in the district which had a sizeable Sikh population. Immediately after discussion with the SSP, I convened a meeting of the Magistrates and the Police Officers and discussed the problem threadbare. We concluded that the residences, the work places, commercial establishments and places of worship of the community would be possible targets of anti-social elements. We concluded that such disturbance would be only in the city and not in the rural areas. Forces were withdrawn from the rural areas to bolster the arrangement in the city. It was also decided to go for massive preventive arrests of anti-social elements. Whereas news of the tragedy was announced in the evening we had received it quite early in the day. This gave us enough time to mobilize and deploy forces and make preventive arrests. Groups of Magistrates and Police officers were formed for intense patrolling and by evening, they were all on the road.

During this unprecedented crisis, the District and Police administration showed exemplary dedication and devotion to duty and we used to work round the clock for 15 days without rest or proper food. The SSP and I with a contingent of forces were always on the move day and night. We survived on murmura, channa and gur (puffed rice, gram and jaggery) and bottles of drinking water stored in our car. These became our life sustenance during that turbulent fortnight.

We noticed anti-social elements were active generally between 11.00 am and midnight and hence started our day at 7.00 am continued to move with our force till 3.00 am the next day. A few interesting instances occurred during this patrolling. While moving with the forces one morning, an old woman came to us and begged with folded hands to save the life of her only son who had received a grievous injury. She said the son was afraid of going to the hospital as he feared the mob might attack him. With the SSP I consoled her and personally took the boy to the medical college hospital. The boy recovered fully and thus a life was saved. When the crisis was over within 15 days, members of the Sikh community and their leaders felicitated me at Guru Ka Tal Gurudwara presenting a sword (Saropa) and a turban. After the felicitation, when I was returning to the car an old woman came running to garland me. When the police prevented her, she uttered, 'Son, probably you do not recognize me but how can I forget you? You have saved my son, please accept the garland.' With tears, she garlanded me and I cannot express what I felt at that moment.

Curfew had been imposed in Agra and Firozabad during the initial days of the crisis. When we received news of disturbances in Firozabad, the SSP and I rushed there, with a contingent of force. The ADM (Firozabad) and CO (Police) were already there on the spot. At that moment, the MLA of that area came there with his supporters. I looked at him sternly and in a thundering voice asked, 'Do you have a curfew pass? If you don't have one, please leave immediately or you will be arrested.' Sensing that we meant business, he left the place immediately. After this incident, we had a review meeting and then it was suggested to the police that a few people of other parties could also be arrested in order to neutralize the fact that a large number of supporters of one party had been rounded up. I rejected the suggestion outright and directed them to arrest whosoever indulged in anti-social activities.

One morning, at about 10.00 am the SSP, SP City, the ADM, City and I were discussing the tense situation in the city when we received a wireless message saying that a mob near Sadar Bazar area was pelting stones. With a contingent of forces, ADM and SP (City) immediately left for the spot, but after some time we received another message of crowd violence. We wanted to contact the ADM and SP City for first hand information but we could not contact them. SSP and I accompanied by force proceeded to the spot. From a distance, I observed that the road was littered with stones and it seemed that the crowd was dispersed by force but were again re-grouping. We had just a few seconds to decide whether to stop the car and talk to the agitators or escape from the place at full speed. The first option was fraught with danger because there was every likelihood of our being seriously attacked. I chose the second option and directed the driver to speed past the spot. We reached the other end safely. This decision might have turned out to be a bad one if some agitators were knocked down by the car but fortunately nothing happened and the situation was controlled. I was fully convinced that some unseen force stood by us to steer us clear of the grave situation. This happens in life. If we are sincere and act selflessly for a noble cause, I am sure we will always be protected by the divine force which will ward off all the obstacles on our path.

The intensity of the crisis had eased out but not ended. Meanwhile, one night I received a telephone message from the Secretary to the Chief Minister that there was a complaint of police excesses against the public in Agra. So a fact-finding delegation, led by the Minister of State for Home, was arriving there the next day. I got agitated and told the Secretary to the CM bluntly, 'Sir, nothing serious has happened in Agra. A city like Kanpur has witnessed more devastation, violence and loss of lives. There is no loss of life in Agra. In fact, the people are watching the hockey tournament in Agra City. If the Government is not satisfied with our work, you rather transfer all police officers and Magistrates, including me and SSP.' The Secretary pacified me and said, 'It is just a fact-finding mission and there is nothing to be worried about. When the officers have worked with sincerity and dedication, we are always there to look after their interests.' The Home

Secretary also assured me in the same vein. I convened a meeting of the police and Magistrates immediately and directed them to inform a cross-section of society viz. political representatives, journalists, student leaders, business communities, intellectuals, teachers, and advocates to give proper feedback to the fact-finding mission. I also personally telephoned many leading personalities to testify about the role of the administration. The next morning, when I went to the Circuit House I was surprised to find a large gathering. The meeting began and the Minister enquired from me about the excesses the forces had committed. I replied, 'Sir, the situation in Agra is more or less normal and nothing much has happened. The situation is fully under control and there has been no loss of life. However, anti-social elements and mischief mongers have been sternly dealt with purely in the interest of maintaining law and order.' From the expression on the Minister's face I felt he did not like my statement. When the delegation came out of the room, the Minister was happy to see a large crowd at the Circuit House. But his smile vanished when they started raising slogans against the mission. The representatives from the crowd clearly asked the Minister, 'Why have you come to Agra when everything is absolutely under control and nothing has happened in Agra? Why did you not go to Kanpur and other places to find out about the loss of lives and properties? Have you come here to create problems?' The delegation left the Circuit House in a hurry. No action was taken against any officer as the Government was well aware of the ground realities here and other districts.

Our firm handling of the crisis earned us much appreciation. Lt. General Nakai of the Army wrote to the Chief Minister appreciating the role of the District Administration in meeting the crisis. Often, I wonder how we weathered out such a grave crisis. Of course, the credit goes to the team spirit, strategy adopted and the missionary zeal with which the staff worked round the clock.

The National Security Act (NSA) is a potent weapon which the District Magistrate needs to use with caution and prudence. I used it against dreadful criminals and anti-social elements indulging in heinous crimes and did not even hesitate to use it against an MLA of the party in power. My action was greatly appreciated by the public and it was approved by the Government as well as by the Advisory Board. This also sent a clear message to the anti-social elements that the District Administration would not hesitate to take tough measures when needed.

I remember just before Eid, I was informed by one of the MLAs about the police misbehavior against a Muslim woman. He said, 'Mishraji unless quick and effective steps are taken this will create serious problem tomorrow on the eve of Eid.' I immediately convened a meeting of journalists at my residence. In the presence of the SSP, SP City and ADM (City) narrated the incidence concealing nothing. By this time, direction had already been given to lodge an FIR against the police official and to get him arrested. I told the journalists, 'Friends, it is a delicate situation and the SSP has already taken effective steps. If you report this incident I am sure it will lead to a riot. If you don't publish it the day after, then there is every possibility of avoiding a riot. Friends, the law and order situation of the city is now in your hands. If you want to avoid a riot, as enlightened citizens, I am sure you will not publish it tomorrow.' They all agreed and I must give them credit for saving the situation. The strategy could have misfired but it worked which further confirmed my belief that if we work for a noble cause, 'the all-pervading divine force' is there to help.

My encounter with Chaudhary Charan Singh, the former Prime Minister, is interesting. During the General Assembly Election of 1985, he was to address a public meeting in Agra City. One day before his scheduled visit, the MLA from his party with his supporters created a tense situation in the area under Malpura Police Station. The SSP and I were present on the spot when there was a lathi-charge to disperse the stone-throwing crowd. Arrests were made, including that of the MLA. When Chaudhary Charan Singh came to Agra, he telephoned me from the Circuit House in the morning and expressed his desire to visit the jail to meet his supporters. I told the former Prime Minister clearly that the District Administration had no objection to his visit but he should know the circumstances under which force was used. I explained the whole situation on telephone and permitted him to visit the jail. The ADM (City) accompanied him. When Chaudhary Charan Singh reached the jail and met his supporters, they complained about the police and the District Administration and shouted slogans. He got angry and told them sternly, 'In politics, you have to bear the brunt of lathi-charge. Your DM has explained me in great detail and I have no grudge against the Administration.' The situation passed off peacefully.

The law and order problems in Agra were quite challenging and I have cited only a few instances. There were others like handling young army recruit deserters, flushing out of anti-social elements from the Agra College hostel and deaths in police custody. These were all dealt with effectively.

I had the rare opportunity to enquire against the DG (Police), a situation so unthinkable. I was surprised to get a letter from the Home Department to enquire into some allegations against the then DG. I thought, probably, in a routine way and without application of mind, the complaint was sent for enquiry. I wrote back to say that probably it was not intended to be enquired by the DM as the DG was Head of the state police organization. But the DG himself wrote to the Home Department that he had full faith in my fairness and that he had no objection at all if I inquired into the allegation. Ultimately I had to do it and submitted my report. This may, perhaps, be the only such enquiry in the administrative history of UP.

In the aftermath of Mrs Gandhi's assassination, strict guidelines were issued by the Government of India as well as by the State Government to ward off any possible miltant threats. Since Lok Sabha elections were to be held, many VIPs and VVIPs used to visit Agra. There were strict instructions about arrangements for their security and safety. On one occasion, the Prime Minister was to come to Kheria Airport, Agra for some time and a powerful Cabinet Minister from Agra approached the District Administration for a pass to enable him and his driver to get to the airport so that he could receive the Prime Minister. The passes were issued for the Minister and his driver but to my surprise, I found that he was accompanied by three others for whom passes were not issued. I instructed the SSP to deploy a guard at the room of the lounge where the Minister's friends were sitting and did not to allow them to come out. I also instructed that they may be treated well with tea and coffee but under no circumstances would they be allowed to come out. The Prime Minister's visit went off peacefully. After he took off in a helicopter, the Minister was furious and said, 'DM Sahib, you have insulted me before my supporters.' I replied, 'Sir, keeping in view the threat perception from militants, there are strict instructions about the security of the Prime Minister. It is our bounden duty to enforce these instructions but, unfortunately, you have violated them and I will report the matter to the Chief Minister as well as to the Government of India and the PMO.' The Minister immediately came to his senses and expressed regret.

In another instance when the Prime Minister was coming to Kheria airport, three Cabinet Ministers were held up at the entry gate that was closed 20 minutes before the touch down of the VVIP plane. The Ministers must have forced the gate-keeper to open the gate, who in turn contacted the Air Force Authority. The Air Commodore informed me of the holding up and asked me whether to allow them in. I asked him point blank, 'What is the rule?' and he replied, '20 minutes before the touch down of the VVIP plane, the instruction is to close the gate.' I said, 'Then the instruction must be complied with strictly.' As a result, the Ministers could not come and they were annoyed but could not say a word as we were firm on enforcing security instructions.

During my tenure as DM in different districts, I observed that the crew of the VIP/VVIP and their supporters created more problems for the district administration than the VIP's visit itself. The Prime Minister came to Kheria airport many times, particularly during election campaign. It was the general practice and drill that the crew of the VVIP used to come a day in advance. Since Agra had a chain of good hotels, the district administration used to lodge them in five-star hotels. The administration always tried its best to keep the crew of the VVIPs in good humour. On one occasion, however, the ADM (Protocol) put them up at the Circuit House. The head of the crew was not satisfied with the arrangement and used foul language against the ADM when he visited them at the Circuit House to enquire about their comforts. He also scribbled and handed over a list of items they needed, like cashew nut in kgs, juice in crates. The ADM came to me crestfallen and narrated the entire episode. I assured him that appropriate action would be taken. I went through the book containing instructions for the arrangements to be made for the safety of the VVIPs and came across a provision that in case there was an airbase the crew had to stay there. If the Officer in Command of the Airbase was not in a position to provide accommodation, then he would request the DM to make necessary arrangements. After a week or so, the VVIP had again to come to the Kheria Airport and I shot off a letter to the Officer in Command of the Kheria Airbase requesting him to provide accommodation for the crew in the Airbase failing which the DM should be requested to make arrangements. Pat came the reply that all arrangements would be made by the Air Force. I told the ADM (Protocol) not to make any arrangements at any five-star hotel. He was nervous, but I assured him that nothing would happen. In the evening, I got a call from the Head of the Crew that the district administration had not made any arrangements for them in the hotel. I told him, 'We are following the rules and the guidelines for arrangements to be made for the visits of the VVIPs. Please go through the instructions and then get back to me.' He replied, 'Mr Mishra, whenever we come, we are all accommodated in five-star hotels but this time it has not been done.' I said politely, 'That was by courtesy of the district administration.' I also wrote a detailed letter to the Ministry of Defence and the UP Government indicating the harassment my ADM (Protocol) had suffered at the hands of the crew.

In one of the slokas, Chanakya says that when a tree is laden with fruits, it bends and likewise a person who is learned remains humble, and shows no arrogance. When I read it as a school student, I could not understand the full import of this but when I met Dr Har Gobind Khorana, Nobel Laureate in Genetics, during his visit to the Taj, I realized its full import. I was fortunate to receive Dr Khorana during my tenure there. He was so full of humility that it was difficult to find such a person in this world of imperfection. I accompanied him through his tour and during lunch, with humility, he said, 'Mr Mishra, instead of wasting your time on me, you may attend to more important duties.' When I replied, 'Sir, it is equally my duty to look after your comfort and security,' he just smiled. As an Administrator, I have observed that a bit of authority and power always gets to the head of the person who then behaves in an arrogant manner. According to Yoga Vasishta, ego itself is a terrible enemy of man and it is the root cause of all miseries. So long as it is there, sorrows and sufferings cannot be eliminated.

I also had occasion to receive Mr George Bush Senior, then US Vice-President during his visit to Agra to see the Taj Mahal. I was in the formal dress. When the Vice President visited the Taj, there was a session for photographs. Every officer present wanted to be a part of the group photo, but I kept a safe distance and closely observed the scene. After the photo session was over, Mr Bush called me and said, 'Well gentleman, would you like to have a photograph with me?' I said, 'Sir, it is a pleasure.' The visit of the US Vice-President was over without a hitch. A few days later, I was pleasantly surprised to receive a letter from Mr Bush enclosing the photograph which I still have as a souvenir.

The civil servant faces many ordeals and pressures in the discharge of his duties. Despite these he must steadfastly stick to ethics, rules and regulations failing which he is likely to land himself in trouble. A famous hotel chain was interested in purchase/lease of a land for building a five-star hotel. The land valuation was to be done by the revenue administration when I was on leave. When I came back, the hotel representative met me in the office and informed me that though the valuation had been made, no further action seemed to have been taken. I called for the file and found, to my utter surprise, that the then ADM (E) had already sent the valuation report which was quite low against the prevalent market price. I examined the file and after analyzing many sale deeds of that area, came to the conclusion that the valuation would be many times more than what had been indicated. Accordingly I passed my order. In the evening, the Divisional Commissioner called me to his residence and asked, 'Mishra, why are you harassing the hotel authority? You have already shown the power of the Collector and now finish the matter quickly.' I replied, 'Sir, do you think that I am harassing them for money? Do you think that I am corrupt?' The Commissioner was taken aback by this reply and said, 'Mishra, I will not believe even if God complains against your integrity.' I returned to my residence and the next day talked to the Secretary, Urban Development and briefed him about the entire episode of under-valuation. I also sent my report. I do not know what happened later, but I had the satisfaction of not buckling under pressure.

I recall a hilarious episode during my visit to Bharatpur Bird sanctuary in winter. It was biting cold and my head-peon (jamadar) Shaitan Singh was in his neat and colourful official dress standing by my side. We were waiting for our turn to board the boat when a foreign visitor came and warmly greeted and shook hands with the peon thinking, probably, that he was from a royal family. I congratulated him on his personality and big moustache, which must have caught the attention of the tourist.

Once I received a call from the Prime Minister's Office about some encroachment in the perimeters of Taj Mahal. The PMO wanted a report within 48 hours from the District Administration. Immediately accompanied by SSP, ADM (City), ADM (E), Sr. officers of PWD and a representative of ASI, I proceeded to take a round of the perimeter. The ASI official showed us two notifications that were issued during the British Raj in the early part of the 20th century indicating the areas of the Taj. The first was modified by a second one. Armed with this information, the team went around the perimeters and found there was no encroachment at all inside the premises. But when we took a round of the perimeters it seemed that the entire market and settlement of Taj Ganj were within the perimeters. How could this have happened; an entire market and settlement had come up around the Taj perimeter? It must have taken more than half a century to come to this stage. The ASI official told me, 'Sir, the old Superintendent of ASI who looked after the Taj, who is now 80 years old, may be able to throw some light.' I went to his residence and discussed the matter. After listening to us, with a smile he pulled out an old book and showed me some portions where it was clearly mentioned that during the British time, the then District Magistrate had settled this area with the people for a paltry sum. I heaved a sigh of relief and sent a report to the PMO, with a copy to the State Government, attaching extracts from the book. Thus ended the fiasco.

My experience in Agra will not be complete without mentioning the Mughlai paratha of Fatehpur Sikri. I had heard of it but had not tasted it. When I went to Fatehpur Sikri on an inspection I stayed at the ASI Guesthouse and promptly ordered the paratha. When it arrived, I was surprised to see its thickness and circumference. It was of many layers and fried in ghee. I found it difficult even to finish one-fourth of it. I was told that during the old days, Emperor Akbar used to have many parathas with more layers.

The work in Agra was hectic and I used to work till midnight. My hair started greying and the long hours adversely affected my health.

After serving as DM for more than seven years, I requested the Government to transfer me to a different assignment that may not be as tiring. The Appointments Secretary persuaded me to continue as DM Agra but with folded hands I requested him to get me transferred from Agra in my own interest and for health reasons. Ultimately I was transferred, in July, 1985, to Lucknow as Director and Special Secretary, Information.

Chapter 16

....✄

Director-cum-Special Secretary (Information)

(July 1985 – May 1986)

The electronic media and social networking
sites with their unprecedented reach, have
redefined the practice of democratic politics.

The Director, Information is considered a key posting as it deals
with one of the powerful pillars of democracy i.e. the media.
Their objective is to provide correct information and facts to the
public, to keep a tab on news and views, to analyze them and to
look into the accreditation and the welfare measures of journalists.
The important decisions the Government makes and announces
at press conferences are also released to the press. On important
occasions, advertisements are issued to the press but these professed
ideals are not always followed to the best of their spirit. No doubt,
the Press and the media had played an important role not only
during the freedom struggle but also in exposing the various scams,
highlighting the difficulties of the public and the weaknesses of the
Government policies. But at times, instead of searching for truth,
they act as a go-between the journalistic world and corporate world
and Government to seek loaves and fishes to further their own
interests. It is heartening to note that the media in recent years have
become fiercely independent. It has also started participating in a

positive way to encourage people's movement as happened during the Anna Hazare Movement for Jan Lok Pal. The electronic media and the social networking sites with their unprecedented reach, have redefined the practice of democratic politics.

Freedom and especially freedom of speech and expression is essential for the development of mankind. It is as natural to mankind as oxygen. So what is freedom? Freedom is essentially a condition of man without which he cannot be at his best. It postulates a set of rights and responsibilities to create a congenial and necessary environment for the full development of the potential of the individual. Lokmanya Bal Gangadhar Tilak said, 'Freedom is my birth right.' During the freedom struggle, Subhas Chandra Bose thundered, 'Give me blood and I will give you freedom.' Bismark followed a policy of blood and iron to ensure the unification of Germany. John Stuart Mill dwells upon the concept of freedom in an interesting manner. According to him, restraint qua restraint is an evil i.e. restraint for the sake of restraint is an evil as it hinders the free flow of energy of the individual and society. But licentiousness is not freedom. He talks of self-regarding and other-regarding actions of the individual. The State can put reasonable restrictions on other-regarding actions of the individual if they go against the interests of society and the State. He even advocates that an individual who is not aware of his real will and real interests may be coerced to be free by putting reasonable restrictions.

We find the concept of freedom enshrined in our Constitution in a holistic manner, emphasizing both the rights and duties of the citizens. The Preamble talks of liberty of thought and expression but at the same time it provides for justice, equality, fraternity and integrity of the nation and the dignity of the individual. Only when these qualitative elements are fulfilled in their true spirit, can the citizens enjoy the freedom in a better way. The rights and duties are sides of the same coin and they are necessary for the enjoyment of freedom in a meaningful way. Therefore the Constitution provides for both fundamental rights and fundamental duties and the people who are conscious of their rights alone, and not their duties, fail the nation.

Freedom is the life blood of any democratic society without which the nation will languish and die. The right to dissent is equally important. Everybody has the right to dissent. According to JS Mill, the entire society minus the lone dissenter has no right to silence the dissenter. This is because if the dissenter is right in his opinion then society is deprived of the truth. Even if the dissenter is wrong, in that event also, society will be the loser because it will be deprived of realizing the truth in a more intensified manner that will emerge out of constant interaction and struggle between truth and falsehood.

Modern developments in science and technology have opened up new frontiers of opportunities as well as challenges with regards to freedom. The internet, blogs, tweets, WhatsApp and the whole range of social sites have enlarged the horizon of liberty. But at the same time, it has become a potent weapon in the hands of anti-social and anti-national elements to foment disorder, instability and hatred in society. A number of instances can be quoted to show how these sites are misused for diabolic purposes. It is also misused by the authority to unnecessarily curb the freedom of expression of the citizen. What is to be done in this respect? Liberty of thought and expression has to be preserved and promoted against all odds but at the same time, we must not allow such freedom to be mis-used to create disharmony. Therefore, the need of the present hour is to strike a balance between these two. The citizens must be educated and enlightened to exercise self-restraint while disseminating information through the social sites. The Government should also come out clearly explaining the situation under which a 'reasonable restriction' can be imposed. The phrase 'reasonable restriction' may be defined and explained so as one to avoid misinterpretation and possible misuse by the authority. I am sure with the passage of time and with the maturity of the Indian citizen, this will no longer be a headache.

The concept of freedom goes beyond merely enjoying a set of rights and discharging a set of responsibilities. In the words of T.H. Green, the Idealistic philosopher, 'Freedom consists in partaking of and contributing to the social good.' In other words, the citizen must be empowered to such an extent that he will not only have a share in the social good but at the same time he must be competent enough to contribute to the social good.

Vedic philosophy postulates the concept of freedom in a spiritual way. Love, knowledge of the ultimate truth and awareness of the true self constitute the very basis of freedom. Love liberates and freedom comes with love. It also comes from the knowledge of the ultimate truth and awareness about the true self. Recognize the God within and be at peace with yourself. Have compassion for one another. It also postulates the principle of the golden mean i.e. the middle path to enjoy the freedom. A spiritual life is the *sine qua non* of enjoying freedom in its true sense.

As Director, Information, I had very cordial relations with the journalistic fraternity. I was always there to help them sort out their problems but I never bowed down to pressure. I noticed the journalists, particularly of the small and medium newspapers, used to frequent my office for advertisements. This was a complete wastage of time and energy from the point of view of both. After mutual discussions, an advertisement policy was formulated indicating the date and occasion when advertisements were to be released to different newspapers. The calendar activities of various campaigns and occasions were listed and the names of the papers which would get the advertisement were also mentioned. It was an open document and instead of coming to the Information Office repeatedly for advertisement, they knew the time and the quantum of advertisement in advance.

The State Accreditation Committee meetings were not held for quite some time. With requests from the Association of the Journalists, I convened a meeting in Jhansi. Some office bearer of the journalists association (maybe Chairman or Secretary) came to me and said, 'Sir, we know, you are a non-drinker. We also know that you have an aversion for it. But since the meeting is going to be held after a long time, we may celebrate it with drinks and dinner.' I said yes to dinner but no to drinking. I told them politely that in the dinner hosted by the Director Information, liquor could not be served. They came out with solution, 'Sir, we know that you will not accept this part of the proposal but we do hope you have no objection if we first drink elsewhere at our own cost and come to the official dinner.' I said, 'I have no objection to that.' Thus, a confrontation was avoided. As Director, Information I refused to pass the bill of entertainment of journalists with liquor by the then Resident Commissioner as it was against the Government policy.

Funds were earmarked for entertainment of journalists as well as for advertisement. The strategy of the Department was to put up the proposal at the last minute for my approval with the suggestion that since there was no time left, it may be sanctioned in favour of the previous agency which had handled it before. I could see through their game to provide undue benefits to certain firms. I always insisted on following the tender procedures as laid down by the Government. During Kumbh Mela in Hardwar, lakhs of posters were to be printed for display and distribution. The proposal was put up for approval at the last moment. Only one name was suggested with a cost of Rs 3 per poster. I could immediately sense that there was something wrong with it and called for immediate offer from other firms also who were recognized by the Department. To my surprise, the cost of one poster came down from Rs 3 to Rs 1. Thus, we saved lakhs of rupees on this account alone.

Keeping in view the important role played by the press, once I suggested to the Chief Minister that the reputed newspapers of National and State standing both in Hindi and English may be entrusted with the task of giving correct feedback about the implementation of the important schemes of the Government by visiting and evaluating them on the spot. The Chief Minister did not agree with my suggestion and said, 'Don't rock the boat.' On a complaint about corruption prevalent in the Directorate of Information, I instituted an Enquiry Committee to look into it. While the Committee was conducting the enquiry, I was summoned by the Chief Minister who wanted to know why the enquiry was conducted when there was no direction from the Government. I replied that even if there was no direction from the Government, being the Head of the Department, I had every right to conduct an enquiry into the allegation of corruption involving my Department. The Chief Minister said, 'You conduct the enquiry quickly and ensure that nobody is harassed unnecessarily.' I assured him that I would ensure justice. The enquiry was concluded and the report brought startling revelations about the corrupt practices prevalent in the Department, particularly in the Publication Wing. The publication materials were not sent to many districts but shown as dispatched by trucks. In the publication of booklets, the officials adopted a subtle strategy of publishing less number of pages than approved for. In many cases, tender procedures were not followed. The estimated loss to the exchequer was about Rs 1 crore. I recommended suspension of the officials of that Wing and suggested a vigilance enquiry. The proposal was approved.

On one occasion, the then Secretary to the Chief Minister communicated a message to me that a particular Information Officer was to be suspended immediately, as directed by the Chief Minister. I told the Secretary that it was not possible to suspend him without knowing the background and the reasons for such action. On enquiry, I came to know that the Information Officer was asked to distribute a truckload of materials of the Government at a conference organized by the political party. Being a civil servant, he refused to distribute the materials at the political gathering. Since there was no written communication from the Chief Minister's office to suspend him and since no reason whatsoever was given, I did not take any action. On another occasion on a complaint from his party men, the Chief Minister summoned me to his residence at night and verbally directed me to give a contract to a particular person. I replied that since he was not L-1, it was not possible to give the contract. If it would be given, there would be audit objection and criticism. Good sense prevailed upon the Chief Minister and he did not insist.

One day, the Information Secretary who was also the Secretary to the Chief Minister directed me on telephone to send Rs 15000 from the Entertainment Fund of Journalists. Complying with the verbal direction, I passed the sanctioned order with a specific proviso that the fund could be utilized for the purpose for which it was sanctioned and the necessary bills and vouchers may be sent to the Directorate for approval. After receiving the sanction order, my Secretary was very annoyed and expressed his displeasure to me on telephone. He declined to take the sanction order. I failed to understand as to what was the intention of the Secretary in asking for funds initially and then declining it. It seems, the Secretary was not very happy with me and wanted to clip my wings. One day, suddenly I received an order from the Secretary taking away all my powers of Special Secretary. After receiving the order, I was angry as well as disappointed. I wrote a protest letter to the Chief Secretary giving details of the works and initiative taken by me. Since I was appointed as Special Secretary, Information by the Appointment Department and not by the Secretary, Information, I raised a legal question as to how Secretary, Information could nullify the gazette notification of the Government by his executive order. I also intimated the Chief Secretary about the scam in the Directorate of Information and wrote to him that instead of getting a pat for the good work, I was getting a kick on my back. The Chief Secretary called me to his chamber where I briefed him thoroughly about the happenings in the Department. The next day, I was surprised to find an order restoring all powers to me.

After a month or so of this episode, I received an order transferring me as Special Secretary, Home. Immediately I handed over my charge. When the Press came to know about it, they stormed into the chamber of Chief Minister and wanted to know the reasons for my transfer even before the completion of one year. The Chief Minister was baffled at the response of the press and ordered the Secretary to cancel the transfer. The Secretary called me and asked me not to hand over the charge. But by that time I had already handed over the charge. There was a stalemate and the Chief Secretary again called me and persuaded me to join back in the Information Department in order to save an embarrassing situation for the Chief Minister. After the transfer was cancelled, in compliance with the Chief Secretary's direction, I was back in the Information Department. I worked for a month or so and thereafter again was transferred as Special Secretary, Rural Development.

Chapter 17

Special Secretary (Rural Development)

(June 86 – Mid October 86)

Had I not taken my mother to different holy places, I would have never excused myself. Had I been unable to fulfill her last wishes, it would have haunted me throughout my life.

The Department of Rural Development at that time dealt with important schemes like IRDP, NREP, TRYSEM, Rural Roads, minor irrigations, rural housing etc. for the development of the rural areas. Mr S.C. Tripathi, a bright and upright officer, was the Secretary of Rural Development. Under his guidance I enjoyed my brief tenure as Special Secretary, Rural Development. I took my job seriously and started holding review meetings and spot inspections. I used to dispose of the files at my level to a great extent. After some time, the Secretary in a lighter vein commented, 'Mishraji, I am left with very few files. Please send some more files to the Secretary.' I replied, 'Sir, I believe the Secretary includes Special Secretary also. As such I did not like to bother you with the heavy burden of files, so that you can concentrate on creative thinking, policy matters, monitoring and quality control. But if you like, I will send almost all the files to you.'

Due to my uprightness and tough stand, there were differences with the Chief Minister. Therefore, the Chief Secretary after consulting me recommended my name for a posting in the Government of India. He further advised me that it was an appropriate time to go on deputation to Government of India so that I could become a Joint Secretary there, after working for two or three years as Director. It would further save me from unnecessary confrontation with the political boss. I readily agreed to his suggestion and in October, 1986, my posting as Director (Youth) in Government of India was issued. Mr S.N. Acharya, the Agricultural Production Commissioner, was not willing to relieve me. I talked to the Chief Secretary who persuaded me to join this Department as it was a new one and enough opportunity would be there to contribute towards development of the new Department.

During my stay in Lucknow, my mother expressed her desire to see a few of the holy places of UP. I was determined to satisfy her wishes and took her to different holy places like Mathura, Vrindavan, Ayodhya, Allahabad, Vindhayachal, Benaras and Hardwar-Rishikesh. After visiting these places, I could see a visible happiness on her face. It was a rare opportunity that I got to look after her. It turned out to be her last wish, as she died one year after her departure from Lucknow. I was grateful for this opportunity that I got to take my mother to different holy places. I would have never excused myself had I been unable to fulfill her last wishes and that would have haunted me throughout my life.

Chapter 18

Director (Youth), Govt. of India & Director General, Nehru Yuva Kendra Sangathan

(October 1986 – May 1991)

What modern science could not give, my faith in God gave me that. Faith and nothing but faith alone can work wonders.

My tenure as Director (Youth) in the Government of India was a significant period, exposing me to the national and international arena. I had the experience of working in the Government of India which enabled me to look at the policy and the problems from the national and international perspective. It was a new Department created under the HRD during the International Year of Youth and it was my good fortune not only to develop it and formulate its plan and activities, but it enabled me to travel to different parts of the world. The day I joined the Department of Youth Affairs and Sports, I went to call on the Secretary, Mr Gopalaswamy. A hard-working officer with a no-nonsense approach, he welcomed me and said, 'Mr Mishra, your Chief Secretary Mr Kalyanakrishnan, has briefed me on everything about you. I appreciate your courage and fighting qualities and hope you will retain it till the end of your life.' From the first day, I struck a positive note with him.

Initially I stayed at UP Bhavan in New Delhi. One Sunday, when I was relaxing in the lounge of UP Bhavan, one person approached me wanting to talk to me privately. So both of us went to a corner and he said, 'Sir, forgive me.' I wondered and asked, 'I do not know what I should forgive you for.' Then he narrated that when I was in Mirzapur, I had taken strong action against his supporters and did not listen to his request. Therefore, he complained to the Chief Minister and taking the name of mother Ganga, had said that I was a drunkard and a corrupt fellow. 'After this false allegation against you, misfortune fell upon me and my family and my business activities went down considerably. My income fell and I also received a bullet injury.' He continued, 'I pondered over my misfortune and came to the conclusion that the false charge against a pious person was responsible for my misfortune.' He had come here to request me to forgive him so that he would have peace of mind. I smiled and said, 'I do not recall the incident you just narrated. Anyway, if you sincerely repent for your behaviour, I forgive you from the core of my heart.' The man thanked me profusely and left the place. I felt that good deeds never went in vain. Repentance is the best form of atonement and forget and forgive is the best policy to march forward on the path of life in a serene and harmonious way.

The Department of Youth Affairs and Sports is a small department with one Secretary, two Joint Secretaries, one for Youth Affairs and one for Sports, two Directors and a few Under Secretaries. There was a Programme Advisor and Assistant Programme Advisor for NSS. The NYKS was an autonomous organisation of the Department looking after the sector of non-student rural youth. Though a small department, it was a very important one as it covered the entire gamut of youth affairs. With its increasing youth population, India is a young nation and not an old one like USA, China or Japan. A young nation with its energetic working population has a big advantage provided that the energies and skills are properly harnessed. We cannot reap the benefits of demographic dividend unless we make the youth educated, skilled, healthy and free from the problems that hinder the free flow of their creative energy. It was a challenging and daunting task, nevertheless under the guidance of the Minister, Ms Margaret Alva, the Secretary, Mr Gopalaswamy, and Joint Secretary, Mr Manavalan, the Youth Department worked like a well-knit team. I should specially name my Under Secretary, Dr K.K. Kirti, who contributed much to the growth of youth programmes.

We used to work long hours after office in a creative and friendly atmosphere and developed many important initiatives and schemes, like the National Youth Day, the National Youth Award, participation of NSS at the Republic Day parade, formation of National Youth Councils, Youth Clubs and co-operatives, formulation of a National Youth Policy, organizing the festival of India in the USSR (youth component) and vice versa, formulation of various manuals for NYKS, establishment of youth hostels, training, briefing and de-briefing sessions for youth delegations, organizing massive national integration camps for rural youth and students, extending help to important and reputed NGOs viz. Bharat Scouts and Guides, Ramakrishna Mission and the Gandhi Gram Rural Institute, organizing adventure camps for youth and preparation of anthology of youth songs etc.

The country is witnessing a historic demographic shift and India's ability to find its rightful place in the comity of nations depends upon how well we can harness the latent power of our young people. India lies on the cusp of a demographic transition, similar to the one that fuelled the spectacular rise of the East Asian Tigers in the second half of the 20th century. However, to tap this dividend, it is essential that the economy has the ability to support the increase in the labour force and the youth have the appropriate education, skills, health awareness and other enablers to productively contribute to the economy.

After the transfer of my Secretary, Mr Gopalaswamy as Secretary (Co-ordination, Cabinet Secretariat), we had the experience of working under another Secretary who, though scholastic, had an entirely different style of working resulting in frustration and stifling of initiative. He was very particular about language, comma and full stop etc. of the draft rather than the contents. One day, he called me and said, 'Mr Mishra, what sort of a draft have you put up? There are so many mistakes.' Politely I mentioned, 'Sir, I was educated through my mother tongue (Oriya) but by the grace of God I scored 80% in the English essay and even when I was a student, I was selected for IAS.' The Secretary did not make any comment.

Militancy in Punjab was at its height and the Youth Department was entrusted with programmes for encouraging youth to participate in different activities so that they would not be lured into militancy. Every fortnight, a report was to be sent to the PMO as well as to the Punjab Governor. A fortnightly draft was prepared for the Governor. From the Secretary's desk, the draft came out with many scratches in red ink. As per the corrected draft of the Secretary, a fair draft was prepared and it was signed by the Secretary and sent. A similar draft was also put up for the PMO. When the draft for the PMO went to the Secretary's office, it came back with corrections and with a remark, 'A very cursory attempt has been made to prepare the draft. Put up the corrected draft.' The Joint Secretary Mr Manavalan, was upset and called me and showed me the observation. I told him, in a lighter vein, 'Sir, you call for my explanation on this and I will give a befitting reply. The Secretary has corrected his fair draft.' The Joint Secretary had a hearty laugh and the matter ended there.

The Secretary used to take a vicarious pleasure in harassing his subordinates and keeping them under tension. Once he was enquiring into the misuse of Government vehicles by officers and summoned me, 'How do you come to office?' I said, 'On foot.'' At which he asked again, 'What?' I said, 'Every day I walk the distance from my residence to Shastri Bhavan and back home.' He did not expect such a reply and said, 'You can go now.'

The Draft National Youth Policy in English was ready for consideration but the Hindi version had not come from the Hindi Cell. As a result the matter was held up. The Secretary called me and asked me to expedite the work. After much cajoling and threats, the Hindi draft was getting ready when the Secretary, getting impatient, again summoned me and asked, 'Mr Mishra, when will the Hindi draft be ready'? I said, 'Sir, in all probability, the work will be done today.' He was skeptical, 'I am sure your Hindi Cell will not be able to complete it for another week,' he said. When I insisted it would be completed that night itself, he directed me to give him the Draft along with its Hindi version, the moment it was completed. My officers and staff worked round the clock and the work was completed by 2.00 am. I went to the Secretary's residence at dead of night and pressed the bell. He opened the door and exclaimed, 'At such an odd hour!' I said, 'Sir, the work has been completed just now and complying with your instruction, I am handing over this document.' He accepted the document and gave me a dirty look.

The Department of Youth had many good schemes one of which was the training of youth for self-employment. They used to finance educational institutions, youth clubs and voluntary organizations to conduct such programmes. Once a group of students from Allahabad University, accompanied by their Professor, G.K. Rai, came and requested for financial help to conduct a seminar and an exhibition at their university. The Project was sanctioned but after a few months, they again approached me for help for another seminar. I refused and advised them to submit a project on 'Training for Self-employment.' They did not know how to formulate a project. So my Under-Secretary, Dr K.K. Kriti, and I helped them to prepare a project. We went to Allahabad, had a detailed discussion with the students, representatives of banks, the Horticulture Department and of the District Administration. After two days of deliberations a project was prepared and a grant of Rs 2 lakh sanctioned for a small processing unit. We advised the professor and students who were carefully chosen to run the project, not to invest unnecessarily on overheads and things like air-conditioners. It was better to make a modest start, from a small room and using a bicycle and a scooter to ensure the supply of processed products like tomato sauce, amla candy, mango pickle, juices and fruit chocolate at the door steps of house-holders at a reduced rate. The name of the society was Purba. It was heartening to know that a project which started with a modest Rs 2 lakh has within a few years attained a turn-over of Rs 2 crore. It bagged the National Productivity Award and Commonwealth Youth Enterprise Award.

My posting at the Centre provided me enough opportunities to tour different parts of the world. These visits gave me good exposure to the understanding of youth problems in an international perspective. The Festival of India in USSR was unique in the sense that hundreds of Indian youth went to different parts of that country and interacted with their youth for about two weeks. We took this event seriously and prepared our youth thoroughly for the visit. Both students and non-student youth, covering a wide spectrum like culture, arts, meditation, classical dance, folk-dance, song, yoga and scholars were selected. All these delegates were called to Delhi for a month's training in different aspects of our country and the Soviet Union. Leading personalities, intellectuals and administrators were invited to interact with them to help them prepare for their trip. I also led a 100-strong youth delegation to the Soviet Union in 1987. We were warmly received, lodged in a hotel and taken to different parts like Moscow, Leningrad, Stalingrad, Siberia, Estonia and Latvia. We travelled by a train specifically designed and equipped with provisions for movie, dining, dancing, exhibition, cultural activities and discussions. I had heard about the 'White Nights'. During this tour I experienced this unique phenomenon i.e. the night was like day. On one occasion our delegation had to perform at the Gorky Park. After the show, I requested my interpreter to show me the way to the public convenience. He escorted me and when I returned asked, 'Mr Mishra, how do you find it?' The urinals were stinking, but I did not want to offend the host and so said lightly, 'It is as good or as bad as in our country.' He had a hearty laugh.

The next delegation to the Soviet Union was led by Dr K.K. Kriti, Under Secretary of the Department. The day before their return journey to Delhi, I got a frantic call from Dr Kriti that Balmer Lawrie & Co. Ltd had failed to ensure their reservation on Aeroflot and as result most delegates would be stranded at Moscow Airport and the visa would also expire within a few days. It was a serious matter and I did not like to burden the Secretary with it. I talked to the Commercial Manager of Air India and met the Secretary (Civil Aviation). The Secretary, in turn discussed the matter with Air India, and gave necessary directions to help the stranded delegates. On his direction, we met the Commercial Manager of Air India who with his untiring efforts succeeded in accommodating the delegates in three flights. My Secretary complimented me, 'Mishra, well done, it is like a good officer taking the initiative and sorting out the problem instead of passing it on to the higher level.'

My trip to Japan was equally memorable. I not only saw the awe inspiring development of Japan but also had a glimpse of their national character. The delegates from different countries were taken from the airport to the hotel by a bus. Since it was a bit warm, I had removed my coat which contained my passport, visa and currencies and put it on the dash board of the bus. When the bus reached the hotel, I got down and after completing the formalities at the Reception, was escorted to my room. Since there was a function in the hotel immediately, I searched for my coat and discovered, to my horror, that I had left it in the bus. I was without my passport, without visa and without foreign currency. I was nervous and took up the matter with the Japanese representative who assured me that within half an hour it would be traced. I was still apprehensive but in less than 20 minutes, the bus was located and my coat retrieved with all its belongings intact. Such a thing is unthinkable in our country. I was impressed by the national character of the Japanese. A nation cannot become great by its economic prosperity alone. It is great because it has a strong national character that is evident in its citizens.

As DG of Nehru Yuva Kendra (NYK) Sangathan, I received an order from the Secretary's office one day that the PMO wanted transfer of some Regional Coordinators from 'x' to 'y' place. This file was marked 'urgent, rush and immediate'. Overawed by the markings, my Director (Admn.) immediately put up the transfer proposal but by then the general election was announced and the poll code of conduct had come into operation. So, I did not take any action and when my Director requested me to do the needful I noted in the file, 'The election has been announced and the code of conduct is in force. It will be considered only after a new Government is installed.' The Secretary was annoyed and warned that I would be responsible for the consequences. I did not budge and nothing happened.

I was empanelled as Joint Secretary and there was a post vacant at that level in my own Department. Since the Secretary was not happy with me, he never recommended my name for the posting or its equivalent in the Department. Friends who were junior in the seniority list were accommodated in their respective Ministries. I was not disappointed but hurt a little. Often, I wondered how long he would prevent me from becoming Joint Secretary. My Minister moved out and the new Minister one day asked me, 'Mishraji, are you empanelled as a JS or not'? I replied, 'Yes Sir, I am empanelled.' Then he asked, 'Why are you not being posted in our Department, when an equivalent post is lying vacant?' When I mentioned that the Secretary had not yet recommended my name, he immediately took up the matter with DoPT and PMO and within two weeks, ensured my posting as DG, NYK Sangathan. This incident made me realize that a vindictive bureaucrat is more dangerous than a politician.

I also attended many youth-related conferences organized by the Commonwealth of Nations. They must have observed my performance at such meetings as they requested the Department of Youth of the Government of India to spare my services to carry out a study on youth of South-East Asian nations. The Secretary sat over the matter for some time. The JS called me and said, 'Mishra, you please meet the Secretary in this respect.' I replied, 'Sir, if the Secretary does not want to send me, it is his business. There is no point meeting him on this issue.' And I did not get the assignment.

During this period, certain things happened in my life which made me become more spiritual. We lost two newborn babies just a few minutes of their birth. Both of us consulted specialists and underwent medical examination and found there was absolutely no incompatibility. My two daughters were born in the normal way and there was no reason why the two miscarriages happened. Since it was a traumatic experience, we decided not to have a third child. But when I came to Delhi to take up my job as Director (Youth), a few months later my wife mentioned that she was in the family way. Both of us discussed the matter and decided to go on a pilgrimage. I applied for a month's leave and mentioned the reason to my JS. He laughed and said, 'Mishra, what medical science could not do, you think your holy trip will be able to do.' We went to the Sufi Saint Sheikh Salim Chisti's Mazar at Fatehpur Sikri. Peerzada Ayazuddin Chisti, alias Rais Miyan, the descendant of Salim Chisti, was a good friend of my father-in-law and he was a nice person and was widely respected and a well-wisher of our family. He was kind enough to usher us to the spot where Emperor Akbar had prayed for a son. With red roses and green chadar, we prayed for the well being of the child. Fom there we went to many holy places like Mathura, Vrindavan, Dwarka, Somnath, Nageswarnath Jyotrilinga and Bhalka Tirth. This journey terminated at Ajmer Sharif. We travelled by train and bus and my wife bore the journey well. It was a unique experience. God certainly had heard our sincere prayers and a son was born through a caesarean operation on Eid Day. First we went along with the baby to Salim Chisti's Mazar at Fatehpur Sikri to offer our prayer and untie the knot we had tied at the Mazar. From there we went to Dwarka for the 'mundan' (tonsure) ceremony of Sushant. What modern science could not provide, faith has bestowed upon us. Can I term it as a mere co-incidence or a miracle? Our sincere prayer had been answered and I took it that way. This experience of mine had further strengthened my conviction about the presence of a superior force who cares for its creation. Faith, faith and nothing but faith can work wonders in this world.

Chapter 19

.... ✂

Commissioner, Sales-Tax, UP

(June 1991 – June 1994)

I had the greatest satisfaction of withstanding the
pressure of my seniors and succeeded in preventing illegal
and unethical decisions.

I was back in Lucknow in June, 1991 and was posted as
Commissioner (Sales Tax), UP. It was an important assignment
as this Department alone was responsible for contributing 60% of
the total revenue of the State. It was a highly technical and sensitive
post and did not have a good reputation among the public. After
interacting with my officers and the feedback I received from the
public as well as from the media, I was determined to bring out
certain reforms. I hit upon the concept of Quality Circle to crystallize
the recommendations for reform. I picked up good and bright officers
irrespective of seniority and had many brain-storming sessions with
them about the reforms. After three months of rigorous discussions,
we formulated the proposals. After the State Vidhan Sabha Elections
in 1993, the new Chief Minister asked for certain proposals and I
handed over the voluminous document we had prepared. Seeing the
documents he said, in a lighter vein, 'Mishraji, who has the time to
go through all these pages?' I replied, 'Sir, the whole document can
be reduced to a few sentences if there is a political will to implement
it. The tax-payers will be given full freedom of self-assessment and

only 15% of self-assessment will be taken up on a random basis for detailed scrutiny. If it is found that the self-assessee has indulged in any evasion of taxes, then he will be sentenced to seven years' rigorous imprisonment.' He replied, with a smile, 'It will rock the boat.' So I had no other alternative but to present to the new Government the reform proposals. A lot of reforms did take place, like rationalization of various rates and reducing them to a few rate-bands, reduction in the number of forms, increase in the self-assessment limit to a much higher turn-over, initiative for introduction of VAT, computerization and monitoring, cadre management to strengthen the Department, removal of stagnation and large-scale promotions and formulation of a new transfer policy. I had the distinction of serving as the last Commissioner of Sales Tax of the state and its first Commissioner of Trade Tax.

I observed that the officers circled round MLAs, MPS and Ministers to get the desired transfer and posting. It was not only irritating but not good for the administration in the long run. I changed the transfer policy by giving each officer the opportunity to indicate three preferences with regard to places and posting. As far as possible, I tried to accommodate them. If there were more candidates for a particular post and a place, we resorted to a marking system by evaluating their last five years performance as recorded in their Confidential Reports. The best officer used to get posted in that place. Thus, we could defend the decisions of transfer and posting of a particular officer. By this process, I was able to accommodate more than 80% of the officers in their preferred places, thus reducing their grievances of high-handedness, nepotism and favouritism in transfer. Still many officers were approaching the Ministers and the Peoples' representatives for a particular post in a particular place. When I got these recommendations from the Ministers and the MLAs, I immediately issued notices to these officers under conduct rules questioning why disciplinary action should not be taken against them for exerting unethical and outside pressure. There was a hue and cry in the Department and the Finance Minister called me to his office.

He politely told me, 'Mishraji, it seems the peoples' representatives have no importance in the management of the Department.' I showed the Minister the relevant provisions of the Conduct Rules prohibiting such pressure and said, 'Sir, these rules are framed by the Peoples' Representatives and it is my duty to implement and enforce these rules. If the rules are changed giving powers of transfer and posting to the Peoples' representatives, I will act accordingly. Moreover, Sir, you occupy a very high position and all of you are concerned with policy formulation.' The Minister just smiled and said, 'Genuine recommendations may kindly be looked into.'

Since, we are functioning in a democratic set-up, recommendations and pressures are bound to come from public representatives. Every recommendation must not be taken as interference in the administration. It must be weighed properly after considering its pros and cons as per rules and keeping public interest in mind. I always followed this principle. Once I was delivering a lecture at the Sales Tax Training Institute in Gomti Nagar to the officers of the Department. Exactly at that time an urgent call came from the Chief Minister's residence to meet him immediately. When I met him he said, 'Mishraji, your Department is harassing this industrialist (pointing to a person standing nearby) for no rhyme or reason. Please look into it.' The Chief Minister directed us to go to a particular room. The industrialist narrated his side of the story. After listening to him, I realized that the raid was conducted on his firm under my instruction. It was a case of illegal transport of cement and falsification of accounts of sale, thus evading taxes. The Dy. Commissioner was enquiring into the whole episode. I could immediately sense that it was going to be a tough problem to be sorted out. I took copious notes in my diary about the grievances of the concerned firm. After one hour, I left the room and met the Chief Minister. The industrialist concerned told the Chief Minister that the Commissioner listened to his grievances very patiently. The Chief Minister directed me to ensure that the person was not harassed. After coming back to my office, I immediately talked to the Dy. Commissioner who was investigating the matter. I directed him to finish the enquiry within a few days. If the firm was prima facie guilty of tax evasion, then he should collect as much evidence as possible to make a strong case. Otherwise, he would be in trouble as the Chief Minister was himself interested in the case. A few days later, at about 11.00 pm, I received a call from the Chief Minister. He was in an agitated mood and told me that the Dy. Commissioner (Assessment) had already imposed a fine of few crores of rupees on the firm. I told the Chief Minister, 'Sir, if the Dy. Commissioner has given a wrong verdict, definitely he will be suspended. I will immediately call for a copy of the judgement, get it vetted by Secretary (Law) and then will take appropriate action.' The Chief Minister replied, 'What will the Law Secretary do? Whatever is to be done is to be done by you and not by the Law Secretary.' I replied, 'Sir, send that industrialist to me, I will talk to him.' The Chief Minister agreed and the next day, the representative came and met me in my office. I told him frankly, 'Gentleman, why are you wasting the precious time of the Chief Minister on such a matter. He has many more important things to do. You know, when a judgement is given, it cannot be changed except through filing an appeal in the appropriate court. Neither the Chief Minister nor I can change this. I will advise you to file the appeal immediately in the Appellate Court.' I added, 'I have no interest whatsoever in this chair and I will just kick it whenever I receive a transfer order. You do whatever you like. Don't waste the precious time of mine and the Chief Minister.' The person left and thereafter I was never bothered.

The Sales Tax Department being a revenue earning Department is very sensitive and proper revenue intelligence is essential to have a positive impact. I always remained alert and sensitive to public complaints, information and feedback I received from various quarters. Once, I was travelling to Mussoorie to attend a seminar on taxation. I had boarded the train and when we were approaching Dehradun, one gentleman who introduced himself as DGM of a reputed computer company of Noida, asked certain clarifications from me with regard to taxability of leasing of computer and its software. Immediately from the discussions, I had a suspicion that the company was evading sales tax on the leasing of computer software. After the seminar, I ordered a raid on this company. My suspicion was right and the company had to pay lakhs of rupees as evaded tax with penalty. It was also my experience that 90% of the complaints I received from the public with regard to tax evasion were correct. Every month, after reviewing the performance of the Department, I used to encourage my officers to present interesting cases of tax evasion and detection. I used to reward the officers who detected the best three cases of tax evasion. This strategy resulted in creating healthy competition among the officers and at the same time yielded the desired result in collection of revenue.

At times deviating from the routine strategy of conducting raids, one has to resort to novel ways. The business houses have their own informers and intelligence system to keep a watch over the policy and the movement of the officers. Many times, the raiding party has to face hostile reaction engineered by the evaders. I had been continuously receiving information about tax evasion by big businessmen of an important market. To avoid violence and to spring a surprise, I first convened a seminar in that particular district and the Divisional Commissioner was invited as Chief Guest. The seminar went on nicely till lunch time. After lunch with all the officers participating in the seminar, a surprise raid was launched in the market taking the evaders completely unaware. The raid was highly successful.

During President's Rule in UP (from December 6, 1992 to December 4, 1993), one of the relatives of the Adviser to the Governor applied for some sales tax subsidy intended to be given for the establishment of new units from a particular date. The proposal was to be considered by a Committee consisting of Director (Industry), M.D. (PICUP), representative from the Deptt. of Industry and Commissioner Sales Tax. The meeting was convened in the PICUP Building and when I reached the meeting, I was told by the Chairman of the Committee that it was a very simple case and it should be recommended. I had already examined the proposal at my Departmental level thoroughly and the proposal was not falling within the categories of giving subsidy as it was not a new unit as per the definition. When I raised the objection, the other Members of the Committee, including the Chairman, who were all senior to me, were annoyed and wanted to pressurize me to accept the proposal. I did not budge and submitted my dissenting note in writing and left the Committee room. I had the greatest satisfaction that I withstood the pressure of my seniors and succeeded in preventing an illegal and unethical decision.

The Adviser to the Governor whose relative's work was not done was not happy with me and he expressed his view before my Secretary that I was not doing well in the Department. When my Secretary, Mr Sushil Tripathy, defended me, the Adviser wanted to see the various works done and published in the newspaper. I collected all the newspaper cuttings and it ran into two huge bags. I sent these two bags regarding the activities of the Sales Tax Department to the Secretary for perusal of the Adviser to the Governor. The Secretary had a laugh and the matter ended there.

Just after the election in 1991, a new Government came to power and certain tax relief and exemptions were given in the matter of sales tax. This resulted in reducing the growth rate of collection of sales tax. In October, the then Chief Minister took a review meeting of the Sales Tax Department in which other important Ministers, Chief Secretary and the concerned Secretaries were also present. At the beginning of the meeting, the Chief Minister wanted to know the reasons for decrease in the growth rate and the names of the officers responsible for this unsatisfactory performance. He wanted me to give three names of Dy. Commissioners who should be suspended for not performing well. I explained the reason for decrease in the rate of growth of tax collection and said, 'Sir, I am the Head of the Department, I owe responsibility for the unsatisfactory performance of my Department.' The Chief Minister was upset by my reply. In the presence of all, he warned, 'Mishra, you always take responsibility on your head to protect your officers. Therefore, I have no alternative but to transfer you.' Very politely I replied, 'Sir, it is your prerogative.' The Chief Minister was put off by this reply and ended the meeting in a huff. There was pin-drop silence. I left my seat and started walking out of the Committee Room when the Secretary Mr S.A.T. Rizvi, and Secretary to the Chief Minister, Mr Yogendra Narain, came rushing and took me to the Chief Minister's room. When the Chief Minister was exiting the washroom, both Mr Narain and Mr Rizvi started to defend me and told him, 'Sir, Prashanta Mishra is an excellent officer of our cadre.' The Chief Minister said, 'Yes, I know that. He is also a very honest officer.' These words encouraged me to say, 'Sir, if you know all these things, why did you show your annoyance with me in the meeting.' He replied, 'Mishra, jis tareeke se aapne uttar diya, usse aapne Mukhya Mantri ko subke samne niruttar kar diya. Yah Mukhya Mantri ke pad aur garima ke anurup nahin hai' (The way you have replied to the Chief Minister has silenced him. This is detrimental to the dignity and position of a Chief Minister). I replied with all humility, 'Sir, it is never my intention to even hurt your feeling. The tradition of our service is that a senior must take responsibility for the failures and must give credit for success to his subordinates.' The Chief Minister laughed and assured me not to be worried. Later, he felt sorry for the incident and extended all support and blessings to cleanse and run the Department with all fairness and justice. I had the highest regard for the Chief Minister. I was also grateful to Mr Rizvi and Mr Yogendra Narain who came to my rescue. Such a situation is unthinkable in the present-day set up. There are no longer the protective hands of the seniors over the heads of junior officers who are sincere and straight-forward. I recollect a skit performed by a group of officers during the IAS Week which portrayed that with the passage of every year, the IAS Officers used to lose one vertebra per year. Thus by the time one becomes a very senior officer, he has lost most of his vertebra and becomes spineless.

Very few people appreciate the fact that but for the departmental officers' efforts to collect taxes, the entire State machinery will come to a standstill. Very often, they risk their lives while discharging their duties. One such incident happened in Gauripur Check Post of Meerut district, where the Sales Tax officer and his staff became the victim of a terrorist attack. The Sales Tax Officer In-charge of the Check Post was fired point blank and one bullet pierced below his eye and came out on the other side. Immediately I rushed to the spot by State Government helicopter. The Sales Tax officer was admitted to the Meerut Medical College and was in a very critical condition. There were two other officials who were dead and whose bodies were cremated that day. I attended the cremation and could sense the agitated mood of the employees and dissuaded them from going on strike. I assured them of the best medical help to the officer who was battling for life. The first operation was conducted in the Meerut Medical College itself. Since he was in a critical condition, we were advised to shift him to Pant Hospital in New Delhi for neurosurgery. It was a holiday. I went to the residence of the Meerut Divisional Commissioner who was a friend, and from there we talked to the PS to the Union Health Minister, who belonged to our cadre. He gave immediate direction and facilitated the admission of the officer to Pant Hospital. We were not sure about his survival. He was in a coma for many months. When I came back to Lucknow, I used to hold community prayers for his health. This continued for more than a week. Distant prayers also have an effect, even when the individual is unaware of it. God was very kind and he listened to our sincere prayers. The officer came out of his coma and survived. It was a sheer miracle. It has convinced me of the presence of a superior force who guides everybody. It has also convinced me about the effect of community prayers. The community is much larger than an individual and the sincere effort of each individual in unison with each other, has more impact than the effort of a lone individual.

The stay in Mirzapur had already laid a deep foundation for my spiritual development. I started reading books on Yoga, spiritualism and religion which greatly helped me in understanding the inner play of subtle forces. When I joined as Commissioner (Sales Tax) in 1991, I had little realization that my maximum spiritual development would occur during this period. What an irony; a Department which deals with money has provided me enough opportunities to move on the path of spiritualism.

Time had passed and my hair had started graying. I had nearly covered 50-55% of my life's journey. But what had I achieved in the spiritual field? What had I done for the society which nurtured me so carefully and affectionately? Didn't I have any responsibility to society and the nation or humanity at large? These were questions which started haunting me and I got increasingly reflective and restless. I had enjoyed enough of material and family life, with prestige, authority, recognition and prosperity. I was not satisfied with my own performance in this world. I should not blame anybody for this. We have come to this world with our samskaras and karmas and we evolve accordingly. Though success is important it is not the end all and be all of life. Birth and death are two fixed points. The game is in between. It's not always important to win every time, but more important is with what aim and attitude we participate.

My longing for spiritualism was getting intense day by day. I studied Patanjali Astang Yoga, Sri Yoga Vasistha, Kundalini Yoga, Sahaj Yoga, Hata Yoga etc. and many other books on spiritualism. Though, theoretically they may improve our knowledge, the Divine force can be felt intensely only through regular practice, discipline and direct experience. Enlightenment does not come through material prosperity or through intellectual activity. It comes through direct experience. A person may be very learned but he may not be an enlightened one. An illiterate person may be an enlightened person through direct experience of the Divine.

I started meditating from 1991 when I joined as Commissioner, Sales Tax in UP, though I had learned various asanas and pranayam through the Divine Life Society (Shivanand Ashram) at the Mussoorie Academy in 1972. As I proceeded, flashes appeared before my eyes, and stayed for a very short while. One night, I dreamt that I was wandering at a Mela and bowed before a boy holding a trishul. At that moment I asked myself, 'Oh God, please manifest yourself.' And I saw a huge brilliant shining light and I also saw a cluster of gods, including Vighnaraj, with brilliant halos around their heads.

As a child, I had read the Ramayana and the place Chitrakoot found an exotic expression in the Epic where Lord Rama, his brother Lakshman and wife Devi Sita spent some time during their vanvas (exile). I had the good fortune of visiting this holy place three or four times in 1993 and had done parikarma of the Kamathgiri. While doing parikarma, I could visualize the ordeal and difficulties faced by Lord Rama, Devi Sita and Lakshman. Along the route, one could see a lot of temples, the place of Ram-Bharat milap (union) and the hillock where Lakshman used to guard Ram and Sita at night. I also visited Gupt Godavari which emerges out of a cave. It is a marvel of nature. It was a unique experience also to go through winding streams of the cave which vanished after a km or so. I also visited the great Hanuman Dhara with the natural stream pouring on Lord Hanuman to cool his body. There were lots of temples and ashrams in and around Chitrakoot. It was a beautiful place and had a tremendous calming effect on the mind due its natural beauty and serenity. The more I visited Chitrakoot, the more I yearned to visit it again. Unfortunately, not much attention has been paid towards the development of this holy place. It deserves much more than it has received so far.

I had read, 'Chitrakoot ke ghat par, bhai Santan ke bheed, Tulsidas chandan ghise, tilak det Raghubir'. (A large number of saints have gathered on the banks of Chitrakoot. While Tulsidas is preparing the sandalwood paste, Lord Rama is applying it on the foreheads of the saints). There is a devotional song on this theme and whenever I listened to this song, tears would roll down my cheeks. I developed a keen desire to visit Ramghat and the Parna Kutir (thatched hut) of Tulsidas. In September, 1993 I visited Chitrakoot and went to Ramghat and the Kutir of Tulsidas. From there I observed an old Shiva temple on a hillock and when I enquired about it, I was told that during vanvas, Ram used to worship Shiva in this temple. This place was also in a bad shape. I expressed my desire to visit this temple. After covering two-third of the steep hill, we stopped near a tree to remove our shoes. I observed a sick person standing on the verandah of the temple. We climbed the steps of the temple and had a darshan of Lord Shiva. We came back and were putting on our shoes when I noticed the same person on the verandah again. He stepped down and came and stood beside me for some time, I gazed at him intently and a strange feeling overtook me. 'Prashanta, he is not an ordinary person; He is a great messenger of God in disguise,' an inner voice said. I immediately rushed towards him and helped him get down the steps and then bowed before him. He blessed me and vanished. I went around the ghat and after ten minutes, I tried to locate him but could not. I did not know who he was but somehow I had the feeling that he was a great soul in disguise. Even now when I recollect this incident, I experience a thrill.

I was getting more and more spiritually inclined often to be seized by vairagya, a feeling of renunciation. At such moments I felt like deserting the family. The atmosphere everywhere in this material world is so corrupt that I often felt depressed. I felt I was getting neurasthenic and often heard the chanting of Namah Shivaya at the back of my head. I was scared and consulted a psychiatrist and experts at the K.G. Medical College and even underwent a thorough check-up, including a CAT scan. But there was nothing adverse in the report and the psychiatrist advised me to take life a little less seriously. I was relieved, but on the other hand it strengthened my spiritual convictions. I started reading spiritual books and was particularly influenced by the magnificent book, by Swami Rama, *Living with Himalayan Masters*. I had the good fortune of meeting Swami Rama at his Rishikesh Ashram in March, 1994. A great scholar and spiritual master, I was thrilled to meet this towering personality.

He said, 'Prashanta, you are very dear to me' and presented me some of his spiritual books.

While in the Sales Tax Department, along with other officers, I had trekked to Neelkanth Mahadev, a distance of 10 km. We covered the distance in four hours and enjoyed the experience. While enjoying the darshan of Lord Shiva, I felt a tremendous vibration. It was an ancient temple under an old tree (Panchtarni) and was supposed to have been discovered, or founded, by Adi Shankara. I was so impressed by the natural beauty and vibration of the place that I visited it three times. Likewise, whenever I went to Hardwar, I used to visit Chandi Devi and Mansadevi which are great Shaktipeeths. One gets a magnificent view of Hardwar and the seven streams of the Ganga from this height. I visited Mukteswar where I met a Mauni Swamiji who had a Doctorate in Physics, the Hanuman Mandir set up by Neem Karoli Baba in Nainital, the Herakhan Shiva temple, Kainchi Ashram, Ghodakhal Gola temple, Chitai temple, the Baijnath temple with a beautiful image of Parvati, and Jageshwar with its complex of 124 temples. Visits to all these places had an abiding impact on me and they further increased my longing for more spiritual experience.

When I assumed the charge of Commissioner, Sales Tax, one Deputy Commissioner, Mr V.K. Chandola, presented me Paramahamsa Yogananda's *Autobiography of a Yogi* a gripping spiritual text which had vivid descriptions of Herakhan Baba and his Tapasthali. It is believed Herakhan Baba was a reincarnation of Maha Avatar Baba. The book was so exciting that I expressed my desire to visit Herakhan, at a distance of 39 km from Kathgodam. When I talked to my Deputy Commissioner, Nainital Mr Jangpani, he dissuaded me as there was a possibility of terrorist presence in this jungle area. A year later, when I again expressed my desire to visit the place he told me, 'Sir, the situation has eased a bit, you can visit the temple but I will advise you to avoid a night halt in that area.' Accordingly, I chalked out a plan to visit Herakhan with my wife and children. From Kathgodam we went by jeep because of the hilly terrain. In fact, we covered quite a distance on the river bed road and walked the last few kms to reach the place. It was evening. We worshipped the Shiv Linga of Herakhan Temple and when I came back after worship, I found an old man standing in the premises of the temple. I touched his feet. He enquired whether I had come here as a tourist. I said that I had read about this holy place and had come here for spiritual purposes. This man, called Fakiranandji, blessed me and handed over some literature to me. After having Prasad, we rushed back to Kathgodam.

Herakhan is a beautiful place situated on the bank of the river Gola which is considered to be the Godavari of Kumaon hills. There are hardly a few huts here and the hill region is dotted with beautiful Himalayan forests, their panoramic beauty and the murmuring sound of the Gola river further enhance the beauty of the place. It was April, 1994. The terrorist menace in this area had ebbed to a great extent. I talked to the Deputy Commissioner, Nainital and expressed my desire to stay in Herakhan Inspection Bungalow for a night. He readily agreed as the situation had improved vastly. On April 3, 1994, I along with my wife left Lucknow for Herakhan via Bareilly and Kathgodam. It was a tiring journey and we reached Herakhan Inspection Bungalow about 7.30 pm after covering a downhill journey of 2 km on foot. It was a beautiful Inspection Bungalow situated amidst the Himalayan forest by the side of the Gola. The evening was pleasant and soon the night was casting its shadow. In the room, there was a photograph of 'Baba Herakhan'. I bowed before it and prayed for his blessings. We rested for the night and the next morning, I strolled along the winding path of the river, enjoying its musical sound. I sat on a rock, meditated for a while and came back to the Inspection Bungalow. Then I, my Dy. Commissioner (Executive) Mr Jangapani, and STO Mr Phartiyal, went to have a bath in the cold refreshing water of the Himalayan river. We enjoyed the bath very much. I came back to the Inspection Bungalow and got ready for darshan of Herakhan 'Shiv Linga'. It was a beautiful Ashram which generally had foreigners who came there for solace and peace. In fact, it was a unique experience to see European women in saris chanting Lord Shiva's mantra, slokas and songs in Hindi.

My wife and I worshipped the Shivalinga with full devotion. When I came out of the temple, the same old man, Fakiranandji, was standing in the premises. When I met him for the second time, he told me, 'I was waiting for you for the last one year.' I replied, 'Fakiranandji, I am a family person, so I cannot come here again and again. The moment I got an opportunity, I came here.' Then he asked, 'Can you stay here for seven days?' I replied, 'No.' Can you stay here for three days?' I replied, 'No'. Then again he said, 'My son, please stay here for at least one day.' I replied in the affirmative as it was possible on my part to accommodate this within my tour schedule. He led me and my wife to his Kutir nearby. He enquired, 'What sort of puja and chanting of mantra do you do in the morning?' I replied, 'Basically I am a devotee of Lord Shiva but I chant many mantras of different gods.' Then in a humourous way, Fakiranandji said, 'I hope you have studied pressure in science. The more the area, the less will be the pressure. Since you are chanting so many mantras and worshipping so many gods, your spiritual energy is frittered away on a wide canvas over a large area. As a result you are not having that penetrating effect in your efforts.' He advised me to concentrate on one God and chant only one mantra of that deity so that it would have penetrating effect. He further enquired whether I was fasting or not. When I replied in the affirmative, he directed me to lie down in 'Savasana' and to concentrate on the presiding deity on the third eye i.e. Lord Shiva with mental recitation of the mantras. He directed my wife to be seated near my right foot. Then he brought a peacock broom and while murmuring of mantras, he started brushing it over different parts of my body for nearly half an hour. Suddenly I felt a quiver at the end of the spine. My body muscles stiffened like a log of wood and I could feel tremendous pain which I had never experienced in my life. Soon, I realized that something warm was moving upwards. After a few minutes, my entire body started trembling and I could feel the passage of a strong current up in my body. It came upto my Ajna Chakra and thereafter I witnessed a vast expanse of light in the sky. After an hour, I woke up from deep slumber and I was feeling a bit exhausted. Fakiranandji gave me a hot glass of milk. When I looked at my wife, uncontrollable tears came down my cheeks. Fakiranandji intervened and said, 'My dear son, you have tremendous spiritual energy but the passage was blocked. I have removed the blockage. Now it is your responsibility to take it further by doing meditation every day.'

It was a unique experience. I was thrown out of gear and was totally dazed. My mind was totally vacant. I was apprehensive about my mental state. Probably my body was not pure enough to withstand the onslaught of the tremendous psychic energy. I thanked Fakiranandji profusely and touched his feet. Much against my wish, I left Herakhan as I had some other engagement in Almora and Berinag. On our way to Almohra, I visited Kainchee temple, established by Neem Karoli Baba. It was a beautiful ashram situated about 20 km from Nainital near a stream. This temple housed a large number of deities. While concentrating before the idol of Baba Neem Karoli, I had a strange experience. I could feel that I was receiving an array of rays from the sky which were being projected into my head. I was thrilled.

We left for Almora and reached by 2.30 pm. After lunch and rest we left for Berinag. On the way, we visited the famous Chitai Temple of Gola Dev. In this temple, the letters of many devotees were hung on the wall for the fulfilment of their wishes. One could see a never-ending stream of ghantis (bells) around the temple. We reached Berinag at about 8 pm. It was a tiring journey.

It was a beautiful morning in Berinag. The cold breeze of the Himalayas, the long range of snow-clad peaks glowing in the reflection of the sun's rays and the occasional sweet notes of birds, made the surrounding much more serene and intoxicating. The morning drive from Berinag to Chakorighat was quite refreshing. From Chakorighat, one can view the whole range of Himalayan peaks. We visited Beri Tea Garden, established by the British in early 19th century. During the British Raj, Berinag Tea was exported to England. It had a typical sweet smell. After spending an hour, we came back to Berinag. We had our Kumaoni-style breakfast which was delicious. I cannot forget the love, affection and care with which Mr Verma, a local resident, treated us to this lavish breakfast.

We left for Patal Bhubaneswar on April 6 at 10.30 am. It was hardly at a distance of 25 km from Berinag. The car went upto the nearest village. One had to walk hardly the last km or so. I was quite excited to see this cave. In 1993, I had read an article about Patal Bhubaneswar. From that day onwards, I had dreamt of visiting it. Now the dream had come true. On the mouth of the cave, was inscribed a sloka from the Skanda Purana. It said that Patal Bhubaneswar was prohibited to human beings till such time that a sage from the South would come and install a Shiv Linga. In fact it was widely believed that Adi Sankara visited this cave and installed the Shiva Linga.

It was a unique experience to visit such a wonderful cave. The entrance is very small and one person at a time can get in by crawling. After crawling for more than 100 feet, one reaches an undulated huge spacious area which can accommodate hundreds of people. One can see a beautiful impression of a huge snake-like image, naturally carved. The local people call it 'Shesh Nag'. One can also see white coloured water dropping exactly on the Shiva Linga from the impression of an udder of a cow. Water also drops from the roof of the cave on Brahma, Vishnu and Mahesh in rotation. One can find the image of a 1000-feet white elephant called 'Airavat'. There is also a long tongue of 'Bhairav' in the shape of a dog. Like this, there are many other things associated with mythology, culture and religion.

It was an unforgetful experience. One may dispute the religious aspect of the depictions in the cave. But nonetheless, it is a wonderful architecture of nature. One cannot but marvel at the slow, steady and silent operation of nature in bringing out such a beautiful cave. The whole place was vibrating with spiritual waves, which I could feel in an intensified manner. I stood speechless in awe and reverence before the Almighty Natural Force. This cave is much more beautiful than Gupt Godavari of Chitrakoot.

After visiting the cave, we went to Mahakali Mandir of 'Gangolihat'. It is said to be the presiding deity of the Kumaon Regiment. After having lunch there, we drove to Pithoragarh for the night. Pithoragarh is a small, beautiful hill station. It is much more beautiful than many other hill stations like Nainital, Dehradun and Mussoorie. We left Pithoragarh on April 7, at 3.30 pm and reached Lohaghat by 6 pm. We stayed at the Inspection Bungalow situated in the thick devdar forests. The next morning I got up early feeling fresh. I went near the stream flowing by the side of the Inspection Bungalow and sat on a cemented bench. The morning air was so enchanting that my eyes automatically closed and I immediately went into deep meditation. After a few minutes, I could feel the tremendous vibration in my body and the rushing up of psychic energy. I was thrilled and immediately rushed to my wife and told her that I could awaken the Energy to some extent myself. I was extremely grateful to Fakiranandji with whose blessing I was able to achieve it.

We left for Mayavati Ashram, at a distance of 15 km from Lohaghat. The ashram was founded by Swami Vivekananda in 1899 and he stayed here for a fortnight in January, 1901. I visited the place where Swamiji used to sit for meditation. The experience brought tears to my eyes. It was a beautiful Ashram from where one could see the snow peaks of the Himalayas. I bought a few books on Swamiji and Ramakrishna Paramahamsa. After spending some time there we came back to the Inspection Bungalow at Lohaghat. After breakfast we started for Banbasa via Champabat and reached there by 1.30 pm. The Inspection Bungalow here was beautiful with a lot of flower plants and trees. The next morning, April 9, 1994, I sat for meditation under a tree and after 20 minutes or so, my body started trembling. I came back satisfied, walked a few rounds, had breakfast and left for Bareilly and reached there by 12.30 pm. Finally we left for Lucknow in the afternoon.

After returning to Lucknow, I remained dormant for a few days. I was apprehensive about my capacity to cope with this psychic energy. Whenever I experienced this awakening, I felt dazed and it took me quite some time to become normal. I was so intoxicated with the unique experience of awakening the Energy that I used to forget my existence. I had complete trust in God that He would protect me from any crisis. Initially I was taking 30 minutes to awaken it, but later it was done effortlessly. Once, in the dead of night I started my meditation. I experienced flashes of lightening and images of gods. This state continued for about four days. I felt that I could bring the Energy upto my Visudha Chakra (throat), but not beyond. But still, I felt apprehensive about the damage it would do, if not done properly. My experience was that when the Energy rose from its deep slumber in the Mooladhara Chakra, the body, particularly waist downwards, trembled vigorously. Thereafter it moved upwards slowly and gradually. One could feel a crawling sensation inside. For me, the most comfortable position was that of 'Savasana'. I felt blissful and could feel the tingling sensation along my spine.

I was so intoxicated with my practice that at 11 pm, it automatically would rise and disturb me. Apart from the usual dancing of Ida and Pingula, criss-crossing each other, I could feel the warm energy flowing through my entire body. On two different occasions at night, I could even smell the fragrance of ittar (perfume) and sandalwood. Light would enter my head from the left side. I would see visions of gods and goddesses. Occasionally even during day time, I could feel the pricking sensation and warmth in different parts of my body. My eyeballs started rolling upwards. On August 14, 1994 night, I could feel that the energy rushing to my brain. I also had the peculiar experience of my mouth widening and my tongue protruding, accompanied with a roaring sound. I was experiencing different moods, shifting from gloom, to bliss and emotion etc. The yogic kriyas continued for a few hours. At the end of the kriyas, I could see a small bluish dot at a close distance. The bluish dot appeared, disappeared and reappeared. I did not know what was happening to me.

I was passing through a phase of metamorphosis, temporary elation and at times depression, anger and frustration. As days passed, I felt the presence of Energy in my body, the feeling of warmth in different parts of the body at different times and this warmth was gradually increasing. Initially there was trembling of the back, waist, hands etc. Now I could feel the shivering in my chest, throat and head. I was getting restless every day. Whether I wanted it or not, the Energy played with me automatically at bedtime and early in the morning. Because of my meditation for long hours, I started getting disinterested in my family, and in the official work. It was becoming unbearable. Such a state of affairs could have landed me in trouble but for the timely appearance of a saintly person at my house on a Sunday morning. He enquired about my health and I told him that I was passing through a bad phase because of my meditation. He laughed and asked, 'How many hours are you devoting to meditation?' I replied, 'Swamiji, every day I practice for about four hours.' He said, 'You are in a Grihastha ashram and not a sanyasi. It is not desirable for a family person to meditate for more than half an hour at a time. If you stick to half-an-hour meditation in the morning and evening, I am sure there will be stability in your mind.' He handed me a book *Chitshakti Vilas* and advised me to go through it.

I enjoyed reading books like *Autobiography of a Yogi, Living with Himalayan Masters, The Inner Government of the World, Light and Fire, Reality at the Dawn, Kundalini Yoga, Hath Yoga, Celestine Prophecy*, books on Swami Vivekananda, Ramakrishna Paramahamsa, Sri Aurobindo and a host of others. During my career, I tried my best to build a library of my own consisting of such rare books. It is a pleasure just to have a mere glance at these books. On May 2, 1994, I visited Lodheshwar Mahadev temple of Mahadeva. It was said that Maharaja Yudhishthira worshipped the Shivling during Agyatvas (living incognito). We also visited Kurukshetra Ashram where the Pandavas performed a yajna after the war. From there we went to see the Parijat tree at Barabanki. I had read about this tree and according to legend, the tree emerged from the churning of the ocean and during Dwapar Yuga, Sri Krishna brought it here from Nandan Kanan. I was surprised to see such a sprawling tree with a 50-feet diameter. It flowers during August-September and each flower weighs about 250 grams. When it flowers, it is white but turns golden when it dries up. According to the legend, Maa Kunti used to workship Kunteswar Mahadev with this flower. The Gita extols it as 'among flowers I am parijata'. I worshipped the tree and felt honoured by touching the trunk of the sacred tree. It is said the tree is unique and the species could not be found in any other part of the country. As far as I remember, there is such a tree in Sultanpur which is very old. We also visited Dewa Sharif, a magnificient structure, a symbol of Muslim-Hindu integration.

My spiritual urge was increasing day by day. I was fascinated by the Himalayas. I was thoroughly enchanted by its beauties and legends. Among all the holy places Shri Kedar Khand has the privilege to be known as the Dev Bhoomi (land of the gods). This place is surrounded by the Panch Kedar, including the Badrinath Dham. The region is also known as Shiv Bhawan (the splendid palace of Lord Shiva). According to the Mahabharat, when the great war came to an end and the Pandavas received back the throne of Hastinapur, Sage Veda Vyasa advised them to go to Kedar Khand to have a holy glimpse of Lord Shiva. This was to get rid of the sins of killing their preceptors and family members and hence get salvation.

Accordingly, they all started for Kedar Khand. At Sri Kedarnath, Lord Shiva used to reside in a meditating state sitting under Mahendra Parvat near the holy Mandakini river. As the Pandavas approached he disappeared from the spot by penetrating his body underground. The limbs of the body appeared at five different places, namely Kedarnath where his buttocks and back appeared, Madmaheshwarnath where his navel appeared, Tungnath where his chest and hands appeared, Rudranath where his head appeared and at Kalpeshwarnath where his locks appeared. All these limbs appeared in the shape of the Panch Kedar Lingas and these are very holy and this region of Panch Kedar is also known as Shiva Palace (Shiva Bhawan). According to Vyas, 'One who remembers these five shrines in the morning, all his sins vanish and he gets salvation instantly.'

The entire Kedar Mandal is a heavenly mansion of Sri Shiva and it is the region of His Lordly sports. Five holy streams of the Ganga descend from the Mahendra Parvat, Umalda Sagar and Vashukital round the holy premises of Sri Kedarnath and it looks as if these merge in the locks of Lord Kedareshwar to perform His holy bath. These streams are known as Madhu Ganga, Kheer Ganga, Swargdwara, Mandakini and Kedar Ganga. Kedarnath is situated in the lap of the lofty Sahyadri Peak of the Himalayas on the banks of the Mandakini where Lord Shiva is incessantly worshipped by the sages, seers, Indra, gods, demons and yakhas.

I had a memorable trip to Kedar Nath, Badrinath and Tunga Nath from May 21 to 30, 1994. On our way to Kedarnath, we first stayed at Shivanand Ashram. After taking the blessings of Swami Premanandjii of the Divine Life Society and Swami Rama, we left for Gupt Kashi on the morning of May 23 by road. Mr N.C. Sharma and Mr C.S. Semwal were with us. These two officers have been my spiritual companions in all these journeys. On the way, we visited Vasistha Cave, Saswat Dham of Swami Adwetanandji of Lachmoli and by the evening, we reached Gupt Kashi. It was a beautiful place. The Mandakini with its crystal clear water flowed down the mountain with a musical note. We stayed at the PWD Bungalow and it was raining very heavily. Sarita fell sick and vomited many times at night and we thought that we would not be able to go to Kedarnath the next morning. We prayed and she became all right the next morning and we were able to resume our journey.

The trek to Kedarnath started from Gaurikund. It was about 15 km. Armed with spiked sticks, plastic covers, water bottles and a first aid box we started walking slowly but steadily towards our destination. It was a beautiful site with the thick forest and river. We had lunch at Rambara at 3.00 pm. We were so hungry that the food tasted like 'Amrit'. From Rambara onwards, it was a difficult climb. We were getting tired but inched forward. Evening was falling and we barely had 2 km to cover. The very sight of the temple 'Kedarnath' overwhelmed me and I sobbed for a few minutes. I told myself, 'Prashanta, you have got what you have come for.' Finally we reached Kedarnath by 8.00 pm. We were all exhausted and at night had a quick Darshan of Kedarnath. We stayed at a house close to the temple. It was very cold and we had to use three quilts. The moon was shining over the snow peaks. It was a sight to be experienced. We got up quite early and had a special Darshan and Puja on May 25. On the Linga, one could find images of Lord Ganesh and Parvati. We also went to Adi Shankara's samadhi.

I was tired and had blisters on my feet. My toe was paining like hell and my legs and thighs had become stiff. The next morning, we left for Dugalbitta and Chopta. The journey from Gupta Kashi to Ukhi Math to Dugalbitta and Chopta was highly enjoyable, as we had to pass through thick forests. Nothing can beat the heavenly beauty of the Himalayas. We reached Chopta Mandaliya Vikas Nigam Resort by 11.45 am. This was the base camp for trekking to Tunganath, which is situated at a height of 12000 ft. Tungnath is on the Gandhamardhan Parvat where thousands of aromatic plants grow and spread their fragrance that thrill the hearts of pilgrims and wipe out their fatigue. The temple of Tungnath is situated at Chandrshila peak and it is the highest shrine among the Panch Kedars. One who goes to Tungnath and Chandrshila is captivated by the enchanting beauty of nature all around. One can enjoy the beauty of the peaks of the Himalayas, Shivaling, Bandarpunch, Gangotri, Yamunotri, Mahendra, Chaukhamba, Chandra Parvat, Nanda Devi and Swetgiri. All these are clearly visible from Tungnath. A virtual paradise on earth, no shrine is so sublime and sacred in the entire world. There is a beautiful temple of Tungnath (Mrikandeshwar) in Makkoomath village where Maithani Brahmins worship Tungnath. It is also said that during Treta Yug, the mighty demon Ravan did severe penance here, sitting on Ravanshila and got realisation of Lord Shiva in the disguise of Chandramauleshwar.

Initially, I was a bit hesitant to trek to Tunganath, as I had blisters. It was a difficult and steep climb of 4 km. Ultimately, I gathered courage and started off. My family stayed back in Chopta. It was a beautiful trek through thick rhododendron forest. Generally burans that flower in most parts of Garhwal Hills are red in colour, but here in Tunganath Valley, one could see a panoramic view of flowers with different hues like red, white, pink, blue and multi-coloured. One could also have a magnificent view of the beautiful Himalayas. It took us 4 hours to reach Tunganath. Shastrijee performed an elaborate puja for us. It was an old Shiva temple and one of the sacred places of Panch Kedar. While performing puja, I started quivering and trembling. I enjoyed every bit of it and after the puja, we returned to the base camp.

On May 27 morning, we left Chopta for Badrinath and reached there by evening. We stayed at the PWD inspection bungalow. Trishul with its snow-clad peak was standing before us in all its majesty and grandeur. At about 9.30 pm, we rushed to the temple to have a darshan before it closed. Thereafter, we had a refreshing bath at the Narad Kund, the hot spring. What a marvel of nature! The hot spring and cold water of the Alaknanda side by side. A bath in the sulphur springs took away all my fatigue. It is believed Adi Sankara recovered Badri Vishal from this Narad Kund. We spent the night at Badrinath and the next morning got up quite early. The moon-lit night was beautiful. I looked at Trishul and got spiritual vibrations. My wife and I went to the temple along with others. We had a special Darshan lasting two and half hours. After breakfast, we went to Manna, the last Indian village on the Tibet border. We also went to Bhim Bridge over the Saraswati river. We came back, had lunch and left for Joshi Math and reached there by 5.00 pm. It was a beautiful small hill town. Tapovan offers a scenic view of the surrounding green mountains covered with step farmlands. Tapovan's major attraction is its hot spring. Visitors also take Tapovan as a trek route to Bhavishya Badri which is situated at 3 km from here. As legend goes, Bhavishya Badri is the place where Lord Badrinath will be worshipped in future when the mountains of Nar and Narayan will be merged together through natural forces. We went to Tapovan, at a distance of 20 km from Joshimath. We had the unique experience of witnessing the gushing of the sulphur hot spring water from a depth of 2500 feet.

May 29 was the birthday of my son Sushant and so we got ready in the morning and went to the Narasimha temple to offer puja. It was a wonderful way of celebrating his birthday. On our return journey, we also worshipped at Kamaleshwar Shiva temple, Shrinagar, Pauri Garhwal. At Munni-ki-Reti, we visited many ashramas like Swarg Ashram, Gita Bhawan and Parmarth Niketan which were situated on the other side of the Ganga in Pauri Garhwal district. It was an unforgettable journey which enriched me immensely in a spiritual sense.

My spiritual practice was proceeding along with the hectic work as Commissioner, Sales Tax. Whenever I got an opportunity to visit a holy place, I invariably made it a point to visit it after work. In June, 1994, my wife, my mother-in-law and I visited Shobhan temple, about 40 km from Kanpur. It was a huge beautiful complex with lots of trees and mango groves. Primarily it is a temple of Lord Hanuman but there are other important deities on the premises. No offering is made at this temple. One can sit quietly and meditate. I met Babaji who was standing under a peepal tree and bowed before him. He enquired about me and asked whether I worshipped 'Maheswar'. When I said, 'Yes,' he said that I had this spiritual inclination due to my previous samskaras.

The place was so magnetic that whenever I came to Kanpur, I used to visit this campus. In March, 1997 during Shivratri day I visited this place after visiting Bankhandeswar Mahadev, Sai temple, Vithur's Valmiki Ashram and Gajanan temple. In Shobhan, after waiting for about one and a half hours, we had a chance to see Baba along with a huge crowd. However, even in the crowd, he recognized and beckoned me. When I went near him, I was overwhelmed with spiritual feeling and emotion. As I approached him, he patted me with love and affection and said, 'Itna bhav kahan se paya re, mujhe bhi kuchh doh.' (Where did you get so much devotion from? Share some with me). He gave me some prasad which he was eating. After the visit, we came back to Kanpur and stayed at my in-laws house. At night I had a strange experience; I could feel the flow of a strong current of energy in my body at the dead of night. Suddenly, I felt that I had come out of my physical body and was circling my wife. I woke up with a start. I interpreted this vision that I was still attached to my wife and I had to first discharge my family obligations.

While coming back from the Shobhan temple to my in-law's house, we had a lively discussion about spiritualism. Mr Dixit, 75 years old and President's awardee teacher, was with us and he commented that we mortal beings were all under the influence of "Maya". The whole world, including family, wife and relatives, was nothing but 'Maya'. My wife got annoyed and said, 'Uncle, why do you term family and children etc. as a product of 'Maya' If, as a mother, I cannot look after the interests of my children and if, as a wife, I cannot look after the interests of my husband, then I am unfit to be called either. It is my duty first to look after my family. Thereafter, I will look after the neighbors and in the process we will expand ourselves to look after society, the nation and humanity at large.' Expansion is life and contraction death.

In the last week of June, 1994, I went to Agra for inspection. It was Monday and in the morning after taking my bath, I went to Kailash Shiva Temple along with my officers. I worshipped Lord Shiva and went to the bank of the Yamuna which was flowing near the temple. At the ghat, on the edge of the wall, I saw a charming child of three years. I got apprehensive with the thought that the child might fall. I was cursing the irresponsible behavior of the parents who had left the child alone. When I proceeded towards the child, he came slowly unruffled and sat near a Shiva Linga. I intently looked at the child and a peculiar joy overwhelmed me. I thought that Lord Shiva was giving me darshan in this guise. After some time, I went to the child, patted him affectionately and told him, 'I cannot wait more for you. It is time that I should leave.' Throughout the journey back to Agra, the face of the child appeared again and again before me.

Chapter 20

❀

Secretary, Institutional Finance

(July 1994 – April 1995)

Sacrificing for a public cause is what helped the
civilization of India to reach its zenith, emitting the light
of knowledge. But where has that spirit of sacrifice
disappeared now?

I had completed three years as Commissioner (Sales Tax) and was
getting tired. I met the Chief Secretary and requested him for a
lighter posting, like Director (Training) of ATI, at Nainital. He smiled
and said, 'Prashanta, I am not going to waste an efficient officer on
a training post. You deserve something better.' After a few months,
I was posted as Secretary (Institutional Finance) dealing with sales
tax, entertainment tax, stamp registration and banks. It was an
important job which required full attention. I never faltered in the
discharge of my duties. Though it was an exacting post, I managed
to take out some time to visit places of spiritual importance. Thus
in July, 1994, I went to Mukteswar, District Nainital to meet the
Swamiji of Mukteswar. The Swamiji encouraged me to go ahead
with my practice and in his words I had been elevated but not yet
established. He blessed me and gave me 'Abhayadan' (blessings
for protection). I came back to Lucknow. I could feel the play of
energy within me quite vigorously. Often in the dead of night, with
the surge of spiritual energy, many Kriyas automatically occurred.
Apart from raising the hand, swirling of head vigorously, I could

notice that Mulbandh, Jalandhar bandh and Uddiyanband happened automatically. The tongue would swirl within the mouth and touch the palate in the Khechari Mudra. While doing my spiritual exercise at night, I could feel a brilliant white light entering the head.

During Dussehra of 1994, I visited Naimisharanya, popularly known as Chakratirth in Sitapur. Naimisharanya is a beautiful place surcharged with spiritual vibrations. I visited Narada Nanda Ashram and paid obeisance to his Samadhi. I also worshipped Sheetala Devi and Devedeveswar Shivlinga and went to Hanumangarhi for worship of Lord Hanuman. As per popular folklore, Vyasa meditated at Naimisharanya (Vyas Gaddi) and conceived the idea of writing the epic Mahabharata. With the help of Lord Ganesha, he wrote the epic continuously without a break. There was a great banyan tree in this place under which the sage meditated. Its prop roots also look like banyan trees. After listening to the local legend, I had a great desire to meditate here at night. In dead of the night, I left the Inspection Bungalow with the driver of my car and came to this place in pindrop silence. I sat under the banyan tree and meditated for an hour and came back. I had an ecstatic feeling which cannot be described. While returning to Lucknow, I visited Misrikh, the Ashram and Samadhi of Maharishi Dadhichi where he meditated and gifted his bones to Indra to prepare vajra (thunderbolt) for the elimination of Vritrasur. My head bowed down before the sacrifice of this great Rishi. It was because of such sacrifice that ancient India reached its zenith emitting the light of knowledge in every direction. But where has that spirit of sacrifice disappeared? Now-a-days, everybody has become self-centered. No wonder society is afflicted with violence, hatred and divisive forces.

I was regular in my meditation and on December 2 morning while meditating, the picture of Maa Vaishno Devi appeared again and again before my mind's eye. Just a week before a retired STO, Mr Sharma, went to Vaishno Devi and had presented me a photograph of Devi alongwith some Prasad. I worshipped the photograph. So I thought that the appearance of Maa Vaishno Devi in my meditation was psychological, little realizing that it was a call by the Mother. The same morning, I quickly prepared myself to go to the Chief Minister's Secretariat for a Cabinet meeting. Since I was getting late, I did not take breakfast and rushed to the meeting. After the meeting, I was coming down and on the ground floor I met the Principal Secretary, Civil Aviation and Tourism, UP who was going to Jammu in the Government plane on official work. He was to also visit Vaishno Devi Shrine. So I requested him to offer prayers before Maa Vaishno Devi on my behalf. He immediately invited me to accompany him if I wanted to go. I thought it was a joke, but he was serious. I was given only one hour to report at the airport at 11.30 am. I immediately rushed back to my residence. My wife had gone to King George Medical College for a dental check up and so was unfortunate to miss this opportunity, I immediately rushed to the airport and boarded the plane. We reached Jammu at 4.00 pm and after lunch left for Katra by road. From Katra, we trekked to Vaishno Devi and reached at 11 pm and at 1.00 am had our darshan. It was a unique experience. It was a mother's call. In 1975 I had visited Vaishno Devi along with Sarita and at that time, the place was not so developed and there was only one opening to the cave. Since then, much development has taken place and the trekking path had been made broad and beautiful. Modern shopping complexes have come up all along the route and the place has changed much beyond my expectation. On January 27, 1995, I went on a tour to village Amaur, Block Bhitargaon of Kanpur Dehat district. I spent the night in the village in a badly maintained PHC and at night, I felt as if my entire body was getting stiff and I was rising slowly. I felt as if I would fly into the space. I was terrified and tightly held on to the edge of the cot with all my might. This was altogether a different kind of experience.

Time was flying and I went to my village Athmallik on February 6 to attend a family function. When I reached the village my joy knew no bounds. A sense of elation overtook me. I met my uncle, Dr I.C. Mishra, the oldest and lone surviving member of the older generation.

He was 84 then. I met my dear childhood friend Sushil Mishra who was a teacher in the village High School. The next morning, I went to the Mahanadi and childhood memories of playing in the water came rushing to my mind. Again, I ruminated over the experiences of my childhood. I was nostalgic. I listened to the music of the flow of the river water. I bathed for half an hour. The same river, the same stream, the same rock, the same jungle, the same Tutu (my nickname), I felt as if I had come back to my childhood. Tears flowed down my cheeks. I saluted the river and the mountain and bid them farewell. It took me about half an hour to reach my ancestral house. I felt a tremendous desire to do puja to our presiding deity 'Rudra Bhawani' (Shiva-Parvati). So I sat for an elaborate puja. Illi, my niece, had made all arrangements. I bathed the Deities and Saligram with milk, decorated the 'Linga' with 108 bel leaves and flowers and sat for meditation. I could feel the vibrations and my body trembled. Though I had seen the Saligram in my childhood days many times, for the first time, I noticed that the shining black Saligram had the mark of the sun with its rays. I was astounded. After a brief vacation in Athmallik, I returned to Lucknow to resume my duties.

Life continued. It was later part of February and Shivratri was approaching. I made up my mind to go to Herakhan Shiva Temple on this auspicious occasion. Initially, I intended to spend three days with Fakiranandji, who had awakened my Shakti in April, 1994. But my Deputy Commissioner (Executive), Nainital, Mr Janga Pani, informed me that Fakiranandji was visiting Delhi and would return only in April, 1995. I thought of cancelling the programme but could not resist the temptation of visiting the Herakhan Shiva Temple. In fact, I was getting restless to go to the lap of nature. I was sleeping at my official residence in Lucknow and at night I heard the hissing sound of a snake emanating from my head. I was startled and apprehensive, but joyful. On February 25, Saturday morning, I left for Herakhan alone via Bareilly and Haldwani. I took a review meeting at Bareilly and Haldwani. By the time, I reached Herakhan it was 8.30 pm. In the darkness, armed with torches we marched on the winding kuchha road leading to the Rest House situated on the banks of the Gola river. It was a beautiful rest house specially designed, constructed and decorated for the Governor in the 1980's. I stayed in the upper suite. Somehow, I got disturbed sleep in this room. Last year, also when I spent the night in this room with my wife, I had a disturbed sleep. I feared that the room was haunted by a good spirit. I felt as if a great snake was around. I was afraid and apprehensive and bowed down before the picture of Herakhan Baba on the table and sought his blessing. I kept the photograph of the Baba in my pocket and went to bed with the lights on. Early in the morning my limbs started troubling me. It was time for meditation. I did my meditation from 5 am to 7 am. At 7.30 am, I went and sat on a rock and gazed at the river and the beauty of the Himalayas. What an unique experience indeed.

February 27, a Monday, was Shivaratri day and as usual I got up at 5 am. I did my morning meditation and again went and sat on a rock, doing meditation from 7.30 am to 8 am. Then we went to bathe in the river. When, I closed my eyes, I could see two deep green circles merging into one another to form a heart-shape figure. It continued for a long time. I got ready to perform puja at the Herakhan Shiva Temple. I worshipped the Linga with Gangajal, milk, honey, sugar, clove, bel leaves, ber and flowers and agarbati. My joy knew no bounds at that moment.

When we were going to the temple, just at the entrance of the ashram, a small handsome boy with hair knotted like Shiva's locks, told us that this was not the road to Kailash. He showed us the road where a great mela (fair) was held every Shivaratri day. Probably, the boy thought that we had lost our way. I was very much impressed by the intelligence of the boy and fascinated by his glow and charm. I thought, Lord Shiva has come in this child's garb. After doing Puja while we were returning, suddenly the boy appeared near the gate. I immediately seized the opportunity and offered him some prasad. He took it with a beautiful smile and disappeared.

It had become my habit to visit various holy places of Himalayas particularly during May and June. I was planning to go to Kumaon hills to visit Almora, Herakhan and Jageswar. But suddenly my transfer order came in April, 1995. My stand on certain taxation proposals was not liked by the Chief Secretary and Principal Secretary (Heavy Industries). A luxury tax was imposed on cigarette and tobacco through an ordinance and in three months, the Department had collected about Rs 20 crores on this score. But the ordinance lapsed and there was no Act in its place. I got a written order from the Secretary to the Chief Minister communicating the latter's direction to return the tax collected to the firms concerned. I smelt something fishy and discussed the matter with my senior officers. The firms were merely the tax collectors and not tax payers. The tax was paid by those who purchased cigarettes and tobacco. Since the tax payers could not be identified precisely, as per the provisions of the UP Sales Tax Act, such amount had to be deposited with the UP Development fund. Moreover, the ordinance, even if it was not replaced by an Act, had the force of law when it was in existence. So I did not implement the order. Instead, I sought an appointment with the Chief Minister to explain this situation. I told him, 'Sir, you are the political executive head and I understand your compulsions. But I am a civil servant and I have a code of conduct to follow. It is just possible that your political compulsion and my principles may come into conflict. In such a situation, you may transfer me.' The Chief Minister said, 'I do not understand what you are talking about. Tell me straight the problem.' I explained the legal position clearly and cautioned that if the tax collected was returned to the collecting firms, this would result in a scandal. The Chief Minister agreed with my suggestion. Without wasting time, I immediately scribbled whatever transpired at the discussions and took his approval on the file itself to deposit the amount in UP Development Fund, and not return to the firms. I must give due credit to the Chief Minister for his understanding the gravity of the case. Quite often, under pressure, we don't put forward our viewpoint in black and white suggesting the appropriate course of action to be taken. If bureaucrats learn the simple technique of giving proper advice impartially, fearlessly and selflessly in writing to the political boss, I am sure that in most cases the political boss will accept the advice.

In another case, some amendments had to be made in the UP Sales Tax Act to provide subsidy/deferment to certain new units which would be established in UP. The Committee of Secretaries, headed by the Chief Secretary, convened a meeting and took a decision to approve and implement the amendment immediately. I requested the Chief Secretary that in the absence of any amendment to the Act, it would not be possible to implement the decision. Later, the proposal was approved by the Cabinet and I was directed to implement it. I brought it to the notice of the Chief Secretary again that it was a Cabinet decision and unless it was reflected in the Act by following appropriate procedure, it would not be possible to implement it immediately. This proved the last straw and I was transferred as M.D., UP Development System Corporation (UP DESCO). Anyway, it was immaterial and I took it stoically and handed over my charge immediately.

Chapter 21

Managing Director, UP DESCO

(May 1995 – July 1995)

The beauty of the Himalayas, the spiritual experience and
the blessings of saintly persons, made me absolutely fearless,
selfless, and ready to take on the challenges of life with poise,
confidence and equanimity.

The UP Desco was often considered a punishment post but
I enjoyed it. I had enough time for reading and learning new
things. I learned to operate the computer, took interest in consultancy
and presentation of reports, and training of the officers and officials
in IT and posting of IT specialists in various Departments. I also read
Shri Narendra Kohli's *Ram Katha,* an interesting book and a novel
interpretation of the epic. It was a good break in terms of content and
the lighter workload provided me a unique opportunity to pursue
my spiritual journey. I visited Jageswar (Kumaon hills), Gangotri and
Gomukh. On the evening of April 25, 1995, my wife and I left for
Almora via Bareilly and reached the place the next day. We stayed
there for a night. At night while meditating I could hear the sound
of the stormy wind and that of the damru. On April 27, we went to
Jageshwar, a quiet place in the lap of nature. The cluster of temples
there is a testimony to our rich ancient culture and sculpture. The
beauty is enhanced by deodar trees and the Jata Ganga which
meanders through. It is an ideal place for meditation. There is a
complex of 124 temples here of which the famous are Jageshwar

Jyotrilinga temple, Maha Mritunjaya temple, Nava Durga, and the Nava Grah Chandi temples. The Maha Mritunjaya temple is the oldest while Dandeswar temple outside the premises is the largest shrine of the complex. We worshipped at both Maha Mritunjaya Shiva and Jageswar Jyotrilinga. While coming out of the premises, we learnt about the existence of Kuber temple in close proximity. We went there to offer prayers and my wife quipped, 'Prashanta, I prayed to Kubereswar Shiva Linga to be kind to us so that even at the worst of crisis, we may not be dependent financially on others.' The place was so enchanting that I visited it half a dozen times. On the way back to Almora, we visited Dandeswar Mahadev and Mritola Ashram.

The Himalayas have always fascinated me and unconsciously, I was drawn and attracted towards this mountain range. I find myself completely transformed, whenever I am in the Holy Himalayas. This time I had planned to visit Gangotri and Gomukh. We boarded the train on the night of June 4, 1995 and reached Hardwar the next day at 11 am. After bath and brunch at the IDPL Guesthouse, Rishikesh, we proceeded to meet Swami Premanandji at the Shivananda Ashram. The Swami advised me to meet four persons during my trip to Gangotri; Swami Hansanandji, Swami Dineshanandji, Falhaari Baba and a Sadhvi who was living beyond Gomukh. The Swamiji blessed me and we started our onward journey to Uttarkashi on June 5, at 2 pm and reached the Shivananda Ashram of Ganeshpuri at about 7 pm. It was a beautiful ashram with all modern facilities near the bank of the Bhagirathi. The surroundings were intoxicating. Swami Premanand Mohanty, an Oriya Sadhu, looking after the Ashram, was indeed a simple person with innocence oozing out of his countenance. He greeted us and lodged us comfortably. I was restless to enjoy the scenic and serene beauty of the Himalayas and the Bhagirathi. At once, I rushed to the bank though it was getting dark. I sat on a rock and meditated for half an hour. I felt as if the whole earth was moving. The sound of the gushing water created awe and reverence. I saluted the river and thoroughly enjoyed my meditation.

The next morning we got up early and I could not resist the temptation of going back to the river to meditate. I meditated on a rock and that made me absolutely serene. I could see energy rings of different colours floating before my eyes. After breakfast, we bade farewell to the Sanaysi and left the Ashram at about 9 am and drove towards Gangotri. On the way, we saw the beautiful fountain of Maneri Bhali Project, the hot spring of Gangwani and the charming place called Harshil, which looked like a fairy land with many streams. We spent about an hour near a stream and reached Gangotri at about 5 pm. We worshipped goddess Ganga and washed our hand, feet and head with the holy water of the Bhagirathi. It was here that Bhagirath had prayed to Lord Shiva, to bring the Ganga to the earth.

Gangotri is undoubtedly a beautiful place, with the river Bhagirathi flowing with a roaring sound. I had visited the place in September, 1972, as an IAS probationer. At that time, there was no trace of such crowds. Now it was much more congested and dirty. After puja, we went in search of Hansanandji, a saint more than 100 years old. When I met and sat down before him in reverence in Vajrasana, tears came in profusion and I was spell-bound. I felt as if I had been associated with this grand old saint in my previous birth. I felt like a child before his august Master. The Swamiji asked, 'Why have you come here. Have you come for power, prestige and authority?' I replied, 'Baba, I have come here in search of spiritualism and brought my family here so that they can imbibe the samskara.' Again he persisted, 'Don't you want power, prestige and authority?' and I just shook my head. Then he asked, 'Would like to have moksha and darshan of God.' To this I nodded in affirmity. Chanting some slokas and mantras, he blessed me and assured me that I would have 'shakshat darshan' (direct communion) of God in this life itself.

We then went in search of Swami Dineshanandji, a Naga Baba, one who remains unclad. My wife was hesitant but I told her that he was a sanyasi and she should not have any inhibition. We reached his Ashram in the evening and the Naga Baba was sitting in such a posture that it covered his nakedness. As I sat before him my whole body was trembling. I told Baba, 'I am disgusted with the present world where only the bad and corrupt thrive and good people suffer. At times, I think of leaving such a society.' On hearing this, he was furious and said, 'We have already left society and come here to meditate. Whatever good thoughts we send through vibrations, should be received by good people living within the society. If such good people also leave society, then everything will be ruined.' He enlightened me on the Gita's philosophy. 'Do your duty honestly and selflessly and leave the rest to Him.' He assured me that since I was following the right path, nobody would dare harm me, 'koi bhi tumhara bal banka nahi kar sakta.'

The next day, we left for Gomukh, which is about 20 km from Gangotri. We started our tortuous but memorable trekking to Bhoj Basa at about 10.30 am. After covering two km, we came across Phalahari Baba's Ashram. Along with N.C. Sharma I met Phalahari Baba who was a devotee of Lord Rama. He advised us about the correct attitude to life. After spending a few minutes in his Ashram, we resumed our journey. It was a difficult trek and a slip of the foot could land you a thousand feet below. We walked with carefully measured steps and took adequate rest at a small dhaba that had come up en route. Not many people were going to Gomukh. Even though the hills were looking bald and denuded, we enjoyed its roughness and the shining snow-clad peaks and the gushing sound of streams. The company also added flavor to it. We made fun, cracked jokes and laughed all the way. We reached Chirbasa at about 3.30 pm. It was an adventure to cross the stream of Chirbasa. We took some rest and started again for Bhojbasa. In Chirbasa, there were chir (pine) trees. Thereafter, it was all Bhoj patra jungle. We were tired, exhausted and at last, we reached Bhojbasa at 7.30 pm. We stayed at the Garhwal Mandal Vikas Nigam's rest house. I was feeling so hot that I removed my sweater at night. Bhojbasa is situated at a height of 13000 ft and all of us had breathing trouble and terrible headache because of the rarefied atmosphere.

The next day we woke up early and got ready by 8.30 am. Sushant, my 8-year-old son, developed high altitude sickness and we had to leave him at Bhojbasa and started for Gomukh at about 9 am. It was not a difficult trek, but the last 2.5 km to the Gomukh Glacier were quite tough. Due to a landslide, there was no sign of the traditional path. As a result we had to grope our way over the big and small boulders and at last we reached Gomukh at about 11.30 am. We were excited and surprisingly, it was not at all that cold in Gomukh. I managed with a woollen pant and a cotswool shirt. But the water was ice cold. We saw a huge iceberg floating down the Bhagirathi. I had a strong desire to have a dip in the Gomukh. In 1972 also I had visited Gomukh, but could not dare to take a dip. This time, I ventured into the stream and felt as if my legs were being cut. I was frightened and came back. The second time, I again went to the water, but again came back. Finally chanting 'Om Namah Shivaya', I took the plunge and felt the greatest satisfaction which I cannot express. I sat for meditation on a rock facing the Shiva Linga peak and within minutes I felt tremendous vibrations and tears rolling down my cheeks. I tasted ice of the glacier. Maybe it was a thousand years old. We spent about an hour in Gomukh and were so exhausted that we could not muster enough strength to trek further to meet the Sadhvi. I bowed in reverence to her from Gomukh.

We returned and stayed the night at Bhairon Ghati and the next morning, left for Uttarkashi and reached Ganeshpuri Ashram at about 3 pm. In Uttarkashi, we visited the Viswanath and Shakti Temple. It was an old temple, with a powerful Shiva Linga. The Shakti temple had a long trishul which was a thing to be seen. Finally we were back in Lucknow on June 12, 1995. While leaving the Himalayas, I could feel the pang of separation intensely. This journey had left an indelible imprint on my mind. The spiritual experience, the beauty of the Himalayas and above all the blessings of the saintly persons, made me absolutely fearless, selfless and ready to take on the challenges of life with poise, confidence and equanimity.

Chapter 22

.... ✂

Secretary, Panchayati Raj &
Youth Affairs

(July 1995 – September 1995)

The Minister has every right to function within the four
corners of the constitutional and legal provisions. But,
he cannot cross the Lakshman Rekha.

*I*n the meanwhile, major political developments had been taking
place in UP. A new Government had assumed office and I was
posted as Secretary, Panchayati Raj and Youth Affairs in July, 1995.
It was a short stint but nonetheless an eventful and important one.
The Panchayati Raj Minister, after making some surprise inspection
in some districts, directed me to suspend the District Panchayati Raj
officers of three districts as the complete handing over of charge from
old pradhans to new ones had not taken place. When I analyzed the
events, I found that in 95% of Gram Sabhas, the complete charge
had been handed over in these districts. I requested the Minister
that instead of suspending the three officers, we may issue show
cause notice to them as 95% of the transfers had already taken
place. Otherwise, almost all the Panchayati Raj officers on similar
performance standard would be suspended. The Minister heeded my
advice and did not insist on their suspension.

On another occasion, the Minister issued an order to me in writing to post particular persons on certain posts which were not in a Zila Parishad. He did not know the procedure for creating posts and the Competent Authority to make such decisions. I put up a polite note indicating the procedure and the Competent Authority to fill these up. In their absence, it would not be possible to implement the Minister's order. Along with my note, I also attached the opinion of the Law Department. I sent the file back to the Minister for reconsideration and returned to my residence. At about 8.30 pm, I received a call from the Minister who was annoyed and said, 'Mishraji, do you think that the Minister has no say in a democratic set up?' Politely, I replied, 'Sir, you have every right to function within the four corners of the constitutional and legal provisions. But you cannot cross the Lakshman Rekha. Since I am your Secretary it is my bounden duty to advise you correctly and as Secretary I will ensure that you will not cross this Lakshman Rekha.' In a sarcastic tone the Minister told me, 'My sat-sat pranam (hundred bows) to you.' I replied, 'Sir, from my side, it is koti-koti Pranam (million bows).' The conversation ended thus.

After this episode, he complained to the Chief Minister that the Secretary, Panchayati Raj was an obstinate officer and he was not implementing the Minister's orders. The Chief Minister called his Secretary and directed him to suspend me. The Secretary knew me quite well and pleaded before his boss that Mr Mishra was an honest and excellent officer. The suspension would send wrong signals to the bureaucracy. The Chief Minister did not listen and, with sarcasm told the Secretary that the bureaucrats only tried to help each other. The Secretary understood the delicate situation and came back. The next day, all officers of the entire Chief Minister's Secretariat, led by the Secretary, went and met the Chief Minister. The Secretary was intelligent and knew that the politician would understand only the language of power and politics. So, he informed the Chief Minister that Mr Mishra was not only an honest and dedicated officer but he was also unanimously elected as Secretary of the IAS Association for three consecutive years. The Chief Minister, a clever politician, understood the tone and the statement and sought only an explanation and not suspension. Thus, the Secretary, by his deft handling of the situation, saved me from suspension.

A few months passed and I continued to experience the magic touch of the energy, the same rushing of energy, stiffening of the body, burning sensation, twinkling light, pressure on the eyelids and lips etc. At times, I had the experience of seeing a capsule-like red, blue and white light. One night, I experienced a beautiful smell for quite a long period. Another night, I could distinctly hear the musical sound of Nupura (anklet) and later it was replaced by thunderous sounds. I was feeling that I was being protected by some unseen force. My Minister wanted to harm me, and poisoned the ears of the Chief Minister against me. But by the grace of the cosmic force, nothing untoward happened. I was overwhelmed and wept profusely as a measure of expressing my heart-felt gratitude to him. He was so kind to me.

One day I got up at about 3 am. After going to the toilet, I again retired to bed, but the music of a devotional song was reverberating in my mind. Slowly, I felt as if I was being seized by a Great Force. I began to chant, 'Om Namah Shivaya' and yogic kriyas started happening. But my concentration was not intense. It was broken from time to time and I realized that due to my past karma, there was something hindering my progress. I remembered great saints like Swami Hansanandji and Swami Dineshanandji of Gangotri, Swami Chinmayanandji, Swami Vivekananda and above all, Sai Baba of Shirdi. I completely surrendered myself to the cosmic force, and invoking these great saints, begged for their mercy and sincerely prayed to them to remove my obstruction. Suddenly, I felt a rush of energy and twinkling light. I could see the room engulfed in soothing rays of light. But I mistook it for the moon's rays. It was actually a revelation to me, this effulgence, but due to my ignorance, I could not recognize my Lord. There was no moon in the sky and there was only darkness. Certainly the Great Force has revealed a bit of its existence and miracle. I was emotionally so charged that I wept like a child.

Chapter 23

....❈

Secretary, Science & Technology

(October 1995 – December 1995)

I do not have any administrative or political mentor
in my life. I have only one mentor i.e. God.

*M*y tenure as Secretary, Panchayati Raj lasted hardly three months and I was transferred as Secretary, Science and Technology which was considered a punishment posting. I immediately handed over charge and assumed the new post. When I called on the Minister, Science and Technology, who was supposed to be a good administrator, he asked, 'Mishraji, how do you like the Department?' When I said that it was a very good Department with a lot of potential, he replied, humourously, that this was the first time he was hearing such a comment. Hardly, one or two files used to land there and practically there was no work. I wanted to create more work and so started interacting with scientists and the scientific institutions and took steps to draft a New Science Policy for the State. I had the good fortune of interacting with eminent space scientists like Dr Kasturirangan. I also suggested to the UP Government the idea of earmarking a particular percentage of the budget for every Department for scientific inputs, as well as steps to create awareness and the scientific spirit and temper among students, by promoting science clubs in educational institutions. There was a total solar eclipse on October 24, 1995 and I took this opportunity to organize an awareness drive, debating competitions and lectures by scientists to enlighten the student community as well as to dispel the superstitions about the eclipse. Special goggles were distributed for the first time for students to observe the eclipse. These efforts of the department were highly appreciated. While in Lucknow, the eclipse began at 7.26 am, I could not resist the temptation of observing it through the special goggles. The TV networks were broadcasting it live from Neem-Ka-Thana (Rajasthan), Diamond Harbour (West Bengal), Iradatganj (Allahabad) and from Delhi. The diamond ring effect of the eclipse was so fantastic that my hair stood on end and tears came to my eyes. The Sun God, the life giving force, showed us a tiny aspect of his grandeur and personality. I stood speechless in reverence, looking at this magnificent celestial phenomenon. I bowed down automatically with reverence to this Great Cosmic Spirit.

I went to Mahoba on November 2, 1995, after 20 years, in connection with some official work. I was feeling nostalgic about the place. I was Joint Magistrate there from August, 1975 to July, 1976 and the experiences and pictures of those days passed through my mind. At that time I used to visit Chandrika Devi, particularly when I was depressed or tense. Visiting the deity after 20 years, I was excited and went to the temple in the evening. The atmosphere was calm and serene and when I saw the deity, I was overwhelmed by the beauty and tejas (glow). I felt a like a child before the mother. I was choking with emotion. I did not feel like leaving the place. Mother was looking so beautiful, benign and kind. But I had to bid farewell with a pang.

When my mood is off, I have no other companion except God to release my emotion. I talk to God like a child and as a friend. It provides some solace to my tormented soul. Quite early in the morning of 18 November, 1995, I got up, finished my morning ablutions and sat for meditation. Slowly and gradually I reached the peak. I saw a small circle of soothing white light in the region of Agnya Chakra. Slowly the mini circle of white light, spread and became enlarged to cover my entire head. I was obliged and overwhelmed.

Work at the Department of Science and Technology was not exacting and I had enough time to devote to the children and family. Such a light posting was a boon in the sense that I could devote more time to the children and read spiritual books. Life was rather smooth when one day I received a call from Secretary to the Governor asking me whether I would be interested to be posted as CEO, Noida. President's Rule was in force in the State and I was hesitant because at this time my transfer would upset the preparations of my daughters for their board examinations. I said 'No' but the Secretary wanted me to hand over a list of honest and sincere officers to be considered for that. I was preparing the list when my wife who overheard the conversation said, 'Prashanta, God is giving you an opportunity. Don't refuse it. Moreover, it will help in the college education of the children as Noida is close to Delhi.' I contacted the Secretary and told him, 'Sir, these officers are honest and sincere, but you tell me whether I will be transferred out of Lucknow.' He said, 'If you are not interested in Noida, you will be transferred as Commissioner, Benaras Division, as you are considered a spiritual person.' I replied, 'Sir, if in any case I will be transferred, then you may consider me for Noida.' Thus on December 8, 1995, I received my transfer order and the next day I took charge.

The CEO of Noida is considered a prestigious and key one and officers exert political and administrative pressures to get this. But in my case, it happened just like that. Never in my life had I approached any politician or administrative boss for transfer, posting or promotion and I do not have any administrative or political mentor. I have only one mentor, i.e. God. He has taken care of me at every step.

Chapter 24

CEO, Noida

(December 1995 – August 1996)

When you are in a position of authority, don't arrogate the benefits to yourself but confer benefits on others. If you follow this principle, no fingers will be raised against you.

*M*y stay in Noida lasted hardly eight months because vested interests could not digest my style of functioning. Noida is always known as the milch cow for corrupt bureaucrats and politicians. My mandate was to clean up the place. This is a place where a galaxy of personalities like artists, administrators, judges, parliamentarians, intellectuals, educationists, defence officers and business persons live. But unfortunately, their services were never utilized to bring about any qualitative improvement in the area. The day I set foot there, I could feel the atmosphere of corruption, it was palpable. Since, the CEO's residence was vacant I was lodged there and was flabbergasted to see elaborate arrangements made for lunch. Dinner too, was elaborate and I got suspicious and asked the attendant as to who was making these arrangements. I also made it clear that I could not afford all this and and very simple food should be served. The attendant replied, 'Sir, the entire management here is looked after by the Chief Engineer.' I was aghast and immediately stopped this practice.

During my short stay, not much could be done but a lot of initiatives were undertaken. These include massive tree plantation, improvement of the Yamuna Front garden with fountains, simplification of procedure for passing of maps and completion certificates, involvement of honest retired officials in the management of Noida, launching of the Smriti Van, installation of Reini well and proposal for Ganga Jal to improve drinking water facilities. I had a grand plan for a botanical garden, science city and an IIT campus as well. I did succeed with my botanical garden project though it faced many hurdles after my transfer in August, 1996. Many of these bottlenecks were sorted out when I became Chief Secretary, UP in 2007. I am glad it is proceeding smoothly. I also got approval for the establishment of a science city in Noida and got a nod from IIT, Delhi for establishing an IIT campus but these dream projects were sacrificed at the altar of residential plots for monetary gain. I also took the initiative for housing facilities for slum-dwellers but this too got stalled after my transfer.

Because of its proximity to Delhi and Gurgaon, Noida had become so important that everybody wanted to have a plot/house here by hook or by crook. This had led to many unfair practices in implementing schemes for allotment of plots and residences. I was directed to enquire into one such allegation and when I enquired, I found that a lot of important and powerful personalities from different walks of life were unduly benefitted. When I brought it to the notice of my Chairman and Secretary to the Governor, they asked me to go ahead with the enquiry and submit a report. I made it absolutely clear that I would not be able to camouflage the enquiry report and it would faithfully reflect everything. After the enquiries, I found that illegal allotments/conversions had been made in 105 cases. And for the first time in life, I felt a bit nervous as the case involved many important personalities. The file was kept with me under lock and key and I was feeling restless. I meditated in the evening to seek guidance and my conscience mocked and said, 'Prashanta, you consider yourself an honest and courageous officer, but now you are hesitating to take a decision. Where is your courage, your honesty?' I got the answer.

That night I wrote down my order in my handwriting and went to the worship room, offered the file to God and prayed, 'Oh! God, I have done my duty, now it is your turn to protect me.' In fact, the cosmic spirit protected me from all attempts made to tarnish my image, as subsequent events unfolded.

I was transferred immediately after I decided to cancel the allotment/conversion of plots made illegally. The transfer order came in the evening of August 16 and though the Chief Secretary and my Chairman were with me in Delhi then in connection with some discussions, they could not muster the courage to break the news to me. When I reached home in the evening, my wife informed me about the order to transfer me to Lucknow as Secretary (Cooperation). I took it in my stride with equanimity and just at that time, I got a call from my successor who said, 'Prashanta, I am sorry, unfortunately I am to replace you as CEO, Noida. When shall I come?' I said, 'Sir, why should you feel sorry about it. It is all part of the game, you can come any time and take charge. If you are already in Noida, you can come just now.' He laughed and said he would come the next day by flight. He was a bit late in reaching office. I had already signed the necessary papers and when he came, I just handed over these to him. While taking charge, he asked me, 'Prashanta, where is the file of that enquiry?' I told him, 'Sir, I have already cancelled the plots and unfortunately, one of the plots belongs to you. ' He laughed again and said, 'It is very difficult to control you.' He did not show any rancor; on the other hand, he was kind and very helpful. At my request, he immediately allotted a house for my family to stay in Noida as my children were studying in DPS, Noida.

I knew, I had charted a difficult path, but these temporary hurdles and sufferings only made me more determined to face such ordeals. Because of my firm nature and zeal to uphold principles, the establishment had got me transferred five times in a short 15-month span! False complaints were foisted just to humiliate me, but I remained unruffled. One of my colleagues leveled malicious insinuations against me and other colleagues at a Press Conference. I was dismayed yet I laughed. Initially I was in a fit of temper but soon I cooled down. For the first time, I realized how venomous a colleague could be. Anyway, it was quite a good lesson and for the first time I realized that at such moments faith in God alone can save you. Complaints were manufactured and I had to face enquiries at different levels. I gave detailed replies to all such complaints. Disturbed with such enquiries, I also wrote a polite letter to the Chief Secretary to uphold the dignity of an honest officer, otherwise the species called 'honest officer' would be extinct. Judicial and CBI enquiries were instituted against those who had complained and conspired against me and ultimately, they were punished. Since truth was on my side, nothing happened to me. My dignity was upheld and the attempt to tarnish my image was rebuffed cosmically.

The Noida posting was considered a prize assignment but for me probably it was the worst posting in my career. Mudslinging has become a potent weapon to humiliate and denigrate a good person. I learnt a good deal from my bitter experience there; that one has to perform on his own strength and not count on any support from colleagues, higher officers or political bosses at the time of crisis. I always keep the sane advice my eldest brother gave, 'Prashanta, when you are in a position of authority, don't arrogate the benefits to yourself but confer benefits on others. If you follow this principle, no fingers will be raised against you.' I scrupulously followed this principle thoughout my career. Though as CEO, Noida, I was entitled to a plot, I refused to take it. Moreover, I did not have the financial wherewithal to deposit lakhs of rupees for this. One important personality of Noida came to my residence and wanted to offer me the help in the form of a gift or, at best, an interest-free loan, but I declined the offer. I told him, 'Mr X, you have not understood the character of P.K. Mishra. You can go.' This approach to life has saved me from a lot of botheration and deflected many attacks against me.

I was feeling restless for quite some time. At night I prayed to the beings roaming the cosmos for guidance. One night I got the answer; 'Concentrate on your own Ishta Devata and go back to the original.' Such guidances certainly helped me and the restlessness vanished. During this time, I visited Vindhyachal, Allahabad, Vrindaban, Goverdhan, Medhmaheswar and Shirdi. Generally, during every Navaratra, Sharad or Chaitra, I used to visit Vindhyachal in Mirzapur to have a darshan of Maa Vindya Vasini, Kalikho and Astabhuja. But this time, I thought that since I was quite far away from Mirzapur, I would not be able to have that darshan. But to my surprise, exactly during the Navratra period, I was invited as an expert by the State Public Service Commission to participate in the interview. I reached Allahabad on March 20, 1996 morning by Prayag Raj Express, met the Chairman, finished my work and proceeded to Mirzapur. The S.P. of Mirzapur, Mr Sabat, took every pain to arrange for my darshan. It was the first day of Navratra and while worshipping Maa Vindya Vasani, I wept. I then met Nara Hari Baba in Astabhuja hill and received his blessings. He also reassured me that I would not fail in my spiritual endeavour. In fact he said that I would make progress by the day. At the cave of the Temple Astabhuja, I met Avadhoot Ram. I thought I had seen him before but could not locate him. He closed his eyes and started predicting about me and told me that I was losing weight because of Sadhana and that I was a 'yogi' in a previous birth. He advised, 'हृदय में बंसी बजाओ.' (fill your heart with divine music). I could not understand the meaning; maybe he advised me to meditate on the heart. Maybe he was advising me to unlock the heart's door to others.

During my stay in Allahabad on March 23, 1996 morning, I visited Hanuman and Shankarcharya's temple. The same evening, with the permission of the Army authorities, I visited the Bata Brikshya (banyan tree) in the Fort, the same sacred Banyan tree which finds mention in the Puranas. It was the abode of Bhardwaj Muni and it was said Lord Rama visited this great tree that had been witness to the deluge (pralay). I was fascinated and did deep meditation for 20 minutes under this sacred tree. I also saw Ashoka's pillar which had withstood nature's onslaught for thousands of years. The Allahabad stay was quite rejuvenating and I returned to Noida on March 24.

Three days later, at about 11 am, I accidently ran into Pandit Rama Chandra Shukla of Sultanpur who was famous for making intuitive predictions. In fact the S.S.P. of Ghaziabad Mr P.K. Tewari was instrumental in arranging the meeting. Mr Shukla predicted that I belonged to a family of 'Sidhas' and had done quite good Sadhana in my previous births. I used to have spiritual experiences every day and it had become a part of life. But something extraordinary happened on the night of April 1, 1996 when I retired to bed chanting my 'Mantra' of 'Om Namah Shivaya'. Suddenly I experienced a tremendous flood of light in the forehead, the brilliance of which I could not bear. I was horrified and trembled fearing that something untoward might happen. I was also gasping. Then the light disappeared but I was breathless for quite some time and became normal after a few minutes.

For many years I had nurtured the idea of going to Govardhan Giri for 'Parikarma,' but that had not materialized. At last, the time came, on May 10, 1996. For some days, I had been toying with the idea of going to some spiritual place on holidays and I thought of going to 'Jamunotri', but this did not happen. One day, Mr N.C. Sharma came to my house and we suddenly decided to go to Vrindavan on the second weekend. On May 10, at about 4 pm we went on the trip. We reached Vrindavan at about 7.30 pm and started our night Parikrama of Govardhan at about 10.00 pm. While praying before Govardhan Girirajji, my body vibrated with the surcharged atmosphere. Along with Mr Sharma, Mr Man Singh (Peon) and Mahadevji, I started the journey, with Mahadevji explaining the significance of each spot. In fact, he was an interesting personality. We enjoyed the 'Night Parikrama'. We completed the 21 km trek with great enthusiasm and spirit. A hot cup of tea in an earthern pot at the dead of night at a wayside shop was so refreshing. There were a few walkers like us doing the parikrama. During the entire period, I kept chanting,

'Hare Krishna'. I was quite surprised to find many persons sleeping on the roadside. I was told that they were 'yatris' who would resume their 'yatra' early the next morning. There were one or two doing the 1008 dandavati. I could not understand what this meant. Mahadevji explained that a few people came with determination to shed their bodies during the Parikrama. Such pilgrims carry 1008 pebbles, prostrate on the road and put one pebble at arm's length. This way they shed all the 1008 pebbles and move to the next place where the same process starts again. It is a difficult journey and takes almost a lifetime to complete. Mahadevji tried to impress us with his knowledge about the areas and their importance. Though we had some blisters, we still continued our journey. On the way, we saw Radha Kund and Krishna Kund. We enjoyed our 15 minutes' rest there. It was about 2.45 am, when we left the Kundas. After covering a kilometer, we found ourselves in the thick of a strong dust storm accompanied by thunder and rain. The only shelter nearby was a school in the jungle. We stood in the verandah of the school. The breeze was cool. We were tired. All four of us did not know when we fell asleep. It was an enjoyable sleep for about two hours. When I opened my eyes, it was 5 am. We thanked Lord Krishna and Girirajji. We thought, as if the same scene of protecting his devotees from Indra's wrath was again enacted in a mini-form here. The morning was cool and pleasant after the shower. We resumed our journey and on the way saw Kusum Sarovar. As per the legend, Krishna used to decorate Radha with flowers on the steps of the sarovar. It was named after Radha's sakhi (friend), Kusum. It was a huge lake with nice arches and bathing ghats. By 7 am, we reached ISKCON's Guesthouse after completing our Parikrama.

We were tired. I took my bath and went to sleep. Mr Sharma woke me up at 9.30 am. We had khichree as Prasad. It was delicious and tasted like Amrit. Thereafter again I went for a sleep and got up at 1.30 pm. We had lunch and again I slept till 5.30 pm. At 6 pm we went to Katyayani Pith, Tatia Ashram of Baba Hari Das Sect, Rangji Temple and Banke Vihari Temple. We had the good fortune of getting the sangat of the old Baba at the Ashram. The Ashram still kept its environment in the same traditional fashion. We came back at about 9 pm and retired to bed. The next morning at about 9 am we left for Noida and reached here at about 11.45 am.

Madmaheswar is one of the Panchkedaras of whole Kedarkhand. Sri Madmaheshwar is situated at Gandhamardhan Parvat at the lower region of Chaukhamba Himalayas. This shrine is virtually a paradise on earth. The lofty peaks of Chaukhamba shine brightly at its head like a silver crown studded with the precious diamonds and gems. A pilgrim who visits there is taken aback to see the enchanting beauty of nature. The temple is a marvelous art of sculpture and carvings. It is said that the Pandavas built this temple at the end of the Dwapar Yug nearly 5200 years ago.

Out of Panchkedaras, Madmaheswar has the steepest gradient. On May 25, 1996, accompanied by my Staff Officer Mr R.K. Sharma and my spiritual companions Mr N.C. Sharma and Mr C.S. Semwal, we started our journey from Noida. That night we spent at Shivanand Ashram of Muni-ki-Reti. We met Swami Premanandji who during the discourses stated that in Western philosophy, they used the word, 'God-fearing man', but why should one fear God? In our philosophy, we love God and don't fear him. Similarly, the Westerners use the word, 'fall in love'. But why we should fall in love. In fact, there should be elevation in love and not fall.

The next morning, I got up quite early and meditated for about an hour. I went to the Ganga to have a dip. At that time, the sun was just rising above the hills of Laxman Jhula. When I did my prayer to the Sun God by offering water, I had a strange experience. In the mind's eye, I could see the rising sun in blue colour. It lasted for a few minutes. We left the Ashram at about 8 am and on the way visited Vasistha Guffa and I meditated for about half an hour there before the Shiva Linga. We left the cave and spent some time in Kaudiyala rafting camp. While observing the running stream of the

Ganga, suddenly I felt as if I was also floating down the stream. We left Kaudiyala for Ukhimath and on the way, visited Saswat Ashram of Swami Adwetanandji of Lachmoli and enjoyed a simple lunch there. After performing puja, we left for Ukhimath and reached there at about 7 pm on May 26. The climate here was pleasant, cool and quiet. It is situated at a height of about 5000 ft. It is a small, nice town situated on the banks of the river Mandakani. We stayed at the P.W.D. Inspection Bungalow. Mr Semwal and his family treated us nicely and we had our dinner at Mr Semwal's residence.

On May 27, after tea, we proceeded for Kalimath, a known Shaktipeeth in Kedarkhand. We passed through the winding hill road for about an hour to reach Kalimath. The river Saraswati was flowing in her pristine glory by the side of this temple. Its water was so clear that I was tempted to have a dip. We may be one of the fortunate few who had taken bath in this holy river. Then we did elaborate puja in Kalimath. The 'Yantra' was worshipped here in all its elaborateness. After Parikrama of the temple, we were taken around various temples. The image of Shiva and Parvati with all their family members and vahans and that too in Sringar rasa was so enchanting and captivating. This image was exactly like that of Shiva-Parvati image of Shiva Dwara of Robertsganj of Mirzapur. It is said that Kalidasa worshipped here and the description of this area finds mention in his *Meghadoot*. The famous 'Kali Shila' on which many 'Yantras' were inscribed, is also situated in this place at a height of 12000 ft. It has been a site of Tantrik Puja since time immemorial. Kali Sila also finds mention in *Meghdoot*. Finally, we met Brati Baba of Kalimath. He was a very old man, devoted completely to spiritualism. He served us breakfast with the love and affection of a grandfather. We had aloo pakoda with fresh butter, halwa and tea. He was a great spiritual person and I considered myself fortunate to have been in his satsang. We came back to Ukhimath Camp by 1 pm. We had our lunch in Mr Semwal's residence and after an hour's rest, proceeded for the trek towards Madmaheswar.

We first covered 20 km by car and reached a bridge from where we had to resume our journey on foot. The gradient was too steep and the terrain rough, tough and dry. By evening we reached Ranshi village at about 6.30 pm and spent the night in that village. The hospitality of the Pradhan and the school teacher made our otherwise difficult journey a comfortable one. We had a lavish dinner arranged by Mr Bhatt and enjoyed it.

On May 28, we got up early, had our bath and went to Ranshi Devi Temple, a Shaktipith. The legend is that the moon was cured of its TB by worshipping the deity of Ranshi. In fact as Brati Baba mentioned, none of the residents of this village suffers from TB. After tea and biscuits, we left the village at about 7.30 am for our onward journey. It was all uphill. We all got tired and exhausted and the road seemed never ending. My feet were faltering, tongue was dried up and my head was reeling. I sat down for a while, and drank a coca cola. The other companions also did the same and immediately we got energized because of sugar and there was no stopping us till we reached Madmaheswar Temple.

What a unique joy I felt at the sight of the sacred temple which stood in a large valley against the background of snowy peaks of the Himalayas. When we entered the holy valley, Aarti had just concluded. We only managed a glimpse. We went to a house and sat by the fire place for some time. Thereafter we went to a house very close to the temple to take rest. It was still raining, the temperature fell and I immediately ducked under the quilt. A lantern was burning. I did not feel like taking anything that night. I had a comfortable sleep. We woke up in the morning of May 29, 1996. From our bedside we could hear the rushing sound of the streams. We took our bath and got ready for Darshan. At about 8.30 am, the priest, who was from the South, came and ushered us into the temple premise. Lord Shiva in his decorative colour was looking beautiful and impressive. He explained to us the legend. Once, a cow of the Tribal Head came to this Shiva Linga in the jungle and offered milk to the Lord every day. The Tribal head was quite surprised to find that the cow was not giving any milk at home. So one day he pursued the cow and found that it was showering all her milk on the Shiva Linga. In a fit of temper, he raised his axe to kill the cow. The cow jumped quickly and the axe fell on the Shiva Linga. As a result the Linga was tilted and had a scar. At night, Lord Shiva appeared in a dream before the Tribal Head and told him to do repentance by building a temple there. The Tribal Head tried his best to build a temple, but it collapsed every time. After many failures, he thought of sacrificing his only son to make it possible for the temple to come up. Lord Shiva got pleased and appeared before him and blessed him. Even today, there are two cows for this temple and the Linga is bathed in the milk of these cows. Another interpretation is that it is Madhya Maheswar, i.e. the middle portion of the body. Therefore, it is curved. In course of time, it became Madmaheswar.

Whatever the interpretation, I liked the place and was engrossed in meditation. Suddenly there was a flash in my mind to remind me that I had forgotten to bring the bottle with Ganga Water which I had brought all the way from Gomukh to Lucknow to Noida to Madmaheswar. I requested R.K. Sharma to rush to my room and bring the holy water. He brought it within no time and we worshipped the Shiva Linga with the holy water of the Ganga. The priest was kind enough to perform an elaborate puja with chanting of hymns and mantras. I was in a different world all together, experiencing the presence of the Great Divine.

After the puja, we climbed about 1 km up to have darshan of Bhairav. From that point, we looked at Budha Madmaheshwar and bowed before it. We came back, had our puri and aloo sabjee (potato curry) for breakfast. I looked around and felt as if I was absorbing all the vibrations of this holy place. While leaving this place, I was feeling sad. We resumed our journey from Madmaheswar to Ranshi Village. The same road, mountains and streams were there, but somewhere in my heart, there was a lurking pathos, the pangs of separation from Madmaheswar.

We reached Ranshi Village at about 8.30 pm and spent the night there. On May 30, we resumed our return journey in the morning and reached Ukhimath by lunch. We had a delicious lunch at Mr Semwal's residence and spent the night in PWD Inspection Bungalow, Ukhimath. The next day we got up early in the morning. In the serene, calm atmosphere of the Himalayas, I felt like meditating. At 6.30 am, we went to Ukhimath Temple. During winter, it houses the Chadi of Kedarnath and Madmaheswar. We worshipped the Shiva Linga and saw the Pancha Kedars in their miniature form, Chaumunda Devi and other deities. After breakfast, we left for Noida and reached by 11.00 pm. Even though it was a difficult trek, I returned with renewed vigour and energy.

After being indisposed for a few days I finally felt fresh, elated and in high spirits. I did not know the exact reason for such a feeling. Maybe rest for about four days, enjoying my solitude and sojourn, being away from the din and bustle of the routine bureaucratic life. Maybe it was the book I was reading. I was reading *Celestine Prophecy* by James Redfield. The book contains secrets and insights that are currently changing our world. Drawing on the ancient wisdom found in a Peruvian Manuscript (500 BC), it elaborates on how to make connections between events happening in one's own life right now and in the years to come. It contains nine insights that unfold the mystery of life. The Third Insight elaborates on the nature of beauty and its full appreciation and perception through which humans would eventually learn to observe the Energy Fields that surround matter. It explains why a good forest heightens our feeling, because the forest with all its beauty, species and splendor, emits energies that affect us. Now I understand why I frequently tend to visit the Himalayas. Whenever I enter the Himalayan Ranges with its snow-clad peaks and rivers, I find myself completely transformed and elevated. This, I realized as early as 1990. Therefore, the insights mentioned in *Celestial Prophecy* are quite relevant to understand the mysteries of life.

Generally I do Yoga with mental recitation of Mantra. In 1995, I got interested in the Sahaja Yoga of Mata Nirmala Devi and Sahaja Marga of Swami Rama Chandraji. Each kind of Yoga is more or less similar with some differences here and there. For some time, I tried to practise all these three systems. But later, I reverted to my original system of Yoga through Mantra. Later, I came in contact with Dr Mohapatra of Mahesh Yogi Institute, Noida. Dr Mohapatra was a doctor at the All India Institute of Medical Sciences in Nuclear Medicine. But he left the job and joined Maharishi Mahesh Yogi Institute. He taught me Transcendental Meditation with Bija Mantra, 'Shiva'. This system of meditation is more or less the same but the mantra is only 'Shiva' and not 'Om Namah Shiva'. Since there was not much variation with my earlier one, I did not find any difficulty in following it. I also did my Antaha Prakshyalana under the guidance of Mr N.C. Sharma. A few days later, a strange thing happened at night. My wife was listening to a devotional song of 'Maa'. I was enjoying it too. The music was so melodious it made me want to dance. My whole body vibrated and danced with the melody. It had such a gripping effect on me that I threw my hands and legs in the air and rolled from side to side. I felt as if a tidal wave of energy was sweeping over me.

Every day I was having some experience or the other. One night, I felt as if brilliant white rays were emerging from my left eye and spreading to the entire brain. On August 6, we were all set to go to Shirdi. By that time, a rumour about my transfer was in the air. My staff officer advised me to postpone the visit. But I declined it firmly. I believe in the maxim that whatever happens, happens because of God and God's action is always in the interest of his creature. I like to flow along with the natural event. For many years, I had been wanting to go to Shirdi. I did not want to miss this godsent opportunity only for a mundane affair like transfer.

At long last, Mr R.K. Sharma, Mr Upadhay and I went to Nizamuddin Railway Station, New Delhi and boarded the Goa Express for Manmad at 3 pm. I was totally surcharged with spiritual feelings. My joy knew no bounds with the excitement of visiting Baba's place. All the time, I was thinking of Baba i.e. Sai Baba and Bhole Shankar Baba. During the train journey, something interesting happened. A beggar with just one hand was begging money from the passengers. At that time, I was thinking of Baba and my first encounter with Him at Chitrakoot. The beggar came to me and effortlessly, I handed over Rs 2 to him. Suddenly, to my surprise, he put his only hand on my head and blessed me. I felt, as if Baba himself had descended to bless me. We reached Manmad Station at 11 am on August 7. From Manmad, we took a taxi and reached Shirdi by noon.

We stayed at the Maharashtra Tourist Hostel which was very close to Baba's Temple. After a bath, we went for our first Darshan of Baba at about 1 pm. There was less crowd and we got a good darshan. We attended all Aartis. We would get up at 4 am to get ready for morning Aarti at 5 am. Then there were Aartis at 11 am, 6 pm and 10 pm. I experienced tremendous spiritual feeling during the Aartis. The chanting in praise of Baba during Aarti created vibrations and often my limbs moved rhythmically to the music. After Aartis, we used to visit Guru Sthan where under a neem tree Baba had meditated for a long time. The most surprising thing about this tree is that its leaves are not bitter. I picked up a fallen neem leaf and bit it and to my utter surprise, it did not taste bitter at all. From Guru Sthan, we went to Dwarka Mai. We saw the stone on which Baba used to sit. We bowed before the original Dhuni (Sacred fire lit by Baba). We saw Baba's bathing stone and Chullah (earthen oven). Just in front of the Chullah, there was a wooden pillar erected by Baba. Legend says that if anybody suffering from joint ache, leans against this pillar, his pain will vanish. I had a nagging pain on my left back and shoulder. I was tempted to lean against this pillar and 80% of my pain vanished in one sitting. I made three sittings and to my surprise, it almost vanished. After Dwarka Mai, we went to Khandoba Temple, where Sai Baba was first addressed as Sai by the priest of the Temple. Thereafter we visited Nava Dweep. Here people worship two trees supposed to have been released from Tree Yoni by Baba. We also visited the house of the old man whom Baba gifted a Black Ganesh idol. I purchased a shawl wrapped around Baba's image for my wife. I should narrate an interesting happening; on Thursday after the last Aarti, I came back to my room at 11 pm but could not sleep till 2 pm. I felt as if a tremendous surge of energy was coursing through my body. I bore with it for some time but then it became impossible to tolerate. With folded hands, I prayed, 'Baba! I am not sufficiently strong and pure enough to receive your energy. Kindly excuse me.' The next moment the energy subsided and thereafter I went to sleep.

On August 8, I purchased two photographs, one of Lord Shiva and the second of Dattatreya. I got the photographs worshipped in the temple. While at Dwarka Mai, Mr Baxi, a fellow pilgrim, was wrapping up these photographs, a saint came, stood near us and chanted a mantra quickly. He told me, 'With these photographs of Lord Shiva and Datta Guru, you are carrying all the powers of Baba.' I wondered how this man knew about the wrapped photographs. I felt as if Baba had come in the shape of a saint. We took his blessings. The next day after noon Aarti, we took farewell from Baba. By taxi, we came to Manmad and boarded the Karnataka Express at 3.30 pm and reached Delhi on August 10, at about 11.30 am.

After visiting Shirdi, whenever I heard devotional songs of Sai Baba, tremendous waves would rise from within. After this trip, I was bubbling with confidence and spiritual energy. I took a hard decision in suspending the Chief Maintenance Engineer of Noida and in cancelling illegal conversions in Sector 43, 44 & 51 for which I was transferred on August 16, 1996. The next day I handed over charge and took over the new assignment of Secretary (Co-operation) on August 23.

Faith in God and spiritual practice had enabled me to weather out many a crisis, whether personal, political or administrative. The loneliness

in my life increased my yearning for solitude and spiritual practices. I started to spend more time in meditation, reading spiritual books and listening to Bhajans. Slowly, I regained my composure. I had started discovering the positive aspects in everybody. Two important developments took place; for the first time, I realized that spiritual development per se only for the development of the individual was totally useless, unless the energy unleashed was translated into action for the welfare of the people. The second development which I intensely felt was the dawning of 'Karuna' (compassion). I read about 'Karuna' and 'Tathagat as Karuna Avatar', but during this short stay in Noida, I felt 'Karuna' intensely and often intense sobs from the core of my heart came up. Very often I felt like blessing the good people whom I know. I cannot give them any material comfort, but certainly I can give them my blessings and spiritual consolation.

Chapter 25

.... ❦

Secretary, Co-operation

(August 1996 – November 1996)

I am sure, by the time I breathe my last breath, I will realize the
Truth and in the process realize my True Being.

I had taken the transfer as a blessing. I stayed in the Guesthouse
of the PICUP Building, Lucknow. Since I was alone in Lucknow,
I was able to devote more time to meditation, bhajans and study of
spiritual books. It was October 2, the birthday of Mahatma Gandhi.
Look at this man. What a frail body, but what a contribution he
made towards development of humanity! I was getting increasingly
philosophical and pondered over the life struggle and contribution of
the Father of the Nation. Not a single area was left on which he had
not said anything. No wonder, Albert Einstein, the great scientist,
commented on Gandhiji, 'Posterity will wonder whether such a man
in flesh, blood and bone has ever walked on this earth.' The irony is
that while the relevance of Gandhiji is increasing day by day all over
the world, we, Indians, are forgetting our own 'Father of the Nation'.
What a shame and what a tragedy! If we emulate only a tiny fraction
of his idealism and values of life, it will transform our country beyond
recognition.

Right from the morning on that day, I was in a reflective mood. I
attended the function organised at Tilak Hall of the Secretariat.
After listening to Bapu's priya (dear) bhajan, I was getting intensely

emotional and thought back on the era of freedom struggle. After seeing the trailor of Shyam Benegal's film *The Making of the Mahatma,* I broke down. The Great Man experimented with 'Truth' till his last breath. I am experimenting with 'Truth' in my own limited way. Life is nothing but an experiment with truth. I am sure, by the time I breathe my last breath, I will realize the Truth and in the process realize my True Being.

Chapter 26

Additional Resident Commissioner, UP at Delhi

(November 1996 – September 1997)

We claim to be the most intelligent species in this universe, little realizing that we do not know what will happen the next moment.

Life in Lucknow was moving placidly. The loneliness of the Guesthouse, particularly at night, made me more philosophical. I enjoyed my solitude and channelled into me the great cosmic energy. Days rolled by and again I was transferred from Lucknow to Delhi as Additional Resident Commissioner after three months. It was not a good posting but on the brighter side, I rejoined my family. Moreover in this posting, I enjoyed much leisure as there was virtually no workload. There were four Additional Resident Commissioners and hardly one or two files would come. All of us would jump to grab the file. Life was peaceful with little interference whatsoever. My spiritual practice continued with full intensity. On January 30, Martyr's day, the fateful day which witnessed the fall of the Father of the Nation at the hands of an assassin's bullet, at 11 am all of us gathered at R.C.'s room to observe silence for two minutes. I was in a somber and reflective mood. I could clearly see the sky from where I was standing. While observing silence, I prayed for the continued guidance of Gandhiji and suddenly I saw flashes of light in the distant sky. I observed not once, but three to four times. Maybe, my prayer was answered.

We were staying in Noida. On February 1, 1997, during our morning walk at the Jamuna riverfront park that day Sarita and I got into an argument. She complained about the cancellation of our programme to visit our friends at the last moment, on account of mood fluctuation, saying that would be considered as an insult to them. She was of the opinion that even if the mood was off, one had to respect the commitment. I was of the opinion that it was better to tell the truth than to spoil the atmosphere by sending negative vibes. As an example, I said, 'We have invited Mr Himanshu Joshi and his family for dinner tonight. If he or any member of his family falls ill, how can we expect him to still come simply because he has accepted our invitation?' The argument was getting a bit hot. So I ended it by saying that since both of us had strong views, let us not discuss it further. I went to the office and came back home in the evening when my wife informed me that the dinner was cancelled as Mr Joshi's son had suddenly fallen ill and was admitted to AIIMS. Slowly and gradually, I realise that the closer one gets to the cosmic spirit, the better one anticipates the future.

I took leave and went to Kolkata on April 12 to meet my elder brother Gama Dada. He came to the railway station to receive us. We went to his residence at Garden Reach. It was a beautiful flat (on the ninth floor) near the river Hoogli and the Botanical Garden was on the other side. The beautiful location of the house, the cool breeze of the Bay of Bengal and the Botanical Garden – all combined had a chastening effect on my spirit. Gama Dada and Sudha Bhabi took special care of me. On April 14, Gama Dada and I went to Dakshineswar and Belur Math. We meditated in the meditation Hall of Belur Math, where Gama Dada had a vision of 'Sai Baba'. Gama Dada also took me to the National Botanical Garden. We enjoyed walking through the garden.

We saw the great Banyan Tree, occupying a few acres. While coming back, I was attracted by a sweet smell. When I proceeded in that direction, I found a number of trees bearing the Shivling flowers. It was a beautiful pinkish colour flower with a small Shiva Linga and multi-hooded serpent. The whole place was filled with its fragrance.

I returned from Kolkata and resumed my routine. Overall life was peaceful. But not for long. On May 20, it was discovered that Chavi had a cyst in her stomach. We were worried and I literally cried. This child had already undergone three operations. Many tests were carried out. We were keeping our fingers crossed and hoped everything would be all right.

More than three months had elapsed, during which I faced my worst personal crisis. We spent half of May 1997 and the whole of June, 1997 in finding out the correct diagnosis of Chavi's problem. We consulted Kailash Hospital, Safdarjung, AIIMS, Apollo, Pant and Anand Hospitals. A large number of specialists were consulted in the hope that somebody would find out a solution without any operation. Almost every specialist recommended surgery. Mentally we were preparing ourselves for the operation and we did Puja in Hardwar, Puri, Vindhyachal and Tirupati for the well-being of Chavi.

Dr Arun Kumar, Surgical Specialist of Apollo Hospitals, was to operate through laproscope. Dr Arun Kumar, was a Professor in London and was a specialist in this field. We could not forget the help rendered by Dr Atul Kaushik who by chance met me in Kailash Hospital, when one night my wife and I were waiting for our driver. It was a strange coincidence. Dr Atul was a highly spiritual person and we clicked. From that day onwards he has been like my younger brother. He ran around and did everything to tie up the operation.

In consultation with Dr Arun Kumar, Dr Kaushik and Dr Mahesh Sharma, initially July 2 was fixed for the operation. Later, it was shifted to July 7. Everything was set for the operation. On that day I went for a morning walk to Jamuna Riverfront Garden and collected Dhatura flowers and fruits which were dear to Lord Shiva. I worshipped with all my devotion for the well-being of Chavi. We went to Kailash Hospital at about 9.30 am. Look at the strange coincidence; it was a Monday i.e. Shiva's Day, the Hospital was Kailash and owner of the Hospital was Dr Mahesh!

Many friends and well-wishers thronged the Hospital. Chavi was not at all nervous and put up a brave face. When she was being taken to the operation theatre in a wheelchair, she waved at us. We wished her all the best, but my heart was gripped by fear of the unknown. The operation started at about 11.30 am and by 1.30 pm, it was over. The cyst and its fluids were taken out successfully. We all heaved a sigh of relief.

This happiness was shortlived. We, human beings claim to be the most intelligent species in this universe, little realizing that we do not know what will happen the next moment. We had consulted a number of institutions and many specialists for two months before choosing the best doctor, then went ahead with the operation, with the hope that there would not be any complication. But something else was in store. Chavi could not pass stool for 3-4 days and she was refusing to take even liquid food. She was not taking anything. If we forced it, she would vomit it immediately. On the third day after the operation, I could sense something was wrong. I told my wife that Chavi might face the same situation, she faced when she was hardly one year old. My wife rejected my apprehension. But my fears came true.

July 11 was the fateful day. Chavi had grown very weak and was unable to speak. On that day her result was declared and she stood third in Delhi University in 1st year Hons in Sociology. I gave this news to her in the evening and she was happy. I returned home, did my evening Puja and meditation. I was preparing to have dinner when at about 9 pm, my wife rang me up from Kailash Hospital to inform me that a tragic thing had happened. Chavi's intestine had burst again. My head started reeling and I felt as if I was sinking. Within minutes, I controlled myself and prayed to God to give me strength and courage to face the situation.

I rushed to the hospital. Everybody was in panic, including the doctors. Dr Arun Prasad was not in town; he had gone to Ranchi. His absence complicated the situation further. No doctor in Kailash Hospital was willing to handle the case. We were advised to shift her to AIIMS immediately. It was 11 pm. We were all nervous. There was no point shifting to AIIMS without making proper arrangements. We desperately tried to contact Dr Arun Prasad in Ranchi. At long last, he came on the line. He advised us not to go for operation in a hurry as nothing serious would happen in the next 48 hours. The doctor told us that it would be better to leave the case to nature to handle and in all probability between 2-4 weeks, nature would automatically heal it. Dr Arun Prasad came back the next day. A few tests were conducted. Since there was no distention of stomach and no fever and since there was bowel movement, he went for the conservative method of treatment by nature. This was entirely a new concept for all of us, including many doctors. Initially, I was skeptical but we had no other alternative. Simultaneously, we also went for Cosmic Therapy, Mahamrityunjaya Japa and Rudravishek. Prayers were offered at Puri Jaganath Temple, Rudra Bhawani of Athmallik (presiding deities of our house), Kali Temple of Garden Reach, Kolkata, Mana Kameswar Temple of Agra and Vindhya Vasini Temple of Vindhyachal. I was overwhelmed by the cooperation I received from the Noida public, Kailash Hospital, especially from Dr Mahesh Sharma, my friends, brothers and relatives. Everybody was eager to help. I informed my in-laws and brothers and they came the same night. My mother-in-law and brother-in-law Prem immediately rushed from Kanpur by road. They reached Noida at about 10 am. The presence of relatives and friends, the cooperation of Noidites and the hospital staff enabled us to tide over the crisis.

It was a nightmare for all of us and a traumatic experience for the child. We had to maintain vigil round the clock. She was on intravenous drip for a considerable time. The Total Parental Nutrients (TPN) was very costly. Every hour she required dressing. It was impossible for us to sleep at night. It was a terrible sight to see Chavi. Her wide expressive eyes begged for mercy. Her expression so touching that it unnerved me.

During this period of crisis, I relied entirely on God and spiritualism. I used to recite Mahamrityunjaya Mantra for hours and offered water oblation to the Sun by chanting seventy of his other names. I always prayed for Chavi's life and good health. I dreamt of my father and mother who gave abhayadan about Chavi. All my prayers and spiritual efforts did not go in vain. In fact my daughter made a miraculous recovery, just when Dr Arun Prasad was planning for further operation. After two weeks of drips, she was put on oral feeding of Recaepex, a medically advised nutrient diet. But the discharge through the leakage was much more than 500 ML. One day, it touched 1500 ML. Dr Arun Prasad was nervous and advised surgery in a day or two. The next day Chavi was to be operated again. During the day when I was resting after lunch, I felt as if, rays of pink colour were emerging from my eyes and were passing over Chavi's stomach. That night at meditation, I literally cried and begged God to come to the rescue of his devotee. The next morning, surprisingly, the discharge had come down drastically to 500 ML from 1500 ML. It was a dramatic improvement and the operation was postponed on doctor's advice. The next day, I got a call from Mr C.B Sathpathy, my friend, guide and a Yogi. He advised me to meet him on Saturday at Sai Temple, Chattarpur area of Delhi. I met him at the appointed time i.e. 5 pm. He blessed me and told me that nothing untoward would happen to Chavi and she would be all right soon. We also put a Rudraksha Mala around Chavi's neck to aid her speedy recovery. She recovered very fast from August 1 onwards. By August 7, the discharge was reduced to 5 ML. So nature had done its job wonderfully. Chavi was discharged from hospital on August 7 and came to our residence. Though she was reduced to a skeleton, I could see a gleam in her eyes. Her big expressive eyes indicated her great happiness. The tortuous moment had finally come to an end. The leakage completely stopped within two to three days. She was slowly coming back to normalcy and started taking solid food from August 25. She attended college two days later. She also realized during the crisis that there was a superior force which controlled everything. She was a changed person.

Chavi's illness had been one of the worst moments of my life. During this one month I learnt a good deal about life. I got an opportunity to save the child, I realized both the utility and futility of the body. I practically experienced the maxim 'Man proposes and God disposes'. It also taught me to have tremendous patience and trust in God. During the period, in my meditation and Puja, I used to have a frank dialaogue with God. I prayed, I quarreled, I argued and I begged for mercy. I felt relaxed and confident after such a session with the Great Cosmic Spirit. He is merciful. He listened to my sincere prayer. The crisis made me more spiritual and a more ardent believer. Often I wondered at my posting as Additional Resident Commissioner, UP in Delhi having very little work. But the crisis made me realize that the planning made to post me on a lighter job was absolutely justified and was in my interest as I was able to devote more time during my daughter's illness. It is better to accept life as it comes instead of cribbing about it. Life frowns at those who always complain about it. Life smiles at those who take life as it comes. Life salutes those who make others happy in life.

Every evening I used to recite the Gayatri and Mahamrityuntjaya mantras. During deep meditation, I used to hear sound of the anklet. Flashes of light occurred and I could see a circle of yellow light changing into white. It appeared as if the white circle was consistently coming out of the yellow circle of light and vice versa. The rush of energy had been a common experience. One night, quite early in the morning I felt that I was travelling in the sky along with some saintly person. I was showing my annoyance with people on the earth as they were not leading a life of principles and honesty. Suddenly I felt as if I was losing consciousness and my prana was leaving the body. I woke up with a start and found myself gasping for breath. I called my wife and when she came closer I felt reassured. I do not know why such an experience happened at all. Is it because too of much chanting of the mantras or does it reflect a weak body and weak mind? Is it a spiritual experience or just a dream?

Chapter 27

Divisional Commissioner, Meerut

(October 1997 – January 1998)

Deeds speak louder than words. Do your duty
sincerely without hankering for publicity or recognition.

I was transferred from the post of Additional Resident
Commissioner, UP, as Commissioner, Meerut Division and took
over the charge on October 3. I worked here for a brief period.
The role of the Divisional Commissioner is not merely to act as a
bridge between the DM and the Government but to ensure proper
implementation of the schemes in the Districts under his jurisdiction
through regular monitoring and by guiding the DMs, but it does not
mean that the Commissioner has to poke his nose into every affair. I
never interfered, but whenever I felt that something was going wrong
or slow I used to caution them. During review meetings, I used to
encourage the DMs and the Divisional level officers to come up with
novel ideas. The idea of implementing Rural Employment Guarantee
Programme to improve the Gram Sabha land and land of small and
marginal farmers were all suggested this way. Works were also taken
up for improvement and renovation of Pandaveswar Mahadev area
and the huge pond near the temple complex of Pratap Pura. The
Chief Minister was particular about the Commissioner's monitoring
meeting and every divisional and district level officer, including the
District Magistrate and the Commissioner, was instructed to keep a
daily diary of the work done. The officers were on tenterhooks. In

one such review meeting, the Zonal Chief Engineer claimed that all the potholes of Meerut-Bagpat Road had been completely filled up. To verify this, immediately after lunch, I took him and proceeded on that road. To my utter surprise, the road was as bad as before. I glared at the engineer. He apologised and asked for one week to complete the task. I warned him that if he failed to achieve the result, he would be placed under suspension. He assured me and completed the job on time. What is more important in administration is not to create an atmosphere of terror but to achieve the intended result.

I will narrate here a meeting with two Cabinet Ministers of the State. They had descended from Lucknow and were staying at the Meerut Circuit House. The District Magistrate came and requested me to meet the Ministers so that his position would be strengthened. I agreed and in the evening, he escorted me to the Circuit House and I was waiting in the drawing room. When the Ministers came, the District Magistrate introduced me to them whom I already knew during my earlier tenure in Agra. During my posting there, I had taken strict action against them. When they saw me, they were embarrassed and immediately said to the DM, 'We all know him from before.' I was embarrassed too. After tea, I retreated quickly from the Circuit House.

During my tenure here, I was assigned the task of inquiring into the firing incident in Muzaffarnagar District resulting in death of a few persons. Muzaffarnagar was not under my jurisdiction but nevertheless, the Government directed me to enquire into the episode. I did it within 15 days and submitted a detailed 500-page report. I observed that the incident was highly politicized and exploited for political gain.

One day, a journalist from Noida complained to me that the Yamuna riverfront area was dotted with illegal farm houses. Along with the journalist I made an incognito trip to the concerned area. Thereafter, I called the District Magistrate and the ADM and directed them to take suitable action. Within a few days, these structures were demolished. The next day, while I was going to office, the media persons congratulated me for the action taken and wanted a brief on it. Instead of taking credit, I feigned ignorance and asked them to meet the DM and the CEO, Noida to get a complete picture. Deliberately, I took such a stand to avoid unnecessary complications and publicity. Anonymity, impartiality and integrity are the hallmarks of a good civil servant and I scrupulously adhered to these ideals throughout my career. I believe in the maxim that deeds speak louder than words. Do your duty sincerely without hankering for publicity or recognition. I always believe in Bhagwat Gita's philosophy कर्मण्येवाधिकारस्ते मा फलेषु कदाचन (do your duty without any expectations).

I stayed in the Circuit House of Meerut for two months. While there, I was not very regular in meditation, as the atmosphere was not conducive but I did regularly chant Lord Shiva's mantra. One night in November, 1997, I woke up with a jolt, after hearing the hissing sound of a snake. I thought as if a great snake was hissing near my head. In fact, it was early morning. I thought it to be a hallucination. But early next morning, I had the same experience. My doubt about the hallunication was over. In fact it was an out and out a spiritual experience with a cool breeze flowing out of my head.

During my short spell here, I had the good fortune of visiting Sardhana, Bilkeswar Mahadev, Pandabeswar Mahadev, Pura Mahadev and Jambu Dweep temples. The Sardhana Church of Begum Sumuru is world famous for its architecture and sculpture. It is said that sincere prayers are invariably answered here. When I entered the sanctum sanctorum of Mother Mary and Jesus, I experienced tremendous vibration. Whenever I visit this church I find myself feeling elevated.

Bilkeswar Mahadev temple is an old shrine. The legend is that Mandodari, wife of Ravana, used to worship Bilkeswar Mahadev. Pandaveswar Mahadev is situated in Hastinapur in an isolated place, uncared for a long time. I visited this temple three times and each time I experienced vibrations. I was dismayed at the pathetic condition of this temple and directed the DM of Meerut to beautify this place so that it could regain some of its lost glory. I believe, it was done by the DM to some extent. Pura Mahadev temple is another famous temple of Bagpat District. It is said that this temple was established by Parasuram. I visited this temple twice and felt spiritually charged. On December 27, we went to Saharanpur to visit Maa Sakambari Devi. It is situated at a distance of 40 km from Saharanpur at the foothills of the Shivalik. While coming down the steps of the temple, a woman in her 80's, known as Mataji, called me and blessed me. I felt as if Maa Sakambari Devi herself was kind enough to shower her love and affection.

Chapter 28

....✄

Managing Director, National Co-operative Development Corporation, New Delhi

(January 1998 – January 2003)

Early in the morning, I felt as if somebody was waking me up with a sweet touch of her hand. I woke up, turned left and saw a lady gradually changing into Goddess Vindhya Vasini.

Though my stay in Meerut was very short I enjoyed every moment of it. I got an inkling from the Resident Commissioner and Chief Secretary at the end of November, 1997 that my name was being considered for the post of Managing Director, National Co-operative Development Corporation (NCDC). On December 31, 1997 I received a call from Mr Kamal Pande, Secretary, Agriculture, Government of India, that finally I had been selected for the post. I was neither happy nor unhappy. However, I felt that probably I would be relieved in March, 1998 after the election. But the Election Commission was kind enough to permit me to join the Government of India. As a result, I relinquished my charge on January 14, and took over as MD, NCDC on January 15, 1998.

I considered this one of the most important assignments in my career. Though a low profile organization, it is an important institution in the field of cooperative development. The approach of NCDC is thoroughly professional and it has an international standing. Its main objective is to finance various activities of the co-operative societies. When I took over, right from the beginning, I had a feeling that there was a lot of factionalism among its officers, particularly among the old guard and the young officers. I counseled both groups to consider themselves as important members of the family of NCDC. I cajoled them, persuaded them and at times reprimanded them. These untiring efforts resulted in resolving issues between the officers and I succeeded in forging a united force.

During my five-year tenure there, many initiatives were taken and the NCDC came out with many new schemes. Promotions of officers had not taken place for years and as a result there was frustration. I took up the cause and succeeded in ensuring promotions to various posts which had been lying vacant for long. The officers were happy and I enjoyed their co-operation. A lot of reforms took place on the basis of the recommendations of the J.N.L. Srivastava Committee. Pilot project schemes had been formulated to strengthen co-operative societies at the grassroots level. Guidelines were prepared for direct financing. One-time settlement of overdues was taken up seriously and to a large extent, the problem was solved. An integrated Co-operative Development Programme was formulated. A lot of welfare measures for the families of the staff were taken in the form of scholarship to meritorious students of the staff, loans for computers and appreciation letters for bright students. A scheme for National Award for good co-operative societies was also formulated. I headed the Central Delegation to Arunachal Pradesh, Karnataka, Orissa, Rajasthan and Jammu and Kashmir to assess the damage caused by natural disasters. The experience gained during these visits immensely enriched my experience in handling natural disasters. During my visit to Jammu and Kashmir, the Central delegation got tight security measures. When I was taking a meeting of farmers in an open field near Poonch, I heard loud sounds of fire in quick succession. The army officer who was also present came to me and said, 'Sir, the

Pakistanis from the other side of the river had started firing mortar. If you wish, we can cancel the meeting and go back.' I told him, 'Well I don't find any sign of fear on the face of the farmers present here. So I should not run away from this place bringing disrepute to the civilian authority as well as to the Government of India.' I insisted on continuing. I took the meeting, listened to their grievances and then after field inspection concluded the meeting.

During this time the profits of the organization went up manifold, from Rs 20 crores to about Rs 100 crores per annum. Likewise, the turnover also increased. In one of the official parties, the then Finance Secretary, who belonged to my cadre, advised me that NCDC should not be dependent on Government resources and grant for financing its activities. I assured him that I would make sincere efforts to achieve this objective. My team of officers and me, guided by Mr JNL Srivastava, Secretary, Agriculture, Government of India, held many brain-storming sessions to thrash out detailed guidelines for NCDC for direct financing. I am happy to note that the NCDC is no longer dependent on the Government for financing its activities.

As MD of NCDC, I was also Chairman of Indian Potash Limited. It deals with potash and other micro nutrients. It is a peculiar organization which is neither Government nor co-operative in character. It abides by almost all the guidelines of the Government and is in close liaison with Ministries of Fertilizer and Agriculture but at the same time pursues its own policy as there is not a single penny invested by the Government in this organization. When I took charge I observed that it had a cumulative loss of Rs 60 crores. At the first meeting of the Board, I told the Managing Director that I would not interfere in their day-to-day functioning. At the end of the day, the bottom line was that he must ensure a profit. I scrupulously followed this principle and had the greatest satisfaction that by the time I demitted office it had not only wiped out the entire loss but accumulated a cumulative profit of about Rs 65 crores. This had been made possible by following a transparent policy, extending all support to the sincere efforts of the MD and by following a policy of non-interference. When the tenure of the MD was over, the Board of Management again selected the same MD as his performance was far better but the Ministry of Fertilizer thought that it was their prerogative to select the MD. The Minister called for the file and as Chairman of Indian Potash Limited, I strongly wrote that the Ministry had no locus standi in the matter as not a single penny of the Government was invested in this organization. Moreover, the MD was quite efficient and his performance appreciable. Good sense prevailed and the Ministry refrained from interfering in the decision of the Board.

The NCDC has been the mother of many good institutions like IPL, IFFCO, KRIBHCO and other co-operative enterprises. As a result, its MD is associated with the activities of these organizations. For six months I also acted as MD, NAFED. As NCDC had earned a good reputation internationally I was elected as Chairman of Network for the Development of Agricultural Cooperatives for the Asia-Pacific Region (NEDAC) with headquarters in Bangkok. It was an NGO floated by the FAO. After my three-year tenure, I was again elected as working Chairman for another two years to manage the affairs of NEDAC. That gave me good exposure to the co-operative activities in the Asian region.

My tenure was dotted with many memorable instances. A few days after I joined, the Financial Adviser came with a proposal for a car allowance for me. I was surprised and declined the offer as I was using the staff car. It had been my experience that often subordinate officers try to test the integrity of the boss. One must be extremely careful about such games.

The Union Agriculture Minister was the President of NCDC Council. When the Minister took charge, I got a message from his APS that the Minister's residence must be fully furnished and air-conditioned and renovated at the earliest by the NCDC. This was the responsibility of the CPWD and not of NCDC. It also entailed an approximate expenditure of about Rs 25 lakhs. I had some reservations and reverted to the PS to the Minister with the request that he must talk to the Minister. The Minister had a good reputation. Within hours, the PS came back and said, 'Sir, the Minister was very annoyed with the APS. His instructions are clear. The CPWD will do it as per their rules and the barest minimum as per rule can be incurred by the NCDC if at all they are required.' Thus a slight alertness on my part as well as my frank conversation with the PS saved the situation. Very often even if we have reservations about the proposal, we do not give proper advice. As a result many bad decisions are taken which are not in the interest of the administration. Free, frank, fearless and selfless advice by the bureaucrats helps in making an informed decision.

In one of the AGMs of NCDC, some Members complained to the Minister that the MD was a miser and deliberately kept the meeting at 3.30 pm so that he did not have to provide them lunch. Further at the General Body meeting, the MD used to provide only a note-book and pencil and not gifts like wrist watches. The Minister laughed and said, 'Mishraji, once in a blue moon, provide a lunch or a dinner to the Members.' But he was terribly annoyed with the suggestion of valuable gifts. He shouted 'Mr Mishra is doing a fine job and he is absolutely justified in providing a note-book and a pencil. You don't require more than this to participate in the AGM. It is a crime to waste money on valuable gifts.'

The Minister of State for Agriculture was the Chairman of the Board of Management of NCDC. Every important decision of investment was taken at the Board's meeting after detailed discussion. In one of the proposals for investment in sugar co-operatives, the Board decided to call for additional information. When the minutes were put up, the Chairman said, 'Mishraji, the minutes may be changed to reflect that the Chairman is authorized to take a decision in this matter.' I was surprised because such a decision was not taken at the Board's meeting. I pointed this out and advised him that if such uncalled for changes were made, there would be complaints in future and we may land in trouble and face CBI enquiries. He didn't insist on the changes.

I also worked as MD, NAFED for six months. At that time the onion crisis was brewing up and I was asked by Secretary, Agriculture to submit a report about the export of onions. I studied the matter and my considered view was that onions should not be exported as it would complicate the domestic situation. The Additional Secretary, Agriculture, who was looking into the matter, called me and tried to be rude. He was not satisfied with my recommendation and said, 'On what basis have you recommended against onion exports?' I said, 'Sir, I have analysed everything in the report and I have nothing more to say. It is for the Government to take a decision and I am not going to change my report.' I believe the export was allowed only for a brief period but when the crisis deepened it was forthwith stopped.

The Government of India took a decision to observe October 31, the birthday of Sardar Vallabhbhai Patel, as National Vigilance Day. A national seminar was to be held and the Secretary asked me to write a paper on 'Corruption' for presentation. I was thrilled as the topic was dear to me. I wrote an article on corruption and steps to counter them and submitted it to the Secretary for approval. In the paper I had made many unconventionnal suggestions. The Secretary said, 'Mishra, it is a beautiful paper but it is written in a journalistic language. There are many things which are unpalatable. If this paper goes as such then my head will roll. Therefore, you make certain changes.' I refused to do that as it was an interference with my freedom of expression. Then he said, 'Well, I need not circulate your paper at the seminar but you can speak at the seminar. Readily I agreed and when in the seminar I presented my views, it was well appreciated and they demanded a copy of my paper. The Secretary was looking at me and I was looking at the Secretary. It was an embarrassing situation. The seminar ended and I sent my article to Mr N. Vithal, Chief Vigilance Commissioner. He wrote back, 'I have gone through your article which contains many unconventional suggestions. I will keep these in mind.'

I visited many countries during my tenures in the Government of India, namely the Soviet Union, Thailand, the Phillipines, China, Japan, Australia, New Zealand, Portugal, France, the U.A.E, Canada, Kenya, Zimbabwe, the Kingdom of Lesotho and Western Samoa. These visits were highly educative and I must specifically mention the visit to China. I went there twice and visited their Commune Enterprises. Though a communist country, China had taken steps quite early to reform the system with the economic principles of capitalism. We visited one of their farmer associations. During discussions, we came to know that the farmer association used to adopt an internationally and nationally famous company by inducting it as a member. It was the responsibility of this MNC to ensure proper delivery of seeds, fertilizers and other inputs for production of the desirable crop by the farmers who would produce as per specification of the company. The company took upon itself the responsibility of storage, processing and marketing of the products. It also established research and development laboratories (biotechnology) for development of agriculture on scientific lines. This was a unique experiment which had immensely benefited China. Forgetting our differences with the Chinese, we must learn from their experience and whatever is good must be adopted.

The annual profits of the NCDC had gone up tremendously and this encouraged my Deputy Managing Director, Executive Director and Financial Adviser to submit a proposal for thorough renovation and modernization of the office of NCDC, including the MD's room, costing about few crores so that it would look like a modern office of a multi-national company. I was amused. When they came in a group to press for the proposal, I narrated the story of Chanakya. He was the prime adviser to Samrat Chandragupta Maurya. Seleucus wanted to invade the Maurayan Empire, and sent his spy to collect information about the state of affairs of the empire. The spy came to Pataliputra and enquired from the people. The people praised Chandragupta Maurya and Chanakya. When the spy enquired about the residential address of Chanakya, they told the spy to go near the bank of the

Ganga where he lived. He came and saw only a thatched house and could not believe his eyes that the prime adviser of a powerful empire could stay in such a hut. Then he saw that a man, after taking his bath in the river, was coming towards the hut. He expressed his desire to meet Chanakya. The man after some time came and said that he was Chanakya. The spy was totally flabbergasted and impressed with the simplicity, honesty and frankness of Chanakya. He went back to Seleucus and advised him not to attack the country where the prime adviser was so simple, honest and straightforward and where the king invariably listened to his advice. Seleucus did not believe it and attacked the Mauryan Empire and was badly defeated. After hearing the story, the officers left my chamber. Again after a few days, they came to my chamber to know about the fate of the file. I said, 'I have already narrated the story of Chanakya. Hopefully, you have listened to it and learnt a lesson.' After this, they said, 'We understand it now,' and quietly left the chamber.

The shift from Meerut to Delhi brought about a decline in my spiritual practice. After the initial euphoria of the new post, my mood fluctuated from one extreme to another. Since I had to attend to my official work at 9.00 am, I used to skip my Puja. I became irregular in my spiritual practices as well as exercises. Naturally I had to suffer the consequences. Healthwise I felt weak. I felt as if my spiritual energy was sagging. The stability of my mind, acquired in the last seven years, gave way to depression, anger and frustration. I realized that it was futile to expect anything from anybody. It was a rat race wherein everybody was looking out for himself. What a strange world indeed! I always prayed God to give me sufficient strength to withstand the onslaught of the world. At times, I felt that some internal changes were taking place within. I became apprehensive about the state of my mind. Often I prayed, 'Oh God! Save me from such disaster. Give me sufficient strength to cope with the problems of life.'

To get some spiritual solace, I decided to celebrate Shivaratri at Herakhan. Alongwith Mr N.C. Sharma and my sahayak (helper)

Mahavir I went in a jeep to Herakhan on Februrary 24. It was raining continuously and was very cold too. We left Noida at about 6.15 am and reached Herakhan by 6 pm. The kuchha road to Herakhan (39 km) was not safe to travel. Anyway, with God in our mind and heart, we managed to reach the place by evening. It was still raining and the chowkidar was nowhere to be seen. It took us about an hour to locate him. Finally, we were comfortably lodged in the Inspection Bungalow. After evening oblation, we set out for the Shiva temple at about 7.30 pm. It was drizzling and quite dark. We reached the temple and enjoyed bhajan sandhya (evening of devotional songs). I was so engrossed and absorbed in Bhajan that I could not listen to a devotee who was offering 'Prasad'. In utter disgust, the devotee said, 'If you have to sleep then please sleep in your room.' I was startled and emerged from my deep absorption. After taking prasad, we came back to Inspection Bungalow.

There was nobody at the Inspection Bungalow to cook for us. So we had to be content with bread, butter and fruits. I slept in the suite on the ground floor. It was all dark. No electricity. Not even a candle and it was cold too. I slept and suddenly early in the morning, I felt as if somebody was waking me up with the sweet touch of her hand. I woke up, turned left and saw a lady gradually changing into Goddess Vindhya Vasini who spoke to me very softly and affectionately, 'Prashanta, I am always with you. Do not worry for anything.' Then the figure vanished. Tears came to my eyes and I realized that my trip had been more than fruitful.

On the morning of February 25, on Shivaratri Day, we did not have a single drop of water at the Inspection Bungalow. So we thought of bathing in the river Gola. Even though it was cold, a bath in the river was quite refreshing. We got ready for puja and went to the Shiva temple and worshipped Lord Shiva. Then we crossed the river to the other side and worshipped a chain of gods and goddesses there. It was the tapasthali of Baba Herakhan. We were touched by the simplicity and devotion of Baba Gaurahariji who was looking after the temples there. Generally nobody was allowed to enter the cave where Baba used to do his tapasya. However, Gaurhariji allowed me to enter the cave and advised me to sit for some time there. Like an obedient disciple, I complied. I entered the cave and so did Mahavir. We sat in meditation for 20 minutes. I emerged from the cave quite elated and composed. We left Herakhan at about 1.30 pm and reached Noida at about 11 pm.

After such a unique spiritual experience, suddenly I became sluggish and lost my zeal to pursue my practices in a rigorous way. It was indicative of the fact that I was gradually drifting away from the discipline and rigour of spiritualism. The stresses I faced every day were slowly piling up. So far I was able to control and channelize these strains, but with the passage of time I was no longer in a position to take these anymore. I turned to God, my protector, to save me from any impending disaster.

As my restlessness grew, my family and I decided to visit Mumbai, Shirdi, Pune, Nasik, Mahabaleswar and Goa to get some solace. On May 4 we visited Triambakeswar Shiv Linga that was a Jyotir Linga. Only here could one have a darshan of Brahma, Vishnu and Mahesh in the same Linga through a mirror. Thereafter, we proceeded to Shirdi and the next morning, visited Shirdi Sai temple and attended the morning Aarti. After darshan we set out for Pune. On the way, we made a detour to the famous 'Saturn temple' of Signapur. Women were not allowed to climb up this temple. They had to watch from a distance and this infuriated Chavi. I wore a saffron dhoti and with bare body climbed the steps of the temple. Since I had worn a Rudraksha mala, many women thought I was a panditji and handed over their puja materials to offer them to Saturn, which I gladly did. Often I wonder why we are so discriminatory in our attitude to women despite the fact that we adore them as goddesses. Whatever the reason, we cannot progress by depriving half the population of their due share in every field of socio-economic, political and cultural life. The problem lies in our attitudes and the reform and empowerment of girl child must start from the family itself. Mere celebration of International Women's Day and launching of some schemes to empower them are not going to help them in any way. We have to change our psyche and start from the family itself.

In July, 1998, I visited Ichal Karinji in Kohlapur to attend a National Workshop on Textiles, organised by the NCDC. During this visit, I had the good fortune of visiting important religious places like Narashingh Gadi – Dattatreya temple, Mahalaxmi temple of Kohlapur and Vitthal temple of Pandharpur. At Dattatreya temple, during puja, I experienced tremendous vibrations and started trembling. It is situated at the confluence of Krishna and Panch Ganga. In this temple, Khadauns (wooden slipper) of Dattatreya are worshipped. I also felt a unique surge of spiritual feeling while feeding the dogs with prasad. On another occasion, I visited Tirupati temple, Kalahasti temple and the famous Shiva temple of Chennai. All these visits made me spiritually charged.

During this period, one positive thing that happened was that I came out of my depressed mood. Sarita went to Kanpur on the eve of Rakhi Purnima and I, along with my daughter Runu, went to Lucknow on August 12 for her admission to the National Institute of Hotel Management. After much discussion, she had chosen this as her career. She had scored good marks in +2 Humanities and got admission in Lady Shriram College, for Political Science (Hons.). Meanwhile, she made into Hotel Management after an all-India written test and interview. After Runu's admission into the Institute of Hotel Management, Lucknow, we went to join Sarita in Kanpur on August 13. That night I felt overwhelmed with a rush of energy and felt that my heart had expanded so much that I could cover the entire world. It seemed as if my heart chakra had opened wide. For the first time in my life, I experienced such an intense feeling of love and compassion.

I came back to Delhi after a brief sojourn in Kanpur. It was October 5, and being a Saturday, I was at home. I was enjoying the soothing melody of bhajans. While doing so I was concentrating on the empty space in the worship room. I saw a circular spot of light pulsating from pale yellow to white light and then vice versa. After a minute or so, I saw a violet circular cloud of light emerging from my eyes and vanishing into the space. Soon the circular cloud of violet changed into green. I enjoyed this hide and seek game of the cosmic light. I had an exalted a sense of elation and ecstasy.

In today's system of families, I am unable to appreciate or understand how they work. It is more like a nuclear family where members pursue their interests in utter disregard of the emotions and requirements of the others. Traditional values are falling apart. Brought up in an atmosphere of traditional values, I was finding myself unable to cope up with the values of this so-called modern society. There is a rat race everywhere, in every field, and spiritual values have taken a backseat. But I am sure one day the society will realize the futility of materialism and good sense will prevail upon its members.

On January 24, 1999 my wife and I proceeded to Pushkar by road. At Ajmer en route we took a brief rest in a beautiful circuit house on a hillock overlooking the lake. It was just a stop-over but to my utter surprise, the representative of Ajmer Sharif requested me to visit the Dargah as it was the birthday of the Peer of Salim Chisti. It was one of the very few occasions during which Jannat Dwar (Swarg Dwar) is opened. We rushed to the Dargah where there was a never-ending stream of people. With much difficulty and police protection we passed through the Jannat Dwar and reached the Mazar. There was so much rush that we were nearly suffocated. Before the Mazar I prayed for realization of my true self. I also prayed for Chavi, Sushant and Runu. Within the premises, I bowed down before the Mazar of Baba Farid. While bowing down, I received several peacock feather swipes on my body from a fakir. This was supposed to be a blessing. From Ajmer Sharif, we drove straight to Pushkar Tirth where Brahma is worshipped. It is the only place in the country where there is a temple for Brahma. We visited Rangjee Temple and

Gaughat for puja and tarpan. Thereafter we went to Brahma Temple and a Shiva Temple in a cave within the premises. Then we came back to Delhi.

I had been in touch with the 'Brahma Kumari' Ashram for some time. I got an invitation first to go to a spiritual conference at their Mt. Abu Institute, which was to be held in first week of Febuary, 1999. I could not make it, as I was heading a Central Team to Rajasthan to assess the drought situation. An invitation came again on February 12 to attend a discourse on 'Shiva' at their Ashram in Delhi. I could not make it to that either. Another day after meditation when I was going through the book *Practical Meditation* published by the Brahma Kumaris, I received a call from the sister of Brahma Kumari Ashram inviting me to attend their function on October 14 at 6.00 pm. Again I missed it as I was proceeding to Bangkok that night. Such invitations were coming but to no avail. I did not consider all these as mere coincidences but I felt there was a design behind these happenings. In fact it materialized very soon when I attended one of their discourses in Delhi. I also visited the Gyan Sarovar of Brahma Kumaris at Mt. Abu.

In February, 1999, I went to Bangkok to attend the Executive meeting of NEDAC, an outfit of FAO. On February 17, along with the project officer of NEDAC, I went to see the great National Palace of Bangkok. Thousands of visitors from all over the globe throng the place. The palace area is vast and expansive and there are 15 to 20 temples and Buddhist shrines within the premises. The entire palace wall is dotted with paintings from the Ramayana. The king of Thailand is always named as Rama, like Rama I, Rama II etc. The most sacred temple here is the Emerald Buddha. My eyes dazzled at splendor, beauty and sanctity of the temple. I sat in meditation for some time and spontaneously started chanting 'Budham Saranam Gachhami' (Following Buddha's path). After spending a few days in Bangkok, I came back to Delhi.

The biting cold of Delhi did not permit me to do early morning meditation. This did not mean that I was not having any spiritual experiences. Some were a mere repetition of earlier ones like flashes of light, hissing sound, rush of energy etc. As years passed by, I felt a distinct difference; I no longer saw images of gods and goddesses. I could feel the movement of energy, flash of light or to be precise, twinkling of bright light. On a few occasions, I could feel as if I was flooded with bright light. I could, in hindsight, see a pattern of the movement of energy. The jerk started with the legs, long back (say in 1991). Then I started feeling the jerk of the energy on my genitals and navel portions. Thereafter I felt it in my chest and in the region of the throat. Later on the movement was transmitted from the throat to the head region (Brahma randhra). I felt as if the energy wave was dashing against the Brahma randhra. There was rhythmic movement of head from left to right and vice versa. I felt a cool breeze blowing on my face and head. When I discussed the matter with my wife during our morning walks, she interpreted that the movement of the energy had started from Muladhar Chakra and reached the Bisudha Chakra. Now the energy passing through the Ajna Chakra was opening the petal one by one of the Sahasrar. This interpretation by Sarita seems interesting.

When Chavi fell seriously ill in 1997, I was advised to worship Surya. This practice of offering water to the Sun god with chanting continued for many years. Whenever I used to have the glimpses of the Sun in the morning, I bowed down automatically, chanting the mantra. Slowly I noticed changes occurring within me. I observed that whenever after bath and puja, I offered water and flower to the Sun, I felt as if a current of energy was rushing to my head. In a funny dream I had at that time, I was visiting a holy place with my friends. We were walking by the side of a kund when suddenly I fell in and got sucked in by the current. I was afraid and started chanting Om Namah Shivay. The moment I started chanting the mantra, the direction of the current got reversed and I was brought back. I woke up and was much relieved.

When Chavi was critically ill after her operation, I promised to visit Shirdi and Kedarnath after her recovery. In May, 1998, we all went to Shirdi but somehow, I could not make it to Kedarnath. This materialized in May, 1999. My nephew Bikan, Mr N.C. Sharma and I proceeded to Hardwar from Delhi on April 24. It was a Monday and that happened to be Ganga Deshara day. We reached Hardwar at about 4.00 pm and stayed in a hotel at the outskirts. We all went to Daksheswar Shiva temple and Paradeswar Shiva temple. Then we proceeded towards Ganga ghat for the Aarti and a dip. Till that moment we did not realize that it was a Ganga Deshara in a Malmas which was considered to be auspicious. We stayed at Hardwar that day and the next day we all went to Chandi Devi by ropeway. It was a Tuesday, the Devi's Day. When I used to visit this place in 1992-92, there were only a few pilgrims. One had to walk. But after the installation of ropeways, people throng this place. There was a tremendous rush at the temple, but the priest recognized me and made arrangements for a special darshan. After visiting Anjani Mata temple and Hanuman temple, we came back to the base and stayed at Parmarth Niketan Ashram.

On May 26, I got up quite early and went for a stroll along the banks of the Ganga. I walked quite a distance and meditated for some time sitting on a rock. The feeling was ecstatic. In the evening, we attended the Aarti led by Swami Chidanand Saraswatiji. The whole atmosphere was spiritually charged and ecstatic. The next day we proceeded to Guptkashi and reached there by 5.00 pm. Guptakashi with its beautiful Mandakini valley looked so charming, that I felt as if I was in a dream world. One could see the panoramic view of the snowclad peaks. We stayed at Guptakashi Inspection Bungalow that night. On May 28 after breakfast we all started for Gaurikund at 8 am and reached it about 9 am. We started our trek towards Kedarnath from Gaurikund. I was extremely elated to trek to Kedarnath on the winding path along the Mandakini. It was a beautiful valley with lot of greenery and hill streams. It was a unique experience to meet people from the different parts of the country and from all walks of life, rich, poor, old and young and children. I was amazed at the will power of the elderly people, who were determined to walk upto Kedarnath, a difficult trek for 10 to 12 hours.

It was my third journey to Kedarnath but every time I felt as if it was my first journey. The Himalayas have so much to offer to mankind, its strength, its beauty, its soothing serenity, its spiritual vibration and above all the feeling of oneness with God. After walking for an hour, we rested in a small shop called Chatti where we had delicious tea. Here we met a group of elderly Rajasthani women and one of them asked me about Kedarnath and whether she would be able to make it. I assured her that, by the grace of God, she would be able to make it. She was a very happy and vibrant old woman and while leaving the shop, she blessed me and I felt as if Goddess Parvati had descended in that form.

We left the Chatti and continued to walk. After some time, I stumbled and fell. My nephew Bikan was worried, but fortunately, except for a minor bruise, nothing happened. It could have been a fatal accident if I had fallen on the other side of the narrow edge. I profusely thanked God. A great danger to my life was averted by this minor accident.

We went on and by 2 pm, reached Ram Bada where pilgrims would take food and rest. We had our lunch and rested for a while. Then it started to rain. We resumed our journey, with a plastic to cover body, when it stopped raining. After a while it started to rain heavily and we got completely drenched. I started to chant 'Om Namah Shivaya' all the way and by the grace of God, the fury of the rain and wind stopped. The trek from Ram Bada to Kedarnath was a steep and difficult one. We took the short cut. I was completely exhausted. I could feel that with age, my strength was sagging. However by sheer will power and trust in God, I made it. Just 2 km before the destination, I had a glimpse of Kedarnath temple. A feeling of elation and ecstacy came over me. I had exactly the same experience in 1993 when I first sighted the temple from this very spot.

We stayed at a guesthouse adjacent to the temple and rushed to the Mandir to have darshan of Kedarnathji, as the mandir was closing at 8 pm. We had a nice, comfortable darshan of Lord Shiva. We spent the night at Kedarnath. It was extremely cold and due to the altitude and rarified atmosphere, I had a terrible headache and occasionally some difficulty in breathing. With no desire for dinner. I just had soup and one puri. Bikan and I were staying in one room. We could not sleep comfortably due to the cold, headache and breathlessness. I slept for a few hours and again got up at 5 am. We took our bath and got ready by 6.30 am. We went inside the temple for a special darshan. We had a good darshan and puja. It was Shiva Chaturdashi, an auspicious day. We never planned for it. It just happened. It was all pre-ordained.

After darshan, I went to the Sankaracharya temple to pray. Very few people visit this temple which is behind the main temple. We forget the Adi Guru who had established the four Dhams for spiritual and national integration. We came back had breakfast and then started our journey to Gaurikund. It was an easy climb down. We spent the night at the Guptakashi Inspection Bungalow.

The next morning we left Guptakashi for Hardwar. On the way, we had lunch at Advaita Ashram, Lachmoli near Kirti Nagar. We worshipped all the 12 Jyotirlingas established in the premises of the Ashram. We reached Hardwar in the evening and stayed at BHEL's Guesthouse. On May 31 morning we left Hardwar and reached Delhi by 1 pm.

Nothing substantial happened in the meanwhile in the field of spiritual experience. I alternated too much between family life and ascetic life. In the present day family, every member and more so the younger generation thinks that he or she is completely independent of the other. They fail to realize that a harmonious, coordinated life is central to the health of the family and society. The disturbed atmosphere prevailing all around, the disrespect shown to elders and the cool relations that exist among members compelled me to have a fresh look at the wisdom of leading a social life. There was no point leading a miserable life. It was better to lead an ascetic life concentrating on self-realisation. I decided to give more attention to my spiritual life. I developed vairagya to a great extent and nearly decided to renounce the world. On that day, I slept in my worship room. Quite early in the morning, I got up and was prepared to leave the house without informing anybody. I went to the bath room and exactly at that time I had a look at the innocent face of my child Sushant who was sleeping beside his mother. That innocent face had a tremendous impact on me. I realised that, since I had accepted grihastha ashram (family life), it was my bounden duty to perform first, the responsibility of a parent in bringing up the kids to be nice human beings with good samskara. It would be criminal on my part to leave the family helpless at this juncture. Moreover, family is not a curse but an asset for the development of many qualities in a person, like patience, tolerance and respect for each other's views, harmony, trustworthiness, discipline and sacrifice. I argued with myself that one could lead a saintly life even in grihastha ashrama. A house-holder who is leading an ascetic life amid all problems of the transitory world with a lot of temptation, is a much greater yogi than a person who has renounced the world. My mind changed and stability restored.

Long back in 1991, I had a desire to visit the Guruvayur temple in Kerala but it took me almost a decade to fulfil this. On August 2, 1999, I went to Thiruvananthapuram to take a review meeting of the NCDC schemes. I stayed at Ashoka Hotel on the Kovalam beach. The hotel is located on a beautiful spot with Arabian Sea lashing at its very foundation. The next morning, I got up at 6 am and went to sit in the balcony for a grand view of the sea. The moment I concentrated on waves and sound, it created a magical effect in no time. I got a tremendous vibe and my whole body started trembling.

On August 5, I drove down to Guruvayur and reached the place by about 6.30 pm. Dressed in just a dhoti and angavastra, I went to the temple. This is the famous Krishna temple of South India and according to local legend, after pralaya and the beginning of a new era, a floating idol of Krishna was fished out of the sea by a fisherman. He took it to the king who in turn built a temple for the idol of Krishna. When I entered the temple, it was time for Aarti. I sat down on the floor and started chanting 'Hare Krishna, Hare Krishna;' immediately I had a tremendous vibration. After the Aarti, the idol of Krishna was taken in a procession on an elephant with the crowd following it. I also joined the procession and completed the Parikarma. It was a nice experience. The visit to Guruvayur temple created a deep impact on the revival of my waning spiritualism. The road to self-discovery is really a long one to be traversed with patience, faith and conviction.

I had a great desire to see the Kamakshi Temple at Kanchipuram and to pay obeisance to the Sankaracharya of Kamakoti Peetham. After attending a state-level meeting with Secretaries of the Tamil Nadu Government on August 18, 1999, I proceeded to Kanchipuram the next afternoon. I met the Sankaracharya. I did not know that the next day, a Thursday, was a very auspicious day, the Guru's day. I was charmed by the tranquil face of the Sankaracharya and his disarming smile. He explained his vision of re-entry into the villages by ensuring all round development in an integrated manner. He advised me to visit the Dakshina Murthy Shiva, the first Guru of the cosmic world, as that was an auspicious day. I went to Govindpur Village (10 km) to worship Shiva. Dakshina Murthy is the presiding deity for learning, concentration, knowledge and spiritualism. In the evening I met a young dynamic saint who was to succeed the Sankaracharya. When I asked him to explain as to where the Samadhi of Adi Sankara was situated, he replied that the Adi Guru was in Samadhi in Kedarnath for a long period and when he emerged, he de-materialized himself, came to the Kanchipuram Meenakshi Temple, then materialized himself and disappeared into the deity. On the morning of August 20 I went to Kamakshi Temple to worship the Mother. It is a magnificent, spacious temple and the Deity is powerful and beautiful.

The day September 3, a Friday, was Janmastami day, the birthday of Lord Krishna. It is a very auspicious day and I was in an elevated mood listening to the devotional music. And at midnight, along with Sarita and Sushant I worshipped Lord Krishna with Aarti and the blowing of the conch. At night I listened to mantras and slokas of Rama and Krishna and did not know when I slept in the worship room itself. At 4 am, suddenly in a semi-conscious state, I found that Mother Kali was taking a round of me. I was terrified and did not know what it signified. Two days later, September 5, was election day in Delhi. In the morning at 8 am, Sarita, Chavi, Runu and I went and cast our votes. At about 4.00 pm there was a great storm with thunder and showers and I was apprehensive that this might disrupt the election process. I prayed with chanting of 'Om Namah Shivaya' to stop it and to enable the people to exercise their right. Lord Shiva seemed to have listened to my prayer and the rain stopped soon.

I would like to mention another interesting experience of mine during meditation. One morning, while in meditation after some time Adi Sankaracharya appeared before my mind's eye. At first he touched his danda on my head and then rays from his right hand pierced my heart. My whole body trembled and after sometime this became unbearable. I was feeling suffocated but when I opened my eyes everything became normal.

The super cyclone of the century hit Odisha in the last week of October, 1999 (October 27 to 29) and ravaged it completely. On October 29, my friend Rajesh Sharma and his wife, Suman, had come to our house at night. We were discussing the Odisha cyclone and the trail of devastation it had left behind. I told him then that I would consider myself fortunate if my services were requisitioned for relief operations. It seems God listened to my prayer because at 11:30 pm the same day, I got a call from my Secretary to fly to Calcutta the next day morning with a mandate to establish a base there for relief operations. I flew to Calcutta the next morning. It was a daunting and challenging task and I was a bit apprehensive about the success of air dropping food packets. But Providence helped me; from 10,000 food packets, the Secretary increased the target to one lakh food packets to be air dropped every day. Help started pouring in from every quarter and even reluctant institutions fell in line. The target was huge and the logistic and supporting institutions were meagre. I was tense and apprehensive. But God's design was different. He planned it in such a way that the networking with different institutions took place in no time.

Mr Pabitra Mohan Rana Vainsha, Deputy GM of Ordnance Factory, whom I had not met since 1965, though he belongs to my village, rang up my brother Gama Dada with whom I was staying in Calcutta. From my elder brother, he came to know about my presence there. When I knew that he was the Deputy GM of the Ordnance Factory, I seized the opportunity as godsent and requested him to help me. He immediately agreed to supply 50,000 packets every day. On his advice, I talked to his Chairman who readily agreed. The Additional Director General, Ordnance Factory, Ms Chaturvedi, who was in charge of supplying the food packets, turned out to be the sister of an IAS officer of the UP cadre who was a friend. Oxfam who helped us a lot, was under the charge of my brother-in-law, Mr Sanjay Awasthi. Hindustan Lever's management person at Calcutta turned out to be the friend of my nephew Srijit Mishra, Marketing Manager in Hindustan Lever, Mumbai. My elder brother Mr P.C. Mishra (IRTS) was a senior Railway Officer. And so there was no problem from the Railways. The Air Force officer from Barakpur Air Force base turned out to be an Oriya and thus the network was complete. The operation of air dropping of food packets went on smoothly. We achieved more than the target and I had tremendous satisfaction in handling this sensitive job. This effort was greatly appreciated by the Board of Management and General Council of NCDC which passed a resolution to this effect. I was overwhelmed and realized that sincere efforts never go in vain. If the objective is clear, intention is noble and efforts are sincere then the Cosmic Force comes to our rescue to facilitate the completion of the task in an effortless manner and case.

When my father-in-law died on December 14, 1999, Sarita and I immediately left for Kanpur by Magadh Express which left Delhi at 8 pm. At 11 pm suddenly I experienced a strong smell which was quite soothing and refreshing. A similar experience had happened in train when my mother died in August, 1987. I failed to reason out how and why this was happening. May be the departed soul visited us at that particular moment. Since the soul is pure and immortal, it brings fragrance by its very presence. Often I have experienced sparkling light during meditation. Once I observed that pinkish and bluish lights were revolving in my forehead. I had also started seeing the bio-energy field of plants more clearly and distinctly.

I had a great desire to visit the Nathdwara temple in Rajasthan and got the opportunity on January 20, 2000. I flew to Udaipur where my Regional Director, NCDC received me. After breakfast, we reached Nathdwara by noon. Generally the temple used to close by 1 pm but unfortunately for me, it was closed by noon that day. For a long time, I had the desire to see Nathdwara, but when the occasion came, I missed the opportunity. But I was determined to visit this temple again. I made an elaborate plan during December, 2001 when my entire family proceeded to Nathdwara on LTC. We stayed at Nathdwara so that we could not miss the darshan. The next morning after bath, we immediately rushed to the temple and had a good darshan of Lord Krishna. A similar incident had occurred to me when as a young Director, I visited Mysore. I made a plan to visit Chaumundi hills. When I reached there, I found the temple closed. The next year again I made an attempt but met with the same fate. In 1991 when I proceeded on LTC with my family to Bangalore and Mysore, I did not have any plan to visit Chaumundi Devi. While leaving Mysore, I saw the hills from a distance and was tempted suddenly to worship Chaumundi Devi with my family. I made a slight detour and when I reached the temple, I found that it was an auspious occasion and we worshipped to our satisfaction. I believe in the principle that man proposes and God disposes. We can plan it out meticulously and make sincere effort to achieve it but the ultimate result depends on so many imponderable factors. Our responsibility is to perform our duties in the most efficient, sincere and honest manner without aspiring for any fruit. This is a very difficult proposition. But nonetheless such a philosophy gives us sufficient strength to meet the challenges of life.

I tried my best to devote as much time possible to puja, meditation, bhajan, pranayam and the study of spiritual books. On February 11, 2000 at 4.30 am during meditation, after 20 minutes, I could observe rays of different colour emerging from my forehead in circles. After travelling some distance, these circles were reduced to a point. It was quite a nice experience where rays emanating from an individual were merged into a point in the cosmos. I experienced this for a few minutes. Thereafter, I observed a small circular illuminated ray at a distance of two to three feet and I was receiving a barrage of rays from this spherical light. The light was never stable; sometimes it moved up, sometimes down and sometimes sideways. I tried to analyse the experience and was not certain about my inferences. Probably in the first instance the individual energy rose up to merge with the cosmic energy and in the second instance, the cosmic energy was coming down to recharge the individual. It is like ascent and descent of energy.

I was spending most of my leisure time in bhajan, meditation and pranayam and study of spiritual books. On the night of February 5, 2000, I listened to devotional music and cried during meditation. I went to bed in the puja room. I had two peculiar experiences the next early morning. I experienced in my sleep that while meditating, I was levitating and soared in the sky for quite some time with my hand in a blessing posture. It is generally believed that such experiences indicate spiritual progress. Peculiar things were happening. I had the experience of contraction of limbs starting down below from the legs. I had also experiences of expansion during meditation. I had the feeling of growing taller with the head extending to the sky. At night and early morning my head used to move vigorously and energy waves hit my brahmarandhra with a thud. One early morning, I was watching the expansive blue sky and suddenly I saw a flash of blue light like a flying saucer and found my mother, clad in a white sari, sitting in my worship room. I saw her like in a dream many years after her death. Once I dreamt that I had gone to a Shiva and Shakti Temple and there was much rush. I was getting a bit nervous. And exactly at that time, a man with a beard came and blessed me. I pondered over it and tried to fathom who that man was. Suddenly it came to my mind, that it must have been Sai Samarath.

One day, I got an invitation from Mr C.B. Sathpathy, E.D, Vigilance, Indian Oil Corporation, to address their senior executives on 'Personal Excellence of Managers through Value Systems.' It was a godsent opportunity to spread the message of the Divine. It was a subject dear to me and I addressed the gathering for three hours. There was pindrop silence and I felt as if Maa Saraswati was inspiring me to talk continuously without a break. The officers said that they had never been exposed to such an excellent value-based topic. A few commented that the whole thing was coming out from the core of my heart. Some others felt that after this lecture, they would be forced to introspect and rethink about their attitude to work and life. I profusely thanked the Great Cosmic Force without whose blessings this would not have been possible.

I was finding some changes occurring silently within me. In the first week of May 2000, one day my wife and I were relaxing in the balcony after our morning walk. Suddenly the sky got dark, wind started blowing with speed and it started raining. My mood got elevated and established a communion with nature. I listened to the music of the wind, the melodious sound produced by the leaves and the rain drops and suddenly I realized that the whole atmosphere was dancing with ecstacy. I prayed with folded hands to Mother Nature, 'Maa, continue to be kind to your ignorant children who do not understand your magnanimity and generosity. Maa, please forgive them for their unhappy acts and give them sat-buddhi' (wisdom).

I have now realized that the principle of give and take operates even in this world. If we receive anything, we have to give it back to him or to somebody else either in this life or in future life. Giving is much more enduring and satisfying than taking. Try your best to give as much as you can and if you receive anything from anybody, try to return it in some form or other to the original gifter or to the needy people. I have also experienced that when I give something, it comes back to me in no time. Accumulation should not be the motive. When one sincerely tries to help others by giving something, it comes back to you in multiples so that more such good works can be done.

I have always had a desire to retreat to the Himalayas. This time, we planned to go to Rudranath. Towards the end of May, 2000, Mr N.C. Sharma and my nephew Bikan went to Hardwar and stayed at Shantikunj for three days. It is a well reputed beautiful ashram founded by Acharya Shri Ram Sharma. The spiritual atmosphere of ashram, the discipline among its followers and the efficient management charmed us all. The simple food offered was tasty. The food in the canteen was cheap; Dosa cost Rs 4/-, Idli Rs 2/- and Jalebi Rs 25/- per kg. The next day, we went to worship Daksheswar Shiva Linga at Kankhal. After a bath in the holy Ganga, I requested Sharmaji to find out whether there was any ancient Shiva or Shakti temple nearby. When they enquired from a sadhu, he replied in a philosophical tone, 'Bacha abhi lagta hai, man sthir nahi huwa hai. Jahan man sthir hota hai, wahin baith jao. Bhatakna zaruri nahi hai.' (Child, it seems you are not at peace yet. Wherever you find peace, settle down there. No point wandering around aimlessly). In a few words, he had explained the entire philosophy of life. We visited Paradeswar Shiva Linga and Brahma Bacharswa i.e. a research institute of Brahma Vidya of Shanti Kunj. We also enjoyed the Ganga Aarti in the evening at Har-ki-Pauri. I had experienced this Aarti many times but each time it felt new and refreshing. On the third day, we went to Chandi Devi by ropeway. Long back, I drew an outline for the development of Chandi Devi Area and I was happy that slowly and gradually, the dream was coming true. Our stay in Shantikunj was comfortable; the food was nice, especially the bonda and jalebi. Mr N.C. Sharma was an interesting person with a lot of spiritual experiences. His anecdotes and lively comments often kept us entertained. When I commented that probably we had come here only to eat, he immediately replied that food was essential to calm down the Jathara Agni (fire element of the belly). Taking food is a Yagna. His presence and sense of humour made the atmosphere lively.

On June 1, 2000 in our onward journey towards Rudranath, we had lunch at Advait Ashram, Lachmolli and spent the night in Rudraprayag at Hotel Monal. The hotel was situated by the side of the river and down below there was an ancient Shiva temple established by Saint Machendranath. We prayed and the Linga was beautifully decorated with Kaner flowers. There was a Baba reading scriptures. We talked to him for half an hour and during the discussion, he gave us some important information about Rudranath.

Mr Semwal had made arrangements for us in Monal. He had instructed Mr Bist, owner of the Hotel, to take us to Koteswar Shiva temple inside the cave. On the morning of June 2 we got ready and decided to have breakfast in the market. At that time, we had no intention of visiting Koteswar cave Shiva temple. We had just come out of the hotel and suddenly Mr Bist appeared from nowhere and insisted that we should accompany him to the temple. We tried our best to avoid him but he came to the main road and showed us the Cave temple on the other side of the river. When we looked at the cave from a distance, it looked so attractive and beautiful that at once we changed our mind and decided to visit the temple. There were hundreds of Shiva Lingas inside the temple. One yogi also took Jal Samadhi in the river at this spot. We came back to the hotel and I reflected over the incident. I came to the conclusion that whatever had to happen, would happen. We tried our best to avoid going to the cave but ultimately fate so ordained otherwise.

We reached Gopeswar by evening and the young District Magistrate of Chamoli called on me at the Inspection Bungalow. We had a hot cup of refreshing tea and I enquired about the journey to Rudranath. He explained that the journey was treacherous with no chatti or human beings on the way. The climb was steep. This advice was quite helpful in our journey. After tea, we went to Bairangana and stayed there for the night in the Inspection Bungalow of the Fishery Department. Bairangana is a beautiful place with streams flowing down with a musical note. On June 3 after a quick breakfast, we started our journey to Rudranath at 7 am. The initial few hours of trekking was quite enjoyable but slowly it became tougher. The climb was steep with lot of lichens on the way. We had rubbed our legs up to the knee joint with mustard oil and salt to save ourselves from their attack. We walked on and on but not a single soul was to be seen, not a single village. There was no proper trekking path either. We had to find our way over leaves and boulders. It made the trekking still more difficult. At about 4.30 pm, we had our lunch of puri, achar and chola.

When we were eating lunch, suddenly a black dog appeared from nowhere. I thought, it was Bhairava Devata (the wandering form of Lord Shiva also known as the Guard of the cardinal points) who had come in the form of a dog. The dog behaved in the most civilized manner and in my mind, I thought, I should worship Bhairava in the form of the black dog. It seemed as if the dog read my mind and came and sat down quietly before me on his hind two legs and the front two legs raised. I bowed down before the dog and thereafter it left the place coolly. It was a strange experience indeed.

It was getting dark and raining. After eleven hours of climbing we had covered just half the way. So we took the decision to spend the night somewhere on the way. We could spot a small army outpost at Panhor managed by a Subedar who called himself the Commanding Officer of the post. He was an interesting character and he proclaimed that we could not enter the makeshift room without his permission. I understood the situation and told him it was he who was to grant us permission. He felt flattered. The army personnel only recognize the DM and Commissioner from the civilian side. I revealed my identity that I was an IAS officer of the Commissioner rank and the other two were of the rank of Deputy Commissioner. After hearing the name of Commissioner, he came to his senses and said that he had not received any such programme of the Commissioner. I explained that originally we were not scheduled to stay here, but inclement weather and circumstances had forced us to spend the night here. I said that we were completely at his mercy. He melted, took our names and addresses and talked to Joshimath on a wireless set for the necessary permission. Then he allowed us to enter the room. This sensitive outpost was manned only by four persons who were from different parts of the country. The Subedar was from UP, the second one was from Rajasthan, the third one from the South and the fourth from the hills. It was truly national integration. The Subedar offered me non-vegetarian dishes and drinks which I politely declined. So he quipped, 'Aap sub ka maza kirkira kar denge' (You will spoil everyone's mood). He was extremely nice and treated us with roti, dal, rice, veg and kheer. They offered us their cots and slept on the ground. The Subedar offered his airtight cubicle to me. The cook in order to please and flatter the Subedar Saheb told me that I was very fortunate to sleep on the cot of the Commanding Officer. I marveled at their attitude and ability to enjoy life even in the most inhospitable terrain.

The next morning, I got up quite early. It was difficult to wash in ice-cold water. The hands became numb. After tea and parantha for breakfast, we set on the onward journey to Rudranath at 8 am. It was a climb up and up all the way. We managed with gram, salt and lemon. We came across a valley that was extremely beautiful with lush fields and snow-clad hills. The different colours of Burans (rhododendron) flowers added to the beauty to the atmosphere which was full of fragrance. We rested for a while on the grass and when we got up we found our bodies exuding fragrance. Every leaf, every blade of grass and every flower here emits that aroma. The water of the stream was pure mineral water.

On the way, was a spot where we have to place a few stones on the hillocks for the ancestors. The place is called 'Pitrudhar'. Placing stones in the shape of a house, it is believed, satisfies the ancestor. It is like the 'Pinda Dana' in Gaya, Allahabad, Varanasi or Hardwar. After Pitrudhar, the climb was a bit easy. The valley was beautiful, full of fragrance and carpeted with lustrous grass called 'Bugyal'. We did have a bit lashing hill rains and subsequent cold. By 3.30 pm, we reached Rudranath. The priest Shri Prayag Dutt Bhatt of Gopeswar welcomed us and lodged us comfortably in a thatched house. Rudranath is situated at a height of 13000 ft. There was no facility for the yatris except for three thatched houses. The Himalayan view from here was magnificent. The natural beauty of Sri Rudranath is serene and sublime emitting celestial bliss. The priest treated us with bread, pure ghee and dal. We were very hungry and relished the simple food. The dal was delicious and when I enquired why, the priest replied that wild plants resembling garlic plants were added to the dal.

We went for the evening Aarti. The self-emerged Linga of Shiva was inside a cave. There were ancient idols and cave-temples all around the main cave temple. Shiva here is in Raudra Roop (incarnation of Anger). The legend is that when Sati sacrificed her life in Daksha's yajna kund, Shiva was meditating in Rudranath. The news was relayed to him by Narad Muni. Shiva got wild and he pulled out one of his locks and threw it over the mountain and Veerbhadra appeared to destroy Daksha's yajna. The Linga was so decorated that it looked very fierce.

The night descended and we lay down on the kuchcha floor covered with wild grass and blanket. I experienced breathing trouble at night due to high altitude. I could not sleep properly. In the morning, when we woke up, we were stiff with the cold and could not dare attempt a bath in the ice-cold water of the stream. We just sprinkled water on our heads as a symbolic bath. We worshipped Narad Muni with wild flowers and then climbed up with much difficulty.

We got ready for the morning puja and went to the cave temple. The purohit, dressed in his traditional robe appeared on time. It was a Nirvana Aarti i.e. the ornaments was taken out one by one till the Linga was exposed. It looked calm and serene in Nirvan Darshan. It was again decorated with much pomp and ceremony. The decorated Shiv Linga looked fearful. Legend says that the temple was built by the Pandavas. The morning Aarti was quite refreshing and elevated our mood. I enjoyed it thoroughly. In fact, Rudra Bhawani is the presiding deity of our family and Bikan and I were the only members from the Mishra family to see Rudra Bhawani in its original place in the Himalayas. We were quite fortunate that way.

After breakfast we started our return journey to the base camp at Bairagana. I did not want to leave the place. The long dangerous journey drained out our impurities and we became Nirvikaras (pure), as N.C. Sharma quipped. He also commented that Narad Muni must be under great stress due to pollution by pilgrims around his Temple. We walked through lashing rain and reached Panahar Army Outpost where the Subedar Saheb was ready with lunch. I was touched by the gestures of our soldiers.

We resumed our return journey even though the rains continued. The path was slippery due to leaves and rain. We walked down slowly maintaining our balance with the help of sticks. I stumbled half a dozen times, but the stick helped me keep my balance. By about 6.30 pm, we reached a flat area, where we took rest and were offered a hot glass of milk from a nearby home. Then we resumed our journey. The last leg, though short, seemed to be never ending. It was getting dark and increasingly difficult to walk. Though we had three torches, we were afraid of wild animals. At 8 pm, Dr Purohit arrived with a gas-light and more torches and helped us find our path. At the bend we spotted two tigers crossing the road. We reached the Bairangana Inspection Bungalow finally at 9.30 pm. Thus, an arduous but nonetheless exciting journey was over. It left an indelible impact on my mind. It cleansed me thoroughly and elevated me to a great extent.

In August, 2000, I went back to Kanchipuram and visited Shankaracharya's Experimental School. Established by the Math, it is a unique experiment of imparting modern knowledge and ancient wisdom, Western science and Indian spiritualism. I was impressed by the students. They started their day at 4.30 am with puja and chanting of mantras. Then they go for yogic practices. During the day, they attend classes where all modern subjects are taught, including computer. The evening is devoted to Vedic yajna and puja. I was impressed by this unique experiment of combining Western scientific methods with our spiritualism.

I visited Kanyakumari first in April, 1991 and then again in September, 2000. It was a unique experience to offer puja to Devi Kanyakumari whose nose ring shines brilliantly at night. I also visited the Vivekananda rock and Adi Kanya Tapasya Sthal. I wondered how the Swami swam across through the waves and reached this rock where he meditated. In January, 2001 while heading a Central team to assess the cyclonic damage to Pondicherry, I also visited Sri Aurobindo Ashram and Auroville International City. While going round the Samadhi of Sri Aurobindo and the Mother, I cried and felt the presence of a tremendous energy. During the same visit while leaving for Karaikal, on the way I offered prayer to Lord Nataraj at Chidambaram and Lord Vaitheeswaran. At Vaitheeswaran temple, I also worshipped Mars and Jatayu. Legend has it that Jatayu died here fighting Ravana and Lord Rama did the cremation here. It is also believed that praying at Vaitheeswaran can cure many diseases. In the evening, I visited the Velankanni Church. The statue of Mother Mary with child Jesus in her lap was enchanting. A tidal wave of emotion overtook me and I sobbed. It is often called the Church of Miracles.

On 20th January, 2001 we visited Thirunallar Saturn Temple. The common belief is that whosoever visits Darbeswar Mahadev and Lord Saturn, will not be tortured by Saturn. Instead he will get a lot of blessings for prosperity and progress. Here we also got the darshan of Marakat Shiva Linga. It is believed that it is worth crores of rupees. We also saw the golden crow, the vehicle of Lord Saturn and enjoyed the morning prasadam. Visits to such places, provided me peace and tranquility and I felt myself recharged. One night, I was experiencing tremendous energy and flashes of light. Quite early in the morning Lord Shiva appeared before me in a dream. He grew so tall that I was reduced to the size of a dwarf.

Summer was approaching and I was restlessly waiting for my trip to the Himalayas. Since, 1993, I had made it a regular habit of visiting the Himalayas in the last week of May or early June. Shri N.C. Sharma, C.S. Semwal and my nephew Bikan were my spiritual companions during this trip. In 2001, we planned to go to Kalpeswarnath and Badrinath. Out of the five Kedars, I had already covered Kedarnath, Tunganath, Madhmeswar and Rudranath. The last was Kalpeswarnath. So this time we decided to complete our Panchkedar trip by visiting Kalpeswarnath. We left Delhi on June 2 in the morning and reached Shivanand Ashram, Muni-ki-reti towards the evening. We went straight to meet Swami Premanandji. My association with him has been since 1979 when I was posted in Tehri Garhwal. He was happy to see us and spent time talking to us for two hours. He entertained us with cold drinks, sweets, namkin and with spiritual discourses. He presented us spiritual books and literature. He was a humorous person and all his talks were punctuated with anecdotes. He said, 'I am the Chairman of my institution' but then he immediately remarked, 'There is only man and no chair.' The sum total of his discussions was, 'Have faith in God, do your duty sincerely and accept things as they come.' On June 3, we left for Heleng, the base camp of Kalpeswar. From there, we had to climb about 15 km to reach the destination. At 10.30 pm we reached Durgam Devastham Gaon where we spent the night. The next morning, after a bath in the natural stream nearby we continued trekking and reached Kalpeswar within 40 minutes. It is a cave temple situated near a river. The holy Hiranyavati flows near the cave of Sri Kalpeshwarnath as if it is creating a holy bath for the Lord. Legend has it that Indra brought Kalpataru (the wish fulfilling tree) here and hence the name. Another legend says the Sage Durvasa did a severe penance sitting under this Kalpataru and was blessed with wish fulfilling powers. Yet another legend has it that Lord Shiva resides here and fulfils the wishes of the people who perform severe penance.

Lord Kalpeswar represents the Jata of Lord Shiva. We went inside the cave and did our puja. There was no pujari (priest). But nonetheless, I had tremendous vibrations. As a group, we chanted and worshipped the Lord. I rang the bells and the whole atmosphere was enlivened. It appeared as if the stage was being readied for Shiva's tandav nritya. Just as we were exiting the cave, an old Bengali saint came in and made us perform the puja and Aarti again. After puja, he gave us tea and ashes. It was said that this saint had been living here for more than 50 years. He advised us to go to Badrinath because after the yatra of Panch Kedars, one must visit Badrinath. We had already planned to go there, even though we did not know this age-old tradition. As God ordained, so it happened.

At Badrinath, we were lodged in the Hotel of Garhwal Mandal Vikas Nigam. In the evening after we freshened up, we rushed to the temple for a darshan of 'Badri Vishal'. Lord Badrinath was in his decorated sringar adored by Garuda, Kubera, Narada and Nara and Narayan. We came back to the hotel through the street which was dotted with shops of many kinds and glittering lights. We had dinner and went to bed immediately. Early next morning I did meditation and witnessed a tremendous vision of light. Thanks to Dharmadhikari, we had the good fortune of attending the early morning puja of Lord Badrinath. It was a unique experience to witness the elaborate ceremony of God Badri Vishal. I had a bath in the hot spring of Taptakund. Here ice-cold water and hot water exist side by side! I also visited Manna, the last village of India at the border, Vyas Guffa, Bheem Pool and the Saraswati river.

I have visited Badrinath many times. It has always had an irresistible attraction within me. My wife and I again visited Badrinath in 2012 when I was Member, UPSC. After having darshan and worship, we trekked to Manna village. We were tired. Suddenly, a tremendous desire overtook me to visit Alka glacier (Vasudhara), the source of Alaknanda. My wife refused to accompany me, but I continued my journey with Mr Semwal and his brother Sarveswar. After crossing one glacier, we were exhausted but had covered only half the distance. We were just discussing about discontinuing the journey when exactly at that moment, an old sanyasi, who had overheard our discussions, commented, 'Sons, the body is perishable but if you have the will you can make it. I am also going to Alka glacier and I will wait for you.' And I thought, 'If the old sanyasi can do it, we can also make it.' We resumed our onward journey and with difficulty manage to reach the place. We did not find the old Sadhu there but we did find a Sanskrit Professor who had come all the way from the South to have a glimpse of this glacier. Look at God's design and grace. The chanting by the professor at the glacier reverberated in the serene atmosphere. The site was beautiful and the chanting of the mantras made it more spiritual. While returning, it was getting dark and we were lashed by rain and snow. My knees were hurting and my legs were faltering. Mr Semwal's brother helped me throughout the return journey. It was a painful journey but I still enjoyed it and the next morning, with the permission of the 'Rawal' (head priest), we had the good fortune of worshipping the original source of the hot water gushing out of a hole and creating a pool in Narad Kund.

Life was going on as usual. Bikan, my nephew who had been a constant companion in my spiritual journeys left Delhi on June 21, 2001 to take up his new assignment in Chennai. The night before he left, I explained to him, the nuances of administration for an hour. His departure left an emptiness in my heart. I was bit sad for a day or two. Life evolves such a mechanism that one learns to adjust to any situation. Our life was moving placidly but suddenly we found ourselves in turbulent waters. Sushant, studying in Class VIII, fell seriously ill with the Guillain Barre Syndrome. We consulted Mahindra Nursing Home (Delhi), Kailash Hospital (Noida), Apollo Hospital, Pant Hospital, AIIMS and NIMHANS (Bangalore). The specialists identified the syndrome, a virus which affects the nerves of the body. The patient recovers slowly and gradually. It was our good fortune that Sushant was affected mildly. But still he faced a lot of difficulties in performance of normal activities. Sushant took it in a positive way and boldly. The tremendous support he received from his classmates and friends enabled him to weather out the crisis. Practically there was no medicine for it; only good food, rest, vitamins and physiotherapy. After consultation with Dr Madhuri Behari of AIIMS, we started physiotherapy from May 12, 2001 at Dr Bela Sethi's Physiotherapy Centre in South Delhi. He was also undergoing acupressure under the care of Mrs Bhati, wife of a colleague. The physiotherapy did wonders and there was tremendous improvement in Sushant's health.

Sushant's illness had driven us more and more to spiritualism and worship. My wife was regularly chanting Hanuman Chalisa and I was doing meditation and mental recitation of Mahamrityunjaya and Gayatri Mantras. After chanting Mahamrityunjaya Mantra for two months, I could feel a lot of heat being generated. In the first week of April I went to Vindhyachal for a darshan of Maa Vindya Vasini Devi. I covered the Trikona i.e. Vindya Vasini, Kailkho and Ashtabhuja, praying at each spot. I met Nara Hari Baba who used to come to Ashtabhuja during Navaratra only. Before going to Ashtabhuja Temple, I sat for sometime with Baba. He enquired, 'ghar mein sabkuch theek hai na?' (Is everything fine at home). I replied, 'Theek hai' (Everything is fine). When I begged his permission to visit the temple, he again enquired about the health of the family and I replied again the same way. After worshipping Ashtabhuja Devi, I came back to Baba and again he enquired sab kuch theek-thaak hai na? I wondered, why he was repeating this question. Tears welled up and I narrated about Sushant's illness. He remained silent for some time and said, 'He will be all right by July'. He gave me some bibhuti (ash) to apply on Sushant. His comforting words gave me a lot of solace. I preformed a havan in Vindyachal and Shiva puja in Rameswarnath temple. The legend says that Rameswar Shiva Linga was established by Lord Rama. It is a Bhabya (captivating) Shiva Linga. It is huge in size and covered with silver. I also visited Tara Devi temple, Preta Shila, Motia Talab, Gerua Talab, Motia Talab's Shiva Linga and Hanuman temple. Few people visit Motia Talab, its Shiv Linga and statue of Hanumanji. In Mirzapur city, I visited Tarkeswar Nath and Pancha Mukhi Shiva Linga. I also visited Sankat Mochan Hanuman temple and Telengswami Shiva temple of Benaras. The whole Vindya region is full of spiritual vibration and I feel it whenever I come here.

This Vindhyachal trip was a great spiritual journey. It not only revived my old association with Mirzapur, it strengthened my spiritual belief and conviction to a great extent and provided me the required psychological, emotional and spiritual strength to face the crisis. On July 1, 2001 early morning, I saw my father in a dream. I was walking along with him. We approached a woman, resembling my wife, carrying a sick baby, my father lifted the baby and cured the baby of his ailments. Thereafter he started off. I followed him for some distance but he told me to turn back, worship him daily and then flew into the sky. It was exciting to see my father in a dream after so many years. The dream augured well for my son who started recovering very fast. God, the Almighty cannot tolerate the sufferings of his devotee for a long period. He has to intervene after some time to establish the fact that there is a supreme force which takes care of every creature, be small or big. I sincerely believe that as long as there is someone in the Cosmos to protect you, there is none on Earth who could harm you.

When Sushant's health problem was sorted out, we were happy, but this was short-lived as Chavi's abdominal problem started surfacing again. I did not know why it was happening to us. Maybe our past deeds were responsible for it. We cannot escape the consequences of Karma. Let us accept gracefully whatever comes in life. Past is history. Future is mystery. Present is in our hands. Let us live in the present and make the best of it. Oh God! Help us in our endeavour and have compassion for us. Be merciful, protect us from dangers and forgive us if we have committed any mistakes. We surrender unto you.

I have made it a habit to visit various holy places. I visited Kedarnath, Badrinath, Vindhyachal, Varanasi, Mathura, Vrindavan, Dwarka, Somnath, Panchkedar, four Dhams of the Himalayas and four Dhams of India, all Jyotrilingas except one, a number of Ashramas including Shantikunj, Shivanand Ashram, Vasistha Ashram and Ganeshpuri, Tirupati temple, Padmavati temple, Meenakshi temple, Kalahasti, Tapkeswar Mahadev of Dehradoon, Belur Math, Dakshneswar Mahakali, Vethur of Kanpur and many other holy places numbering over 250. Despite my disciplined life, from time to time I experience health problems. I have pondered over it, but could not come to any definite conclusion. Maybe, I am dissatisfied with social, organizational and family surroundings. Maybe I am the odd man out in the present society. Stress is accumulating into my system for a long period. Probably this is why I have taken recourse to meditation, bhajans and spiritualism. But my doctor had advised me to discontinue meditation and worship for some time. Meditation is often prescribed as an effective way to de-stress, whereas in my case, they advise me to leave it! I just could not leave meditation on doctor's advice, surely. What an advice to give! I am sure, there must be a way out, there is always light at the end of the tunnel. I know that I have the potentiality to move much faster on the path of spiritualism, but held back because of the worldly pull. Some day it will be over.

March 25 was a Monday and Muharram. I was relaxing as it was a holiday. At 9.45 am I got a telephonic message from the NCDC gate that a sadhu from Mirzapur was insisting on seeing me. On enquiry it was revealed that he was a disciple of Kali Kamali Baba and when I was District Magistrate, Mirzapur, I had met him in Ashtabhuja. I directed the guard to bring him in. The saint came at about 10.30 am. He went for a bath at the servant quarters and when he came back I met him in my drawing room. He was more than 80 years. He immediately embraced me and invoking Maa Vindya Vasani, blessed me and my family. He went on explaining the meaning of life and how creation was made. He said that 400 years ago I was born as a daughter in his family. He specifically came here to see that nothing untoward happened to me and my family and that there would be prosperity and health for us. He advised me to write in Red Ink 'Om Sad Guru Narayan, Narayan Swami' on five pieces of paper and paste them on the wall. He also whispered a mantra and advised me to whisper the same into my wife's ears. I brought some fruits which he worshipped with Ganga water and distributed them. He had his meal and at about 12.30 pm left my house. He did not accept even a penny. He had specifically come here to bless me after going to Lucknow and from there to Delhi. Indeed, it was quite surprising.

On March 27, 2002, Prof. Edward from Boston University, accompanied by Sister Sangeeta of Brahma Kumaris, came to NCDC to address our staff on spiritual techniques for relieving stress. When the Professor asked me about the NCDC, I replied that it dealt with co-operation which was the very basis of our existence. We are all born out of co-operation. We function efficiently due to co-operation of our vital limbs. Likewise society, nation and humanity each functions on the basis of co-operation. Even the entire cosmic world operates on this principle. Hearing this definition of co-operation, the Professor was surprised and said, 'We Americans are not human beings but working beings and need persons like you.' He delivered an interesting talk and we were quite impressed by his approach to release tension.

Somehow I have a feeling that I am protected by an invisible force. But for His help and blessings, I would not have been able to manage the relief operation mounted during the super cyclone in Odisha. I would not have been able to make a record achievement of sanction and release of funds. During my tenure ar NCDC the profit reached dizzying heights. The miraculous saving of Chavi's life twice and the speedy recovery of Sushant were also due to His grace.

As narrated, Vasistha Guffa is a great sidha place. Its call is irresistible and I have made countless visits and encountered interesting experiences here. During one visit after dinner and a chat with Swamiji, I retired to bed. I could see the Ganga from my room. I started to concentrate on the melodious sound of the flowing river. It must have been more than two hours when I started to hear many sounds and, in particular, a peculiar sound seemingly of an animal. I also heard a carpenter's hammering and sound of a bell. The image of Swami Purushottamanandji came to mind again and again. In the midst of all these experiences I did not know when I fell asleep. I got up at 4.45 am and meditated on the Ganga and the Himalayan range and felt as if mother Ganga was emerging from the water with the abhaya mudra to bless me. Tears welled up and I was choked with emotion for this great river. The Ganga is the creater, promoter and sustainer of our great civilization and if you remove this river, life will be drab and uninteresting. If you destroy the Ganga, you are destroying the country's spiritualism and that means the virtual death of India. It is time that we took urgent steps to restore the pristine glory of mother Ganga. Mere slogans and lip service will not do. A few schemes here and there to clean the Ganga will not make any dent. We need Bhagirath Paryathna (efforts) and we need a Bhagirath in every household.

We have made tremendous progress since 1947. But the pace of development could have been much faster and more qualitative. We failed in discipline, we failed in character and we failed in realizing our own 'Sanskriti' (culture). The political leadership has failed and more so the intelligentia. The blind imitation of Western culture and values has created a crisis, particularly for the young. We imitate the West only in their dress and their promiscuity. But we are not at all serious in cultivating their positive qualities like discipline, punctuality, hard work, scientific spirit and honesty. Modernity and progressiveness do not consist in aping the West. We do not hesitate to ridicule our culture, but forget that this culture has been a great one for thousands of years. In this respect I would rather be an Oriental Conservative rather than a superficial Occidental Westerner. The Westerners are now turning to our way of life, but we are eager to ape their way of life. 'I will open all the doors and windows of my house so that fresh air can come in from all directions, but I refuse to be blown off my feet,' said Gandhiji. Scientific spiritualism is the only answer to all ills of the world.

What a world it is! A world where innocents suffer, a world where honest and straight-forward people are humiliated and a world where corruption and selfishness thrive! In such a world, how can one have peace of mind? Whenever, I feel that I am at peace with myself and with my surroundings, suddenly something will happen to disturb my peace of mind. It has happened on many occasions and I have gone into a spin. But each such incident which disturbed my peace of my mind, taught me some lesson or the other, in the study of nature and character of human beings and the world in which we live. Each such occasion cleansed me and brought me closer to the Great Cosmic Spirit. This world is a great experimental churning place, a place of great learning and a place of leveling down. I am learning the nature of this world and the truth underlying it, in a hard way.

On our annual trip to Himalayas in 2002, we started for Yamunotri in the first week of June. The narrow path, the rain, the mud and the stink made the trek very uncomfortable. But the valley was beautiful. We reached Yamunotri at about noon. The sight of the Yamuna originating from Yamunotri glacier, with all its crystal clear bluish water, left an undelible impact. What a difference between the Yamuna at Delhi and the river at Yamunotri. Side by side with ice-cold water of Yamuna, we have the sulpher hot spring. In fact the Surya Shila, the source of the hot spring is the main attraction and everybody worships Surya Shila. We took a refreshing bath in the hot spring and did our puja at Surya Shila. Then we worshipped Mother Yamuna and Sankat Mochan Hanuman. The image of goddess Yamuna was really beautiful and automatically attracted the attention of the worshippers. It was a fantastic experience.

In July, 2002, accompanied by my wife, I went on an official visit to Indore. We stayed at a beautiful hotel. In the afternoon, we left for Ujjain Mahakal Temple. We were fortunate to get a good darshan of Mahakal. It was about 5 pm when the Aarti was scheduled for. I was allowed to enter the sanctum sanctorum of Mahakal. Sarita was asked to see it from a distance near Nandi. Sringar of Mahakal is really an art to be performed by an expert. It was a unique experience to witness the sringar of Mahakal. The whole place was vibrating with tremendous energy and I could feel it. I was there for about 45 minutes. After visiting Mahakal, we were advised to visit Kala Bhairava temple which was at a distance of 12 km from Ujjain. The tradition here is to worship Kala Bhairav with wine. The idol was really impressive and the wine just evaporated when a plateful was offered to the Deity. We were witness to it and we were just flabbergasted at this incident. Wine was offered as prasad. Since I was a teetotolar I was advised by the priest to touch it to my eyes. I did it and sprinkled a small droplet on my tongue. Look at the effect. I could feel the rush of energy in the tongue, mouth and palate. It was just like Khechadi Mudra. It continued for half an hour or so. Merely a droplet of wine as prasad would not have this effect. It was something else.

On the same trip we also went to Omkareswar. It was a four-hour drive through a winding, ghat road. We visited Omkareswar Shiva temple situated on the banks of the Narmada. It is said that the valley is in the shape of 'Om'. It was a pleasant experience to cross the river by boat to approach the temple. We had a good darshan and puja of Omkareswar Shiv Linga. Then we came back by boat and worshipped

Mamaleswar Shiva Linga. It is said that both are Jyotir Lingas and a visit to Omkareswar is incomplete without a visit to Mamaleswar Temple. On the morning of July 17, 2002, we went to Bhojpur to see a huge Shiva Linga of 21 feet supposed to have been worshipped by Raja Bhoj. The temple had collapsed and in its ruins, there is a resemblance to Konark. It is an archaeological monument. The place was serene, uncrowded and peaceful and left a calming effect on us. From Bhojpur, we went to a nearby place where we could see a big image of Lord Mahavir. It was a place of Jain Tirth. Thus, my desire to worship both Jyotir Lingas of Mahakal and Omkareswar was fulfilled during this trip.

Long back I read an article on Ramana Maharshi's ashram in the South and I had a tremendous desire to visit that place. That chance came on August 23, 2002 when I went to attend the General Body Meeting of IPL. After attending the meeting at Chennai, I went to Kanchipuram to meet Shankaracharya who blessed me with a smiling face saying 'My blessings are always with you'. He also said, 'I feel happy whenever you visit the Ashram'. These blessings elevated my spirit. We talked about development, character and the co-operative movement and welfare measures to be taken for the downtrodden. I gave him the idea of adoption of co-operatives by the Math so that they could be run efficiently. The Shankaracharya advised me to witness the Aarti of 'Sphatic Shiva Linga' of Adi Shankara. I felt blessed to have been able to witness this worship by the Shankaracharya. I fixed my gaze on the Linga for some time and suddenly I observed a circle of multi-coloured lights surrounding the Linga. I thought it was due to reflection of light. So I deliberately broke my concentration and then focused again. But I could not see the multi-coloured lights any more. How could you explain this experience; was it mere reflexation, or was it hallucination? Or was it a manifestation of the Linga in the form of light?

On the morning of August 24 we left for Thiruvannamalai and visited Ramana Ashram which was at the foothill of the Arunachal hills. It was a beautiful Ashram where serenity prevailed. I meditated for some time in the meditation hall as well as in the meditation room of Ramana Maharishi. Now it was time to go to the temple. The temple was huge with a large sprawling space extending to few kilometers. It is believed that Shiva Linga exists here in the form of Agni. It was in this Arunachal Hill that Shiva manifested as a great pillar of light whose top and bottom could not be fathomed. It was from here that creation started. A tremendous spiritual power overtook me and I lost myself in a reverie.

After dinner we embarked upon the 'Pradikshana' (circling round) of Arunachal Hill. Generally people do that on bare foot. It had just rained for half an hour and this was considered an auspicious sign. It was a parikarma of about 16 km. Bubbling with energy we ventured upon it barefoot. We started the journey at 8.30 pm all along discussing, gossiping and joking. There were 52 places to be seen during the parikarma and about 21 lingams. We did puja at a few important places and worshipped Agni Lingam, Kuber Lingam, Varuna Lingam and Aishanya Lingam etc.

It is said that many Siddhas are there in Arunachal Hill and appear in different forms during the journey. We came across more than half a dozen Yogis. On two to three occasions, I felt that they were Siddhas and messengers of God. On the way, we also saw a small snake crossing the road. The initial 7 to 8 km, we covered with enthusiasm. Thereafter, I started feeling pain in my sole. The pain started increasing at every step. But I started joking with them so that we might not feel the pain. I told them the Sai Baba story. Once the Guru of Sai Baba took him to a well, tied his legs and hung him upside down. After four hours, when the Guru asked Sai Baba how he felt, he replied, 'I am experiencing happiness beyond senses.' So jokingly, I said, 'We are also enjoying Atindriya sukha'. The last leg of the journey of 2 to 3 km was extremely painful and I felt as if I would fall down. Walking on the Lingam road was very painful. But with God in mind and accepting the pain as prasad of Arunachal Hill, we covered the distance in four and half hours. I returned to Delhi but my mind was still wandering in the Arunachal Hills. The journey to Kanchipuram and Arunachal Hills had a profound effect and I started feeling the presence of God in everything. A transformation was taking place within. I was having communion with the unknown force, may I term it as Cosmic Spirit. It is unknown in a sense that though it is our own swarup (self), we do not recognize it due to our ignorance. Once the dirt is removed, we may have instant interaction and communion with the ever resplendent spirit.

I read a book, *Divine Revelation* and inspired by it, started experimenting with the dynamic meditation concept described in it. On September 29, 2002 at about 4.30 am I started meditating and had tremendous vibrations. This continued for half an hour or so. Thereafter, I started gazing at the sky and stars continuously. Suddenly, I observed that a star twinkled brightly for fraction of a second and then disappeared. I thought it was a falling meteor. After a few seconds, I observed in a different place a star twinkling brightly for a few moments. At every pulsating of the star, I felt a tremendous sensation in my heart and crown. This happened four to five times and then it stopped. The next day, I tried again but nothing happened. I did not understand the reason for it. Maybe an invisible cosmic force was trying to guide me.

In November, 2002, I made a trip to Gangtok. This is a small, neat hill station with a population of less than one lakh. All hill towns look alike, and their problems, customs, and traditions and ways of life are all the same. On November 9 after breakfast, we went to Changu Lake, a sacred lake for the Sikkimese people situated at the height of 12400 ft. We took a round of the lake. After lunch I proceeded to the Rumtek Monastry, one of the largest Buddhist monasteries and learning centres in Asia. It came into prominence after the dispute over the property and the fleeing of a boy from China to India who claimed to be the Karmapa of Rumtek. The road to Rumtek was bad and it took us about an hour to reach it. It was a magnificent, beautiful monastery. I stood before the golden coloured statue of the Buddha and a tidal wave of spiritual feeling swept over me. Then we visited the site of ruins of 16 Karmapas and the chatra (rod) they used. I also visited the great Buddha statue at Gangtok. As legend goes, the statue is growing in height and as a result the roof of the room has had to be pierced to make way for it.

After returning from Gangtok, life was proceeding as usual. On the night of November 18, 2002, something strange happened. After dinner, Pinku, my nephew, and I were deep in discussion on the origin of the expanding universe, the concept of string and multi-universes. When I was talking about the relationship of mind and Universal Mind, intelligence and Super-Intelligence, consciousness and Universal Consciousness, suddenly I felt a tremendous rush of energy, originating from the base of the spine. I started gasping. It was out of control and to calm myself I started repeating, 'I am in control', 'I am in control'. The rush of energy subsided and after a while I became calm.

One evening while strolling with my wife I asked, 'Tell me Sarita, what is common between us?' She thought for a while but could not give any answer. I quipped, 'Morning and evening walks are common to both of us. Otherwise, we are poles apart.' She had a hearty laugh and said, 'We may differ on many things yet we have managed to create a nice family life for such a long period.' I pondered over the matter and found she was correct. Though we differ widely on many things, we believe and share the same core values, like truth, honesty, integrity, faithfulness, sense of justice, fair play and compassion. Every individual is unique and one should not expect entirely the same attitude, the same pattern of behaviour and response from the other person. One must respect each other's view point but the core values must remain the same. Otherwise family life will be ridden with dissent, disagreement and discord. The period from 1991-2003 was an important phase of my life because during this time I was at the peak of my spiritual practice. This phase was marked by intense spiritualism, study of spiritual books, visits to countless holy places, interaction with sadhus and saintly persons and ecstatic experiences. Marked charges in my personality, physical, mental, psychological and spiritual, did occur during this period and these brought out a sea-change in my attitude towards life, society and humanity at large.

Chapter 29

Principal Secretary, Bureau of Public Enterprises, Food & Civil Supplies and Commissioner, Welfare, UP

(April 2003 – January 2004)

Frequent transfer is a convenient weapon in the hands of the political masters not only to discipline bureaucrats but also to harass them so that they fall in line.

I came back to Lucknow after completing my Central deputation in March, 2003. The period between 2003 and 2013 was essentially one of more administrative experiences than spiritual ones. I held many posts. I worked as Principal Secretary, Bureau of Public Enterprises, UP for two months. During this time, nothing much was achieved except in two important matters i.e. (a) Transfer of assets and liability to Uttaranchal State Government with regard to UPSRTC and (b) up-dating the balance-sheets of PSUs and removing audit objections. When I took over, I found that the transfer of assets file was moving in circles for the last 2 to 3 years but nothing substantial happened except raising objections by the Secretariat babus. I took it as a challenge and convened a meeting of all concerned including Finance and Transport Departments and CMD, State Transport Corporations. After two to three meetings, we were able to sort out all the problems and the whole matter was over in one week. I have observed that the Secretariat, and more particularly the Finance

Department, is fond of raising objections and queries and that too in phases. It takes a lot of time as the file has to move up and down in the corridor of the Secretariat. It is my conviction that such procedures are dilatory and defeat the very purpose of the speedy decision-making process. After the initial round, it is always better to have meeting of the concerned Departments, including Finance and Planning, to sort out the problems and queries in one go.

In June, 2003, I was transferred as Principal Secretary, Food and Civil Supplies and worked for three months. During this period, I was primarily busy with procurement of foodgrains. Again in September, I was transferred as Principal Secretary and Commissioner, Welfare. It was a Department where good work could be done for the marginalized sections. I concentrated on effective implementation of the special component plan and formulated a scheme for physically challenged persons for their integration with the normal students. It can be observed that I received three transfer orders within nine months. I had the same experience when I was transferred frequently in 1995 and 1996. It is a common feature in the State that the Sword of Damocles (transfer in this case) is always hanging over the head of bureaucrats. Frequent transfer is a convenient weapon in the hands of the political masters not only to discipline the bureaucrats but also to make them fall in line. It is also a convenient mode of extracting concessions and favours in an illegal manner. Often it is alleged that transfer is an industry where no investment is required to earn money. Every State has a transfer policy but it is observed more in the breach than in observance. It is a tragedy that the political masters do not understand the disasterous effects of such transfers. It not only adversely affects the moral of the officer and the bureaucracy but at the same time jeopardizes the prospects of good planning, proper implementation and good governance. We must remember that corruption thrives due to bad governance and the only remedy is good governance. The sooner they realize it, the better.

Chapter 30

Additional Secretary (Defence), Govt. of India

(January 2004 – November 2004)

Don't confuse me as a body. I am a soul and I have unlimited power of access.

I was empanelled as Additional Secretary in the Government of India and waited for orders. In January, 2004, I received the order to join as Additional Secretary (Defence). I took charge on January 17, 2004. Since I didn't have any experience in this Ministry, initially I felt out of place but I accepted the challenge and went about in a professional manner, learning through meetings, briefings and presentation to get a grip of the functioning of the Ministry. Though my stay here was hardly for a year I learnt a good deal.

Interestingly, in other Ministries, the double file system is prevalent but in the Ministry of Defence, it is the single file system that prevails. At times, this creates difficulties and if anything is missing then it becomes difficult to retrieve it. During this period, I had the good experience of associating with preparations for the Republic Day parade and Independence Day celebrations. It was quite an uphill task but due to established practice, discipline and repeated rehearsals, these had always come out with flying colours. The Defence parties are a class apart. It is quite colourful, elaborate and enjoyable. Everything is arranged meticulously. The Defence personnel know how to celebrate and enjoy life even in the most arduous of circumstances and places.

My tenure here was hectic as every file seemed time-bound and urgent. I tried to give my best but on occasions I was at loggerheads with my Secretary. The Defence Secretary used to take review meetings every Monday. On one such occasion, he asked me to clear a particular file immediately. I had already recorded my reservations but when the Defence Secretary expressed his annoyance, I told him politely about my inability to proceed in this file further for reasons recorded in it. He was not happy with my statement.

On another occasion, he wanted me to get some information from the Ministry of Parliamentary Affairs on certain procedural matters. I talked to the Deputy Secretary as he was very thorough about these matters and got the information. In the evening when I met the Secretary he asked, 'From where did you get this information?' When I replied that I got these from the Deputy Secretary, Parliamentary Affairs, in a sarcastic tone he said, 'Do you have access to Deputy Secretary only?' I could understand this loaded statement. I replied, 'Sir don't confuse me with just a body. I am a soul and I have unlimited powers of access.' He was taken aback and didn't say anything.

An important meeting was to be held at the PMO to discuss the increase in FDI limit in the defence sector. The subject was not in my jurisdiction but the Secretary directed me to attend the meeting. When I went through the file, to my surprise, I found that there was no viewpoint of the Ministry of Defence with regard to increase in FDI in Defence Sector. So immediately I convened a meeting of the concerned Wings of the Ministry and at that meeting the view was to oppose it as it was fraught with danger and had serious implications. I recorded the views and personally took the file to Defence Secretary. He didn't give any direction. Time was running out and I had to attend the meeting. Unless I knew the exact viewpoint of the Ministry, how could I effectively participate? I could guess that the Secretary was not in a mood to give any direction. I immediately rushed to the Office of the Defence Minister and informed him about the meeting and wanted to know his view. When I explained the views that emerged from the meeting, he closed his eyes for a minute, and said, 'Oppose it.' This clear-cut direction from the Minister saved the day.

My relation with the Secretary (Defence) was not cordial and he requested the then Cabinet Secretary to shift me to some other Ministry. I was on leave at that time and when I came back, the Cabinet Secretary called me and said, 'Prashanta, your Secretary has requested for a change. Do you have anything to say?' I replied, 'Sir, absolutely I have no objection and no hesitation if a decision is taken by the Government. But I must clarify the position. Many times my straight and honest approach has not been appreciated. Moreover, the style of functioning of the Secretary results in considerable delays. If a decision to transfer is taken, I will not take more than a minute to hand over charge.' The Cabinet Secretary said, 'You are an excellent officer and the change will be to an important Ministry.' Within a few days, I was transferred as FA and Additional Secretary, Ministry of Civil Aviation, Tourism, Culture, Forest and Environment. After receiving the order, I went to Secretary and thanked him. As per usual practice, he wanted to give a farewell party which I politely declined. I also went to meet the Defence Minister who enquired, 'Will you like to stay back in the Ministry of Defence?' I said, 'Sir, since it is an order of the Government, I will rather abide by it without wasting any time.' Thus, my brief period in the Ministry of Defence ended.

Chapter 31

$\mathcal{FA}$ & $\mathcal{AS}$ (Civil Aviation, Culture
& Tourism and Environment &
Forest)

(December 2004 – July 2005)

Strength of the pound is built upon the strength and accumulation of the penny and as such I cannot throw them into a dustbin.

$\mathcal{I}$ was posted as FA & AS (Civil Aviation, Culture, Tourism and Enironment & Forest) in December, 2005. The country was in the throes of momentus changes in the field of civil aviation. The open sky policy initiated by the Ministry, acquisition of new fleets for Indian Airlines and Air India, modernization of airports and privatization of Delhi and Mumbai Airports were some of these activities undertaken with far-reaching consequences. I can say from my experience in the civil service that whenever far-reaching reforms are undertaken requiring huge investment, we must be pretty sure that many objections will be raised in the post-implementation period. Therefore, one has to be careful, honest and straight-forward to proceed; otherwise one is sure to land in trouble facing allegations.

I faced many hurdles while handling many important matters. The acquisition of fleet for the Indian Airlines had been pending for a long time. While on a tour of Jaipur I was summoned back by my Secretary to Delhi immediately to process the file. I rushed back and was given hardly 24 hours to process an important file with huge financial implications. My style of working was different. Generally I used to take decisions only after taking the view points of my officers in a meeting where they had the freedom to express themselves frankly. I had detailed discussions with the Director (Finance), Under Secretary and the staff and jotted down the relevant points. After discussing for about 3-4 hours, I went on dictating my observations. By about mid-night, the file was ready. The Secretary called me the next forenoon and after discussions, sent the file to the Minister. The Minister was not happy about the observations. He convened a meeting of the concerned officers of Civil Aviation where I was also present. He commented that the observations were not objective. I replied that in my long career, I had worked with all sincerity and in an objective manner. Nobody had raised a finger against me. Even I had to fight and write to higher authorities to include the observations, in the note prepared to take a decision in this matter by the Competent Authority. After further negotiations with the Airbus by the Empowered Group of Ministers, a final decision was taken.

In the privatization of Delhi and Mumbai Airports, I put my foot down and recorded my dissenting note with regard to final selection of the bidder. There were heated discussions at the meeting and the views were evenly divided. The matter was referred to the Group of Secretaries, headed by the Cabinet Secretary. While having the meeting, the Cabinet Secretary summoned me. After my briefing and detailed discussions, the matter was referred to the Sridharan Committee for expert opinion. My views were supported not only by the Group of Secretaries but also by the Sridharan Committee and later by the judiciary.

One experience with regard to finalization of procurement of Aerobridges and their installation is worth recalling. Global tenders were floated and after technical scrutiny, the financial bids of two companies were opened. L-1 was not considered on the basis of a report from the Ministry of Home Affairs highlighting the security hazards involved. There remained only one firm i.e. L-2. The difference between the two quoted prices was enormous. Despite pressure, as Financial Adviser, I advised that we should go for a fresh tender. If the Government thought that it was very urgent and absolutely essential to public interest, the price of L-2 must be brought down to that of L-1. I observed that any pressure in this matter should be firmly dealt with. The file never surfaced.

I advised the Government that the revenue intelligence system should gather information/intelligence with regard to purchase/sale of planes, Aerobridges and other costly implements. Since the manufacturing firms in the civil aviation sector are extremely limited, it would be better to build up a thorough information/intelligence input bank on such purchases and sales so that it can help in negotiations to arrive at just and fair decisions. An integrity clause and a fall clause in the agreement were also suggested. Hopefully, the Government would have considered these suggestions.

One had noticed an indifferent attitude on the part of officers towards prudent expenditure on quality. The blatant instance was of an invitation card at a cost of Rs 200 per card. This was brought to the notice of the Secretary and his intervention resulted in reducing the cost to Rs 20. Similarly, there was a project of film-making and bids were invited. Probable cost of it was coming to Rs 30 lakhs. When this was referred to the Film Division, they said that it should to be pruned down. A meeting was convened by the Minister (Tourism) and there were heated discussions. One of the high profile personalities retorted that the Financial Adviser was penny-wise but pound-foolish. This comment from an outsider was outrageous and he had to be told that the strength of the pound was built on the strength and accumulation of every penny and as such, could not be thrown into the dustbin. As far as I can remember, the cost was scaled down substantially.

Chapter 32

---- ✄

Secretary, Parliamentary Affairs, Govt. of India

(October 2006 – June 2007)

Indians are not only argumentative but see politics in everything, forgetting their responsibility towards society and the Nation.

Empanelment in the Government of India is a much talked about system. One has to be empanelled at various stages of the career like Joint Secretary, Additional Secretary and Secretary. Though important from the point of view of career development, the system so far prevalent is opaque, secretive and at times shrouded in mystery. Though I did not face any difficulty at any stage of empanelment, I felt that the system needs positive changes to make it more transparent. The criterion for the empanelment is shrouded in mystery. They are never posted on the website. The criteria change from time to time and when an officer is not empanelled, he is not informed about the reasons. Such a system naturally creates bitterness and demoralization in the civil service. The Government may think of associating the Union Public Service Commission, known for its integrity and credibility with the empanelment of the officer. The opaque system of empanelment and subsequent posting should be made transparent to ensure efficiency in administration.

After taking over as Secretary, Parliamentary Affairs on October 31, 2006, I called on the Cabinet Secretary who probably thought that I had come to request for a change of posting. When he asked me about the purpose of the meeting I said, it was just a courtesy call, he seemed puzzled. Never in my life, have I flouted the order of the Government with regard to my transfer. Whenever my transfer order had come, I took just a minute to hand over charge and to proceed to the new assignment.

At one time my Minister, during my absence, directed the Joint Secretary to provide gifts during the budget session. When the Joint Secretary mentioned this to me, I asked for the precedents in this respect and its financial implications. When the Joint Secretary said there was no such precedent and the financial implications could be to the tune of few crores, I went to the Minister with this information. When I brought these facts to his notice, he pondered over it and directed me not to proceed with his direction. I thanked him profusely and appreciated his informed decision.

It has been my belief that if proper facts are brought to the notice of the Minister in black and white, the political boss is amenable to rational advice a civil servant gives. The Ministry of Parliamentary Affairs is an interesting Ministry. When Parliament is in session, it has to work round the clock but when it is not in session, there is much free time to study and think. This posting provided me enough opportunity to observe the working of Parliament, the debates and the way the House functions. It also provided an insight into the functioning of its various Committees. Frequent disruption of House proceedings is a case for concern and these have been expressed on the floor of legislative bodies and other national fora. Resolutions have also been passed from time to time to maintain the dignity of Parliament and Legislatures. But despite all these efforts, there had not been much improvement in this aspect.

Mr Jagmohan mentions in his book, *The Soul and Structure of The Governance in India*, 'How could there be good governance in a country where Parliamentarians are unable to conduct themselves in an orderly and disciplined manner and where pledges solemnly taken in the highest deliberative body of the land and by the chosen representatives, are broken soon thereafter with extremely narrow ends in view and without having any regard for the overall interest of the nation and general welfare of the people themselves. How right was John Stuart Mill when in his classic essay on Representative Government, he wrote: 'How can a representative assembly work for good if its members can be bought, or if their excitability of temperament, uncorrected by public discipline or private self-control, makes them incapable of calm deliberations.'

Indians are not only argumentative but they bring politics into everything. There is politics over dead bodies, on language, on campus happenings, on castes and religions and even regarding our heritage. Politics per se is good for society, but this should not be at the cost of national interest. While Parliamentary proceedings get periodically disrupted one finds lively debates in the media and learned articles being published in newspapers and magazines. After the din and bustle, we find that the various suggestions of intellectuals and constitional luminaries to improve Parliament's functioning, are not being acted upon.

I often toy with the idea of creation of a Union Political Service Commission on the pattern of the Union Public Service Commission. Those interested to take up political service as a career option should pass a written examination conducted by the Commission. Only those who successfully clear the examination will have the opportunity to contest elections. We must devise a proper syllabus. After the election, the successful candidates must go through a training course of at least a year. At the end, they should pass the examination to be eligible to take the oath as a Member. When I disclosed this plan to friends, they termed it as highly elitist, thoroughly impratical and utopian which cannot be implemented in this imperfect world.

Chapter 33

Chief Secretary, Uttar Pradesh

(July 2007 – May 2008)

What is more important in life is not how long you have
stayed at the crease of life, but how fast you have scored in life.
Always keep up 'Principles of Life' which are more important
than mundane pecuniary benefits of the service.

The Presidential election was round the corner and the Ministry
was busy. After attending a meeting when I came back to my
room, I was informed by my PPS that three telephone calls had
come from the UP. Chief Minister's Office. In the evening, the UP
Cabinet Secretary called me on telephone to say that my name was
being considered for the post of Chief Secretary, UP. He sought my
willingness but I refused. On hearing this, he said, 'Prashantaji, the
newly-elected Government is in absolute majority and is in search
of good officers to bring about a positive change on the law and
order front as well as development. As an excellent officer with a
good reputation, the Chief Minister had zeroed in on you.' Again, I
politely refused and said, 'I am enjoying my tenure as a Secretary to
Government of India and have absolute peace of mind. UP politics
is unpredictable. I do not like to lose my peace of mind. Moreover,
the experience at the Centre is more interesting and challenging.'
The next morning, the Appointment Secretary (UP) got in touch
and persuaded me to take the charge in UP and I again refused. A
group of officers of the UP cadre descended on my residence the
next evening and persuaded me to accept the offer in the interest of

administration as well as in restoring the dignity of the institution of the Chief Secretary. There was some strength in their argument but I did not make any commitment. I talked to my seniors and well-wishers Mr Nripendra Mishra, Mr Sushil Tripathi and Mr Yogendra Narain and they all persuaded me to take up the challenge. After a day or two, the newly-elected UP Chief Minister personally talked to me on telephone and said. 'You are a very good officer and you have been working for many years in the Government of India. The new Government also wants good officers to implement the State Government policies.' When I politely told her that I was happy in the Government of India and that UP's scenario was unpredictable she said, 'I know, you are an honest officer and I will not put any pressure on you to do anything illegal. Moreover, your posting will fit into our concept of social engineering.' On this assurance I expressed my willingness to take up the job.

The Chief Minister announced my name at a press conference in Lucknow. After this I was flooded with hundreds of calls congratulating me for being posted as Chief Secretary in the country's most important State. I was to take charge on July 1, 2007 but before that I went to my hideout i.e. Vasistha Guffa to get the blessings of Swamiji and the presiding deity, Lord Shiva. Swamiji was happy but cautioned me to be careful. The Chief Minister had come to Delhi on some work and I was asked to meet her the next morning. When I met her, she enquired about my plan and when I said that I had booked a ticket by Indian Airlines to go to Lucknow, she in her indomitable style and despite my protest, directed the Secretary to take me by the State plane. So the next day at about 10 am I left for Lucknow by the State plane.

The ordeal started immediately after touchdown at Lucknow. I got a taste of bureaucratic intrigue. While getting into the staff car, the Staff Officer to the Chief Secretary came running and wanted to brief me about some important happenings. 'Sir, it is my duty to bring certain facts to your notice. As per my information, the Cabinet

Secretary is quite eager to occupy the room of the Chief Secretary and you are likely to be shifted to some other room. The floor of C.S. room has been dug up for repair and renovations just a few days back. This will compel you to shift to some other room. In fact, you will be requested accordingly.' I was not unnerved but could sense the intriguing part. Arriving at the VVIP Guesthouse, I called for Mr J.S. Deepak, the Appointment Secretary, and Mr G.B. Patnaik, two outstanding officers of our cadre, to give a feedback. They both briefed me along the same line. It was a tricky situation and I hit upon a strategy to weather it out. I decided to take charge at the adjoining conference hall of the Chief Secretary's Office which was intact. At the appointed time, I went to the meeting and took charge in the presence of a few important officers. The media was also invited. The media asked two questions: a) How do you look at the creation of a Super Chief Secretary called Cabinet Secretary? b) What will be your policy in a nutshell? I could sense that they were trying to trip me so as to create a controversy and a rift between the Chief Secretary and the Cabinet Secretary. I said, 'We are all partners in the same organization. To achieve the desired result, all of us have to work as a team. The creation of the post of Cabinet Secretary has added one more Member. I am sure he will act with dignity and with team spirit.' As regards the policy, I said

सर्वे भवन्तु सुखिनः सर्वे सन्तु निरामयाः
सर्वे भद्राणि पश्यन्तु मा कश्चिद्दुःखभाग्भवेत।
ॐ शान्तिः शान्तिः शान्तिः।।

(May all be happy and prosperous.
May all be free of illness.
May all be good and spiritually uplifted.
May no one suffer.
Om Shantih Shantih Shantih!!)

It is like 'Sarvajan Hitaya Sarvajan Sukhaya' (Good for all, happiness for all) policy of our Chief Minister.'

In the evening, a function was organized by the Civil Service Institute to welcome me and to bid farewell to the out-going Chief Secretary. During the dinner, I gave a bit of my mind to the Principal Secretary (Secretariat Admin) who pretended to be ignorant about the digging in the Office. I mentioned that as Principal Secretary, he ought to have known this development and he had failed in his duty. The officers of the Secretariat Administration came to me the next day and requested me to shift to a room at the ground floor. I told them to finish the work in three or four days and that I had no difficulty in working from the conference hall. Thus their plan to grab the Chief Secretary's room was frustrated. The situation was handled so deftly that it did not create even a ripple.

Thursday was the day fixed for Cabinet meeting. I was informed that after the creation of the post of Cabinet Secretary, my predecessor would not attend the Cabinet meeting. He was not even invited. After taking over, it was quite surprising that I was not informed or invited to the first Cabinet meeting. This seemed like a deliberate attempt to have a parallel power centre. The Chief Minister took it seriously and gave a thrashing to the then Cabinet Secretary. She called me to her residence and enquired about the episode and when I narrated the entire story she restored the prestige of the institution by directing the Cabinet Secretary not to commit any such mistake.

The first review meeting by Chief Minister was to take place in August, 2007, but just a day before the meeting, at midnight, the Cabinet Secretary came to my residence wanting to finalise the list of officers who were to be suspended just after the meeting. I was shocked and refused as such a practice would demoralize the officers who hadn't even been given enough time to show results as the financial sanction had been released in the first week of August. Moreover, the practice of targeting officers for suspension even before the review meeting was repugnant to all canons of good governance. It had been the practice in UP for some time to suspend officers at the drop of a hat. There is an instance of the Chief Minister making a surprise inspection and discovering that a few bricks of a newly laid road had come apart, in a rage, she ordered suspension of the Divisional Commissioner which was immediately broadcast through the media. I came to learn of the suspension from the television that evening. I was surprised and enquired from the Divisional Commissioner about the reason. He explained, 'Sir, I have also come to know of my suspension from the TV news, and frankly I don't know the reason.' I advised him to collect the necessary information. After one hour he informed me that he was suspended because of the missing bricks. The announcement of suspension had to be formally approved in the file by the Chief Minister. The file came to me without any analysis of the circumstances under which such a senior level officer was put under suspension. I noted that the person was a good officer without any blemish in his career. He was also going to retire in a year or so and if such a senior officer could be suspended for such a reason, then no officer could escape suspension. I requested the Chief Minister to reconsider the case. She accepted my advice and the officer was reinstated immediately and posted to some other Department. But in the process, his prestige had taken a nose dive. There were many instances of senior officers being subject to suspension and humiliation on flimsy grounds. I discussed the matter with the Appointments Secretary, the Cabinet Secretary and the Chief Minister and came out with detailed guidelines for such suspensions. As a result, the spree of suspensions came down substantially. In one case when I pleaded for not suspending a high-level officer, she said sarcastically, 'Chief Secretary Saheb, you are very kind and don't recommend suspension of any officer.' Despite such taunts, I stuck to my principles. I had tried my best to protect good and honest officers even at the cost of incurring the displeasure of the Chief Minister.

In another case, the Chief Minister wanted to suspend a senior Principal Secretary as she was annoyed because of the news reports that despite the drought situation in Bundelkhand, the officer was holding a party and fashion parade at his residence. She summoned me at 10.00 pm to her residence where a few senior officers were also present and wanted to suspend the officer. I requested her not to do so without knowing his side of the story and without seeking an explanation. The officers also supported my view. The Chief Minister ultimately changed her mind and directed that the officer be shifted to another department. In the same breath, she asked, 'Chief Secretary Saheb, do you also organize such parties at your residence?' I replied, 'Madam, whenever anybody comes to my residence, he will hear nothing but the sound of the conch, the recitation of mantras and the chant of bhajans.' She was taken aback and said, 'People say, you are a very religious person.' It is often alleged that she subjected officers to humiliating treatment but she was never harsh to me and always treated me with courtesy.

The Chief Secretary's job, I was pretty sure, was not going to be a smooth affair. The complexity of UP politics coupled with administrative and political intrigues and caste considerations added to the political instability prevailing there since 1989. Right from the beginning, I was determined to adhere to principles and administrative ethics. I chalked out a road map and presumed the first three months would not to pose any difficulties, the next three months would witness differences within a tolerable limit, the following three months the differences would be at their peak and the last three months would be for survival. The situation developed exactly as I visualized. In the first three months, the political leadership listened to my advice and things moved smoothly. Plans of action and phases of implementation were chalked out, divisional meetings were held regularly to monitor and streamline the administration. Every review meeting was followed by a discussion on the value system. I introduced the system of writing monthly D.O. letters to all District Magistrates and Commissioners highlighting the policy, initiatives taken, status of implementation and expectation from the officers. I also used to take daily review meetings of departments. A think tank was set up to advice the Government; surprise inspections by Group of Senior officers and even by the Chief Minister, were introduced. One could see the visible impact of these review meetings and inspections.

After the initial burst of enthusiasm, I could sense some disquieting features in the administration. Many important files were stuck with Ministers for long for reasons best known to them. I started getting negative feedback about the functioning of the Government Departments. I met the Chief Minister and briefed her about the situation and she assured me these files would be cleared soon. In fact within a few days, all pending files were cleared. This demonstrates that she was the undisputed leader whose diktat nobody dared flout. From time to time, I also informed the power centre about the decline in the popularity and image of the Government. On many occasions, I came in conflict with the establishment. I had serious reservations, particularly on the proposal of UP Control of Organized Crime, the proposal for empowering the Cabinet Secretary to write CR of all IAS officers, construction of the Ganga Expressway and leasing out about 70 acres at an insignificant price for establishment of a private university. The proposal on control of organized crime contained many draconian provisions about surveillance, phone tapping and rigorous punishment to the derelict officers to which I had serious reservations. I was determined to resign if my advice not heeded. I conveyed my feelings and this had a chastening effect.

One evening while disposing of files, the Appointment Secretary came with a file and said, 'Sir, the file is with regard to giving power to the Cabinet Secretary to write the CR of all IAS officers (excluding Chief Secretary) and the matter had been discussed with the Chief Minister.' I replied, 'Mr Appointment Secretary, the proposal is both illegal and mischievous and so long as I am Chief Secretary, I will not be a party to such a proposal. If it is approved, I will quit service immediately.' He asked me, 'Sir, what shall I say to the Cabinet Secretary and to the Chief Minister?' I told him that 'whatever I have said, you tell them exactly that.' I did not sign the file and the proposal did not see the light of day.

The Ganga Expressway was an ambitious plan, with a project cost of more than Rs 40,000 crores. I was not consulted about its details or the financial implications. Just two hours before the Cabinet meeting, the Cabinet Secretary came personally clutching the file and requested me to see it. I refused as the time was short for examining such an important proposal. The most interesting part was that the proposal was later approved by the Competent Body with a rider that a Committee of Secretaries, headed by the Chief Secretary, should also look into it. After the approval, there was nothing left to give it a second look. The decision was communicated to me in writing. In compliance with the decision, I held the meeting of the concerned Secretaries and technical experts for 10 days continuously. For hours we used to discuss in detail the various provisions. After such discussions, the Committee suggested far-reaching modifications. The Cabinet Secretary got wind of it and came to my meeting with a bidder. The bidder complained, 'Sir, you are putting us in the gallows by suggesting such modifications and alterations.' I replied, 'Mr Bidder, you have no locus standi at this meeting. Moreover, so long as P.K. Mishra continues to be Chief Secretary, he will ensure that the UP Government will be safe and will not be in the gallows.'

Many a time because of such alertness and sticking to principles, such embarrassing situations had been averted. Once I had to attend a marriage ceremony of my relative in Calcutta and applied for 3 days casual leave. I had booked my ticket by a commercial flight to Calcutta. The Cabinet Secretary telephoned me to say that I could fly to Calcutta by the State Government plane to review the status and conditions of the UP Government Guesthouse there. Thus, it would be an official trip and using the State plane could be justified. I laughed at the idea and told him that it would be highly unethical to use the Government plane for a private purpose. Moreover, I would make myself a laughing stock if I reviewed the condition of the UP Government Guesthouse there to justify use of the state plane. When I returned from Calcutta, my PPS put up a TA bill for my signature, and when I asked about it, he said the Chief Minister had approved it as an official trip and, therefore, the reimbursement would be made to me. I was furious and refused to sign it. This was a small incidence which could have snowballed into a crisis if somebody had leveled allegation of the misuse of official aircraft.

There is no denying that the formation of the unconstitutional post of Cabinet Secretary created a parallel power centre. It not only demoralized the bureaucracy but also sent a wrong signal to the public. There was little respect for established norms and procedures and everything was governed by political considerations. Even many central projects were obstructed. There were groups and cliques in the bureaucracy and one could feel a perceptible politicization of bureaucracy. This trend is ominous for every State. The politicization of bureaucracy, the criminalization of politics and the unholy nexus between bureaucrats, corporates, politicians, police and anti-social elements poses a grave danger to national unity and even its very existence.

All said and done, I must say the Government functioned with speed, clarity, firmness and efficiency though there were allegations of corruption. The positive aspects were political stability, undisputed leadership, unity of command, quick decisions, firmness in handling law and order situation, elimination of dreaded dacoits, development of Ambedkar villages, a lot of urban development activities in Lucknow City and Noida, building of gigantic smaraks, initiative taken in e-governance, computerization, e-tendering, computerization of scholarship, survey for metros in KAVAL Towns, decision to take the metro link to Greater Noida, handling of the drought situation in Bundelkhand, the proposal for construction of the Ganga Expressway, inviting scientists of international repute to study and report about possibility of generating artificial rain in Bundelkhand, floating the concept of Food and Fodder Banks in drought-hit areas and giving prosecution sanction in 300 cases. The most important achievement was in the field of law and order which was handled with firmness and speed. The goondas (louts) and the bad elements were put in their place. The urban development of Lucknow, Noida and Greater Noida was such that passing through some of these areas one often wondered whether he was in a foreign country. The tragedy of UP, since 1989, was that it had been suffering from political instability, till it was broken in 2007. Primarily UP was governed by either the Samajwadi Party or the Bahujan Samaj Party with the minor exception of the BJP for a short period. When the BSP was in power, it was felt that the previous regime was better and, ironically, when the SP came to power it was felt that the BSP regime was better! This is a peculiar situation where the two important national parties have not been able to do much in the complex political scenario of UP. Ultimately, it is for the people of the state to decide which way to go. I am sure, only political alertness and maturity of the voters will ensure a stable and prosperous UP by voting for enlightened leadership and good governance. In fact, they have shown their political maturity and wisdom in the recently held Assembly election.

I had good relations with the judiciary as I was serious about decisions and observations made by the judiciary and monitored the implementation of their important decisions from time to time. On occasions like dismantling of the PDS, sanctioning of funds and installation of equipment for security of court premises and shifting of shops from Kanpur City to the newly constructed Mandi, I felt that whenever correct facts and inputs were presented before the courts, they had not hesitated to grant the necessary relief. Judicial activism has become a common phenomenon in the country now. One can appreciate the fact that many good things have happened and many initiatives taken in various fields, be it environment, health, sanitation, safety or security because of judicial activism. But judicial over-arching or over-reaching may not be desirable in the long run, as it militates against the principle of separation of power and checks and balances. Therefore (a) Judicial activism is good and welcome; (b) judicial over-arching or over-reaching is bad and (c) Judicial in-activism will be the worst.

I had tried my best, as Chief Secretary, to improve the situation, to protect the good officers and ensure proper implementation of development programmes and to provide a transparent administration. The differences with the power centre however continued and the creation of a parallel power centre in the form of Cabinet Secretary, frequent transfers and postings, the suspension spree, scanty respect for established norms and procedures, administrative intrigues and politicization of the bureaucracy, all had cheesed me off and made me sad and disappointed. The last straw was when a proposal was submitted for approval of the Competent Authority for leasing out about 70 acres of Government land at a throwaway price to a private organization. The proposal also contained a provision of a few crores for construction of boundary walls etc. for the safety and security of the institution. The Law Department and the Finance Department had no objection to the proposal but I was not convinced, and put forth my observations which were unpalatable. At night I was summoned to the Chief Minister's residence and was asked to change my observations which I refused. The next day, I got a hint from the Cabinet Secretary and my colleagues that I would be changed. The Cabinet Secretary wanted me to accompany him to meet the Chief Minister, but I declined it on the ground that I had not been asked by the Chief Minister to meet her. I got the wind of change. I came home for lunch, narrated everything to my wife and took her into confidence before taking a decision on immediate voluntary retirement.

At 3.00 pm, the Appointment Secretary and the Cabinet Secretary wanted to meet me urgently and I could guess the purpose. I told them not to bother to come to my residence but merely send the order of my change so that I could comply with it immediately. They still insisted and came to my residence at about 4.00 pm. They informed me about the decision of the Chief Minister to shift me. They offered me a number of posts and went to the extent of offering me the Chairman of State Public Service Commission in November when it would fall vacant. At the fag end of my career, I did not want to leave the office with my head bowed. So I decided to take voluntary retirement with immediate effect and directed the Appointment Secretary to prepare the necessary papers. At 5.00 pm, I reached my office. The decision to take voluntary retirement was kept a closely guarded secret and only the Appointment Secretary, Cabinet Secretary and my personal staff knew about it. The Appointment Secretary and my staff officers came to my room and pleaded with tears but I had already taken the decision and asked the Appointment Secretary to comply with it. I had no regret at all in quitting the post of Chief Secretary, UP. I took these developments with equanimity and stoic patience. But I am happy that later the Government had to retract its steps in this matter.

Before quitting, I wrote to my colleagues:

Dear Colleagues,

'He who would accomplish little, must sacrifice little;
He who would achieve much, must sacrifice much;
He who would attain highly, must sacrifice greatly.'

I enjoyed working with all of you who have always stood by me and extended all cooperation in the discharge of the affairs of the State. Life is never a straight line. It is not a bed of roses nor is it a mid summer night's dream. At times it becomes a tempest or a winter's tale or you take it as you like it.

What is more important in life is not how long you have stayed at the crease of life, but how fast you have scored in life. Always keep up 'Principles of Life' which are more important than the mundane pecuniary material benefits of the Service.

May God bless you,
Sd/-
23.05.2008

I signed the letter seeking my VRS with immediate effect. I preferred to quit the coveted post rather than to dance to the tune of politicians. In my own way, I had maintained the dignity of the office and also preserved the dignity of the profession. A person is known by the qualities of his head and heart and not by the powers or the riches he possesses. Reputation is not built overnight. It takes years of dedicated service and sacrifices. The reputation travels faster than the person. A successful life is a life of duty, honesty, integrity, perseverance, self-sacrifice and service regardless of material rewards. The inner character is a far more significant factor in the success of a person. The key to success is to align ourselves to unchangeable principles and stop taking detours. I quit not to impress anyone or for cheap popularity. I did it just to live up to my own standards and principles of life. Thus ended my administrative career, spread over 36 years.

After signing the paper, I came back to my residence. Slowly and gradually officers, journalists, friends and people came to know about it only through scroll news on TV. Honest and good officers started trickling into my residence with anguished faces. I maintained my equanimity and took life in its usual course. They were surprised to see my stoic acceptance of the situation. I received more than a thousand calls from my well-wishers, friends and sympathizers. At the dead of night, I was surprised to find an emissary from the Chief Minister's Office to meet me in my residence. He requested me not to make it an issue. With a smile, I assured him that it was not in my nature to create unnecessary controversy. It was the prerogative of the Chief Minister to change the Chief Secretary and as a civil servant it was my prerogative to take appropriate steps to uphold my dignity and dignity of the Service. So the matter ended.

The next morning, i.e. May 24, 2008, I was reading the newspaper over a cup of tea with my wife. The Security staff of the Chief Secretary's residence informed me that a large number of media persons had gathered to meet me. I talked to one of the senior media persons on telephone and enquired about their purpose of visit. He said, 'Sir, you kept your resignation so secret that we came to know about it only late in the evening. We want to take a 'bite'.' I replied, 'Look, Prashanta Mishra never bites.' He said, 'Sir, you always say that you are a disciplined civil servant bound by a code of conduct. Since you have retired, there is no bar on you for expressing your view point.' I said, 'Friends, PK Mishra was a disciplined civil servant while in service and continues to be a disciplined retired civil servant.' He had a hearty laugh and I invited them for a cup of tea. After spending half-an-hour or so, I thanked them all for their cooperation rendered during my tenure as Chief Secretary. I told them that voluntary retirement was my personal decision. I did not like to discuss the reasons behind it. I would like to say that I served the State and the country with all sincerity and integrity for 36 years and had no regrets.

I was flooded with telephone calls from visitors, friends and relatives and letters from different quarters. Of the many messages, I like to mention here letters from my daughter Pragya and from a retired officer which moved me.

'This is a mail to my dearest father to tell him that he has made all of us very proud today with his extremely tough decision. Today I am so proud to be the daughter of Prashanta Mishra. The decision was a decision which only a person like papa can take. Papa has once again proved that NOTHING is more dear and important to him than the principles on which he has led his life for so long. Never to give into any pressure, he has shown through his action once again that NO ONE can make him do anything which is against his integrity.

I am upset not because papa took VRS, but because of the circumstances that led to his VRS. It is not his loss but the loss of the Chief Minister and the State of UP that they did not value a human being who fights for the truth. My respect for him has gone up a few notches after this incident.

I'm reminded of the lines by Harivansh Rai Bachchan: 'मैं हूँ उनके साथ खड़ी जो सीधी रखते अपनी रीढ़' (I am with him who stands upright). He could not have written a more apt line to describe papa. We, as a family, are solidly behind his decision. Thank you papa for being what you are. We all love you very much and respect your decision.'– Pragya Mishra.

'Inspired by the letter of Pragya Mishra, the voice of young India, I will like to place, in your website Forum, my admiration for Prashanta Mishra, former Chief Secretary, Uttar Pradesh, for his decision to quit, thus upholding the honour and dignity of All India Services. The only matching example I can recall was that of the then Union Home Secretary Godbole who also believed that principles of life were more important than the mundane pecuniary benefits of service. We in the bureaucracy blame the politicians for politicalisation of services as a stratagem to smokescreen the deterioration in the personal values and principles of the members of the services that was once the solid material of the 'steel frame' of governance. It calls for introspection by the members of All India Services to answer to their conscience whether it is our own doing to set our priorities wrong by placing mundane pecuniary material benefits of service before the principles of life or it is the doing of politicians. Once the mundane pecuniary material benefits become the primary goal of All India Services, then in its pursuit, while in service and even later for getting post retirement crumbs, the focus shifts from good governance to pleasing the political masters who obviously are always too happy to have such a bundle of subservient, pliant and compliant members of 'All Ineffectual Services.' We are proud of such officers, though a rare species nearing extinction and hope that this generation of AIS will get some inspiration from such exceptional examples worthy of emulating and be of the same mind to reach a consensus on the values and principles of life. I show my solidarity with Mishra and his family.'

Mr Jagmohan writes in *The Soul and Structure of Governance in India*, 'The officers have either been perceived as friendly or hostile by the political masters. While the former have been pampered, the latter have been subjected to humiliation. Civil servants are woven into a corrupt network and even some of them are willing to play a collusive role. Such a state of affairs in public services was unthinkable in the early period of independent India. Over the years, the number of officers who were willing to become partners in the predatory activities of the politicians began to increase. By design or by default, they allowed themselves to be exploited by the politicians. Quite a few of them even became active collaborators.' The steel frame has de-generated into a form of moth-eaten bamboo structure. What is required is a wide range of reforms. In the words of Swami Vivekananda, 'I want root and branch reforms. You must go down to the basics of the things, to the root of the matter.'

One of the important suggestions Mr Jagmohan has made is that there is a need to set up a Ministry to be named as Ministry of Ethics and Social and Cultural Reforms to be headed by the Prime Minister. This Ministry will be advised by a quasi-judicial Commission, to be called as a Reform Commission. This may be a small step but it will be in the right direction to discover the destiny of India.

Public money provided for development is to be spent judiciously and with integrity. Anonymity, impartiality and integrity are the hallmarks of civil service and I expect all my colleagues and members of the service to strictly adhere to these principles. But often for short term gains, we lose sight of our principles. Money is not the be all and end all of life; there is something beyond it. The organizational ethics, public interest and social responsibility must be in our mind while taking decisions. It is time for introspection, reflection and action. Friends, we have many challenges ahead to put our state on the fast track of development. Utmost efforts have to be made to establish a fear-free and corruption-free society where everyone gets his due. It is time that all honest, right-thinking and courageous people must be organized to fight against corrupt and bad elements at every step. Unless we make sincere effort to fight these elements in whatever form they are and wherever they are; we will not succeed and we will suffer humiliation at every step. Once we organize ourselves and make a determined effort to face these anti-social and bad elements courageously, they will run for cover.

Soon after quitting office, I dashed to my hideout i.e. Vasistha Guffa, to meet Swamiji and to meditate. I told Swamiji that I had quit service and now I was a retired person. When I expressed my desire to devote myself to spiritualism full time the Swamiji shook his head and said, 'You will serve another five years at the Centre.' I was surprised at this prediction as I had already taken voluntary retirement.

I was now master of my own programme and my first priority was to get the pension papers ready. In less than a month, I got my Pension Payment Order. The residence of the Chief Secretary was an earmarked one and I didn't like to stay there any longer. In the last week of June, I vacated the place and flew to Delhi. During the flight, my wife posed a question, 'Prashanta, with your long experience in the IAS will you be able to get any consultancy assignment?' I said that definitely I would get one but that was not my priority. I had worked for 36 years and I needed to rest and enjoy my retired life for at least six months. We reached Delhi and while Sarita was busy unpacking, I decided to rest a while. At about 5 pm she roused me for my sleep saying that there was a call. I asked her to take down the number so that I would call later. She replied, 'Prashanta, it is a call from the PM's Office.' I immediately took up the call and talked to Secretary to the PM who was at the other end. He asked, 'Sir, what are you doing at present?' and when I replied that, 'I am enjoying my retired life', he posed a question, 'Will you mind taking up an assignment with the the Government of India?' Both of us were overwhelmed with this response. I told my wife, 'You were asking for a consultancy and God has immediately responded to your request. Let us go to the worship room and thank God.'

Chapter 34

·· ✀

Member, Union Public Service Commission

(August 2008 – August 2013)

Any attempt to dilute the importance of UPSC and its Constitutional mandate even in an oblique manner must not be tolerated.

*N*ever in my wildest of dreams did I expect to be made a Member of the Union Public Services Commission. But the Cosmic Spirit operates in a subtle way of rewarding a person who has deep faith in Him and His principles. In August, 2008, I got the order appointing me as a Member of the UPSC, a coveted constitutional post. I joined the UPSC on August 18 and the next day went to meet the Prime Minister to thank him. He was courteous enough to receive me at the door of his room and affectionately patted me. He said, 'This is the least I can do for you for the sacrifice you made as Chief Secretary of UP' I was overwhelmed by the gesture as well as the courtesy and simplicity the Prime Minister displayed.

I am proud to be a Member of UPSC and we must be grateful to our founding fathers that they have conceived such a Constitutional Body for the recruitment, promotion and disciplinary proceedings of officers who play an important role in shaping the future of the nation. An institution is never built in a day. It requires long years of sustenance, efforts, sincerity, devotion, fairplay and justice to acquire the reputation that it enjoys. An institution is not merely a conglomeration of brick and mortar. It is not a congregation of isolated individuals having no organic emotional link. An institution like the UPSC, in the ultimate analysis, is an organic whole embracing within itself the deep-rooted past, the challenging present and an expected future with all its ramifications. It has a mind of its own, a psychology of its own, its own culture, custom and tradition providing necessary sustenance, security and opportunity to its Members who dedicate themselves to the service of the nation according to their potential and talents. The day its high traditions, culture and independence are tinkered with that day will be disastrous not only for the institution but for the entire nation. So what is more important is that at every stage, at every moment and in every decision, we must supremely be guided by national interest and its constitutional mandate. Any attempt to dilute its importance and Constitutional mandate, even in an oblique manner, must not be tolerated.

I enjoyed working here for five years. The work culture, traditions and freedom given to its Members to express freely, fearlessly, but selflessly suited my temperament. I learnt a good deal which I had not experienced in my entire career as IAS officer. I find lively expression of democratic experience in its working, particularly, in the Commission's meetings and decision-making process. The freedom given to the Members in decision-making process enables them to understand the various dimensions of a problem by getting inputs from different directions and thus the decision arrived at is enriched beyond doubt.

There has been an increase in knowledge which I have never experienced before. The interaction with learned advisors and candidates has expanded my mental horizon greatly. The thoroughness with which a problem is analyzed has really impressed me. You will not find such tradition and attention to minute details in any other government department. During this time, a lot of initiatives had been taken, particularly in the field of examination reform.

When I joined the UPSC, I was dreaming of introducing a paper on administrative ethics, morality and value system in the Civil Services Examination. I discussed it with the Chairman and other colleagues. I requested the Chairman to speed up the examination reform so that I could leave the institution with a sense of satisfaction. I was extremely happy that it happened before I demitted office.

As a Member I not only had to take interviews on administration, development, civil services etc. but had also to take interviews on technical subjects like engineering, medicine, IT etc. Well before the interview, we were informed about the services/disciplines for which we have to take the interview. Whenever, I got such a message from the Chairman's Office, I used to read a lot, consult annual reports, the latest policy of the Government, various schemes and books from the UPSC library which is very rich in its collections. I used to make brief notes and build up a question bank. Every night, I used to read for two hours to get myself updated with the latest facts and information. The philosophy of UPSC is not to harass the candidates but to bring out the best in them through friendly interactions. With my long experience in UPSC, I can legitimately claim that there was no interference whatsoever from any quarters in the selection process.

I have enjoyed every moment here. It is not merely an institution, it is a great Constitutional Body, selecting and shaping future administrators. Its corridor is not one of power and authority but of empowerment, empowering every section of society in a just and fair manner to serve the nation in a dignified way. It is a great institution incessantly working for a great cause.

I demitted office on August 6, 2013. At the time I felt nostalgic about it and also a pang of separation. This was an appropriate occasion to recall Nehru's farewell speech at Harrow. He said, 'I do not know when tears came to my eyes; I do not know how it came to my eyes and why it came to my eyes. Probably, we Indians are susceptible to tears and bit of a sentimental and emotive type.'

Chapter 35

Post Retirement Life

The powers that we had and the facilities that we enjoyed during our service must not go to the head. Otherwise one will face a lot of trouble and psychological problems.

I retired de jure on May 23, 2008 when I tendered my voluntary retirement but de facto I retired on August 6, 2013 when I demitted the office of Member, UPSC after completing the five-year tenure. The day after demitting office, my mind was totally vacant and I did not know what to do. I embarked upon the idea of weeding out my old files which occupied much space of my house. The 'operation file cleaning' went on for a week and to my utter surprise, I discovered that 90% of the files were utterly useless. In our life we have developed a tendency to cling on to many things that are useless and have outlived their purpose. One will find heaps of files, books, journals, old clothes and other articles fit to be consigned to the kabadiwala. It is better to examine these articles periodically so that they could be weeded out in time. The same principle applies to one's inner life as well. Unnecessary things, experiences and thoughts get deposited in the inner life in a subtle way. Therefore, it is important that from time to time, one introspects, reflects and resorts to the internal cleaning process through meditation.

I have collected a library of spiritual books, like the Vedas, the complete works of Swami Vivekananda, books on Ramakrishna Paramahamsa, the works of Swami Rama and Osho, the Ramayana, the

Mahabharata, the Gita, many management and motivational books, Swami Shivananda's books and Sri Aurobindo's works, numbering about 400. Since my house in Noida is very small constructed on an area of 125 sq.m it has no space for my library. It has only three rooms. I did not want to part with these books and my wife did not have a room to spare. I hit upon an idea of donating these books to the Noida Public Library on the condition that whenever I wanted to consult a book, I could borrow it. Thus I donated 350 books and retained the reference books.

Since I was putting up in a Government accommodation in Delhi which was to be vacated within six months, we started the renovation of our residence in Noida. It was very difficult to commute between Delhi and Noida to supervise the renovation work. The work of renovation was taken over by my wife. Since I did not have a car, she had to commute by autos and public transport. Very often in Noida, she had to use rickshaw to reach the destination. But as good luck would have it, Deepika who was in-charge of renovation, turned out to be the daughter of my ADM (City) when I was District Magistrate in Agra. So much of our headache was over and we took it as god's blessings. The renovation was over by the end of January, 2014 and we shifted on February 4, 2014. I was back in Noida after many years to finally settle down as a permanent resident. I did not have much social connections initially. It is said that the public know everything and in fact the public of Noida knew everything about me and my family and my principles. They have tremendous respect for me. Thus, it has become easier for me to mingle with them and be a part of them.

Post retirement life may prove to be a boon or a bane depending upon how one is able to adjust to the new situation. To fall from 'a life full of activities to a life of nearly zero activity' is a tremendous psychological shock which must be faced boldly. When we get older, some of the worst traits can get exaggerated. It is only a spiritual person who is able to achieve equilibrium under such stress. Take life as it comes and live it fully without getting bogged down with the past. Be physically, mentally and psychologically prepared to lead a life of a common citizen and I am sure you will enjoy your retirement life most. However, a word of caution is here. Health becomes the paramount importance in the old age and one must be very particular to maintain a good health so that you can enjoy your retired life. One must not hesitate to do routine chores like shopping for vegetables, milk, cleaning of utensils and premises, watering of plants and entertaining guests etc, but you must enjoy doing these chores. I am a retired person but not a tired person and have tried to help my partner in my own small little ways. My wife is a sharp and intelligent person with artistic taste. She has taken every pain to make the house beautiful and since she is computer savvy and capable of discharging many of the functions, I am personally leading a blessed life. I have kept myself busy teaching 3 or 4 children belonging to marginalized sections. It is good that more or less every month the UPSC invites me to preside over ad-hoc board that keeps me not only busy but mentally alert and compels me to read new things so as to conduct the interview efficiently.

Since I have a lot of leisure time, I devoted myself to study of books and writing. Various organizations invite me to participate in their meetings and seminars. But still there is something lurking in a corner of my mind that I have not been able to fully justify my retired life. The society has given me so much that now it is my turn to give it back. Therefore, I not only devote myself to the task of teaching children of marginalized sections but at the same time I don't miss any opportunity to interact with the student community. My craving for social activities landed me in Noida Lok Manch, an NGO.

I find a great level of satisfaction in social work for the NGO. I could see the dreams in the eyes of the children whenever I interact with them. In my own way, I have tried to help this organization. From time to time, I have given new concepts and ideas to NLM. I would like to mention the idea of organizing the Rashtriya Chetna Shivir for

about 430 students in October, 2015. The aim was to inculcate among them a sense of national values, patriotism, discipline, confidence and to facilitate the development of their full potential. It aims to ignite their minds through interaction with leading personalities of the region in different fields. We invited well known personalities/ experts/renowned scholars to interact with the students on important topics like environment, motivations, patriotism, yoga, meditation, personality development, participation of youth in nation-building activities, stress management, creative education, morality, values in life, spirituality, the Indian Constitution – fundamental rights and duties of the citizen, social responsibility, swatchhta abhiyan and health and hygiene etc. The discussions were through interactive mode followed by question answer session. Students liked the 'interactive discussion session' and got an excellent opportunity to meet distinguished personalities. The Yoga Session in the morning by the Art of Living and the extra-curricular activities in the evening were useful and interesting. They were taken on a visit to Akshardham Temple and Science Centre at Pragati Maidan for exposure to spiritualism and the scientific temper. The camp had been a grand success.

Now I feel that post-retirement life is perhaps one of the best periods of my life. I am a free bird. I am the master of my own programme. No tension, no boss and no interferance but enough leisure to devote my time to study, social service and to persue my interest in spiritualism. I love to live an ordinary life of a common citizen, devoid of power, authority and glamour of the service. To lead such a life does require an extraordinary effort and a positive attitude to life.

Chapter 36

Conclusion

I will like to fly even beyond the frontier of the Cosmic World.

I have lived my life as a child, as an adolescent, as an adult, as a family person and now I am in the late autumn of my life ready to hand over all my responsibilities and work to the younger generation. I am chastened, I am subdued and I am calm. To quote from 'Ode to Life':

'In the hush of dawn
The beauty of the rising sun
Sets ablaze the heart
With light, hope and happiness
In the quiet of the evening
The slanting rays of the setting sun
Bring in their wake
Peace, tranquility and bliss
For an enlightened soul
Both are important
For the wisdom of the message they convey.'

'In the twilight of our life, when we look back over the years, what will shine forth and stand out as milestones of our sojourn on earth will not be the wealth that we have accumulated, or the power and pleasure that we have enjoyed; but will be those acts of love that enabled us to render a healing touch to our fellow humans in pain; those acts of courage that empowered us to become agents of justice and liberty; and those acts of self-sacrifice that gave us a glimpse of our eternal glory as children of God.' Ultimately, the whole life is nothing but a search for truth, a journey to realize one's true self.

We mortals, ignorant about our True Self, concentrate merely on the body. In our journey on earth, we never even reflect on the true self. Greater than the greatest and smaller than the smallest, the ever-luminous 'Indwelling Spirit' is present in the heart of everybody, but we ignore it at our own peril. It must be our honest endeavour to realize it. When we live the life of spirituality, strength comes to us, our consciousness begins to expand, sympathies grow and widen and we become better and better. We must realize the dreams of Sri Aurobindo to move from an ordinary human being to a super human being and from an ordinary consciousness to a supramental consciousness. Dwelling upon the process of evolution, the mystic sufi saint Hazrat Jalal-ud-deen Rumi says:

I died as mineral and became a plant,
I died as plant and rose to animal,
I died as animal and I was man.
Why should I fear?
When was I less by dying?
Yet once more I shall die as man,
To soar with angels blest;
But even from angelhood I must pass on ....[1]

I do not know whether I will be able to realize my true self in this life time. I do not know how many births I will take to go back to my original source of energy. But I am sure that one day, may be in this birth or may be in a subsequent birth, He will reveal Himself to me.

'It is but few who hear about the Self.
Fewer still dedicate their lives to its

Realization. Wonderful is the one
Who speaks about the Self; rare are they
Who make it the supreme goal of their lives.
Blessed are they who, through an illumined
Teacher, attain to Self-realization.'

'The Self cannot be known through study'
Of the scriptures, nor through the intellect,
Nor through hearing learned discourses.
He can be attained only by those
Whom the Self chooses. Verily unto them
Does the Self revel himself.'[2]

The entire life is a pilgrimage, a pilgrimage to discover your true self, to steadfastly proceed from falsehood to truth, from darkness to light and from mortality to immortality. We are all part of the Great Cosmic Spirit. We are born out of it and will dissolve back into it. Hence we are all pure and infinite. Let us realize the infinite potential of our True Self during our pilgrimage. 'I am born with potential. I am born with goodness and trust. I am born with ideas and dreams. I am born with greatness. I am born with confidence. I am born with courage. So, I am not meant for crawling. I have wings. I will fly. I will fly and fly'[3]. I will like to fly even beyond the frontier of the Cosmic World.

Om Shantih Shantih Shantih!!

---

[1] Balkrishna Pandey's book 'Personality'

[2] Excerpts from the Katha Upanishad as translated by Eknath Easwarn

[3] Dr APJ Abdul Kalam